1 MONTH OF
FREE
READING

at
www.ForgottenBooks.com

By purchasing this book you are eligible for one month membership to ForgottenBooks.com, giving you unlimited access to our entire collection of over 1,000,000 titles via our web site and mobile apps.

To claim your free month visit:

www.forgottenbooks.com/free483355

ISBN 978-0-332-97380-7
PIBN 10483355

Surrey
Archæological Collections

Relating to the
History and Antiquities of the County

published by the
SURREY ARCHÆOLOGICAL SOCIETY

VOL. LI

PRINTED BY E. W. LANGHAM, FARNHAM

FOR

THE SURREY ARCHÆOLOGICAL SOCIETY
CASTLE ARCH, GUILDFORD

———

MCML

The COUNCIL of the SURREY ARCHÆOLOGICAL SOCIETY desires it to be distinctly understood that it is not responsible for any statement or opinions expressed in the COLLECTIONS, the Authors of the several communications being alone accountable for the same.

GIFTS AND LOANS TO THE SOCIETY

Members and friends desiring to give or lend books, documents or objects of antiquarian interest to the Society, for the Library or Museum at Castle Arch, are earnestly requested to send such gifts or loans to the Hon. Secretary, Surrey Archæological Society, Castle Arch, Guildford, with a covering letter stating whether the objects sent are a gift or loan to the Society. As regards articles intended for the Museum, these should be accompanied by full particulars, such as where found, date of finding, etc.

Members wishing to leave money, books or articles to the Society by Will are asked to make use of the following Clause :

"I GIVE to the Surrey Archæological Society of Guildford free of duty the sum of £ (words and figures) (for books or other articles, a description is necessary). AND I DECLARE that the receipt of the Treasurer or other proper officer of the said Society shall be a complete discharge therefor."

The Honorary Editor will be glad to receive contributions of county interest, either in article form or as notes, with appropriate illustration. Copy, preferably in typescript or very clear manuscript, should be complete in every particular and quite ready, in every detail, for publication.

CONTENTS

	PAGE
REPORT OF PROCEEDINGS FOR 1948	vii
STATEMENT OF ACCOUNTS FOR 1948	xvii
OFFICERS AND LIST OF MEMBERS	xxi
SOCIETIES, ETC., IN UNION	xlvii
LIBRARIES	xlix
RULES	1

ARTICLES :

Romano-British Cemeteries at Haslemere and Charterhouse. By JOHN M. HOLMES ... 1

The Fourth Century Romano-British Pottery Kilns at Overwey, Tilford. By ANTHONY J. CLARK ... 29

Investigations on Walton Heath and Banstead Common. By J. M. PREST and E. J. PARRISH ... 57

Roman Villa at Sandilands Road, Walton-on-the-Hill. Excavations of 1948-49. By A. W. G. LOWTHER, F.S.A. ... 65

Some Surrey Wills in the Prerogative Court of Canterbury. By HILDA J. HOOPER ... 82

The Stained Glass of Guildford Guildhall. By BERNARD RACKHAM, C.B., F.S.A. ... 97

An Experiment in Local History. By JOHN H. HARVEY, F.S.A. ... 102

Old Houses in Epsom, Ewell and Cuddington. By CLOUDESLEY S. WILLIS, F.S.A. ... 110

The Grotto, Oatlands Park, c. 1778-1948. By J. W. LINDUS FORGE, A.R.I.B.A. ... 134

NOTES :

A Macehead of Igneous Rock, Ranmore	141
A Diorite Axe, Kingston	141
A Polished Axe from Titsey	141
Three Stone Axes from Ashtead	141
A Neolithic Flint Mine, East Horsley	142
Cast Bronze Ornament, St. Catherine's Hill, Guildford	143
Iron Age Pottery, Weybridge	144
Stane Street	147
Saxon Spearhead, Cheam	151
A Saxon Pot from Thursley	153
Coin of Ptolemy IV, Lingfield	153
Coin of Constantine, Ewell	153
Compton Church : The Oratory	154
Pepys and Guildford	156
St. George's Church, Crowhurst	156
A Scold's Bridle	156
A 1792 Dorking Bequest	156

REVIEWS AND NOTICES	157
INDEX	160

PAGE

NOTES :

Stone Axes from Ashtead   142

Ornament of Bronze Age Date   143

Iron Age Pottery, Weybridge   145

Iron Age Pottery, Weybridge   146

Section of Stane Street   148

Plan of a Stane Street Section   149

Linch Pin and Metal Object   151

Saxon Spearhead, Cheam   152

Plate XVIII.   (A) Neolithic Flint Mine, East Horsley.   (B) A
               Saxon Pot from Thursley .   .   .   *facing*   152

Plate XIX.   (A) Coin of Ptolemy IV, Lingfield.   (B) Coin of
               Constantine, Ewell .   .   .   .   *facing*   153

REPORT OF PROCEEDINGS

1949

THE NINETY-FOURTH ANNUAL GENERAL MEETING was held on 28th May, at the Guildhall, Guildford, by kind permission of His Worship the Mayor, and was presided over by Sir Frederic Kenyon, G.B.E., K.C.B., F.S.A., President of the Society. The Minutes of the last Annual General Meeting were read and confirmed, and the Accounts and Report of the Council for the year ended 81st December, 1948, were presented.

Report of the Council

for the year ended 31st December, 1948

THE COUNCIL OF THE SURREY ARCHÆOLOGICAL SOCIETY has much pleasure in presenting its NINETY-FOURTH ANNUAL REPORT, with the ACCOUNTS FOR THE YEAR 1948.

PUBLICATIONS.—Volume XLIX of the *Collections* was issued to members during January. Volume L was printed and would have been issued during the year but for difficulties concerning binding. It is to be issued to members during February, 1949.

Research Paper No. 1.—The Council agreed to the initiating of a series of special papers, devoted to items of research concerning the archæology of the county. These were designed to relieve the shortage of space which would be occasioned if they were included in the *Collections* and also, by producing them in a large (Crown Quarto) "format," to enable them to include larger illustrations than is possible in the annual volume, except by the use of "folders."

The first of this series, entitled "A Study of the Patterns on Roman Flue-Tiles and their Distribution," by the Hon. Secretary, was published in November, and may be obtained by members from the Assistant Secretary, price 2/6 for members, 5/- for non-members. Postage 3d.

The second Research Paper, "A Mesolithic Survey of the West Surrey Greensand," by the Honorary Editor, is in course of preparation.

LOCAL HISTORY.—The Local History Committee was formed to take over the functions of the former Sub-Committee of the G.P.C., in 1948. It is hoped that the Committee's first publication, *Blechingley : A Short History*, by Mr. Uvedale Lambert, will soon

vii

be ready. Other texts are being considered by the Committee for publication in this new series of histories of Surrey parishes.

The Society's transcript of Leatherhead parish registers has been re-typed and indexed by the Society of Genealogists, and an indexed copy is now in the Library ; a complete transcript of the Charlwood registers has been made by our members, Mrs. Lane and Mrs. Sewill.

Photographic copies of a map of Ashtead of 1802 by James Wyburd, the property of Mr. A. R. Cotton, and of Lord Hylton's map of the Tattershall Estate in 1764 (parishes of Gatton, Merstham, Chipstead and Chaldon) have been made, and on the Committee's recommendation the Society has purchased the original map of the Manor of Pendell in Blechingley in 1622, by William Boycot.

The Committee has given advice or assistance to members and others carrying out research in the parishes of Charlwood, Chipstead, Coulsdon, Cuddington, Elstead, Horley, Malden, Merstham, Oxted and Thorpe ; and has been instrumental in securing the gift or loan to the Society of documents and transcripts : in particular, two important collections of manorial and estate documents relating to Oxted and neighbouring parishes have been received on loan from the owners, Captain C. E. H. Master and the Barrow Green Estate Co. respectively, and deposited in the Croydon Public Library. A calendar of these documents by the late Mr. F. C. W. Hiley and Mr. Clarence G. Paget, is in progress.

Records of Commissary and Consistory Courts of Surrey.—These records, which relate to the whole of the old geographical county, were transferred entirely to the new Diocese of Guildford in 1927. For many years they had been stored at Southwark Cathedral, and since 1905 in an underground room there. This accommodation was most unsatisfactory, and in 1946 Mr. H. V. H. Everard found the bundles of Parish Register Transcripts only partially sorted and in some cases covered with mildew. At his instance the Society investigated the condition of the records, and was finally able to arrange for their transfer to the Southwark Public Library, which generously provided accommodation. This applies to all classes of records except those relating to Tithe Apportionment, which have been transferred to the County Record Office, Kingston-upon-Thames. Mr. Everard has not only supervised the packing, transfer and unpacking of the documents, but has since completed their sorting and rearrangement. It should be noted that the documents are still technically in the custody of the Guildford Diocesan Registrar, 1, The Sanctuary, Westminster, S.W.1., to whom applications should be made for permission to inspect records. The records include marriage bonds, transcripts of parish registers, visitation papers, proceedings before the ecclesiastical courts and licences for various church officials and for meeting houses.

The Council draws the attention of members to the classified bibliography : *Local History Handlist*, published by the Historical

Association (21, Bedford Square, London, W.C.1 ; price 1/1 ;
interleaved, in stiff boards, 2/- post free). The first edition is
still available, but revision is in progress : corrections and suggestions will be welcomed by Dr. J. F. Nichols, F.S.A., 15, Minster
Road, Godalming.

VISITS AND LECTURES, 1948.—The following were held during
the year:—

Visits

13th April. To Chertsey Church and the remains of Chertsey
Abbey, followed by a visit to Thorpe Church, all of which were
described by Mr. E. A. Freeman. At the end of the day some of
the members walked over to see the Elizabethan House, "Great
Fosters," at Egham.

15th May. Ewell Church and village, conducted by Mr. Cloudesley S. Willis, F.S.A. The members visited the site of Nonsuch
Palace, which was described by Mr. S. R. Turner, F.R.I.B.A.,
on the site of the Banqueting Hall. An old cottage in Cheam
and the 16th century houses in Park Lane were also noted. The
memorials and brasses in the Lumley Chapel, Cheam, were
described by Miss Müller.

22nd June. By permission of Lord Ennisdale, the members
visited the 16th century house at Baynards Park, near Cranleigh,
where a most interesting account was given by Mrs. Montagu
Skinner. From there to New Park Farm, where Mr. A. B. Johnston showed the 15th and 16th century parts of the house. Thence
to St. Nicholas Church, Cranleigh, which was described by the
Rector, the Rev. H. R. L. Johnston.

10th July. Annual "out of the County" visit to Chichester.
The Rev. C. Gordon conducted the party round the Cathedral.
Other buildings seen were Pallant House (1712), the Greyfriars
Church (here Dr. Wilson, F.S.A., met the party and lectured on
the antiquities kept there), St. Mary's Hospital, where again Dr.
Wilson was the guide, and No. 20, St. Martin's Square, described
by Miss H. Johnstone, Litt.D. The "Pudens Stone," one of the
most important Roman inscriptions in the country, was also
inspected.

17th August. The Churches at Stoke D'Abernon and Fetcham
were described by Mr. R. Morrish, F.S.A. Slyfield Manor House
was visited, where the members were conducted by Mrs. Hitchin.
The arrangements for later in the day, viz., a visit to the excavations at "The Mounts," Leatherhead, had to be cancelled at the
last minute owing to a sudden change in the weather.

11th September. Warlingham and Farleigh Churches were
described by Mr. H. Everard, and at Addington the Church and
Churchyard were described by Mr. K. A. Ryde, A.L.A.

Lectures

28th February. At the Technical College, Stoke Park, Guildford. In the morning, Miss M. E. Wood, M.A., F.S.A., lectured on Norman Domestic Architecture. In the afternoon, Mr. E. Yates, F.S.A., on Wealden Iron-Working.

9th October. Also at the Technical College, Mr. C. D. Hawley, F.R.I.B.A., gave a lecture in the morning on the appreciation of beauty in old buildings, and at 2.30 p.m. Mr. J. H. Harvey, F.S.A., lectured on Gothic Builders and the County of Surrey. All these lectures were illustrated by lantern slides.

The "Register of Interests" meetings also took the form of lectures with slides, as follows:—

3rd January. Flint and Flint Implements by Mr. W. F. Rankine, F.S.A., Scot.

7th February. Monumental Brasses by Mr. R. H. Pearson, Secretary of the Monumental Brasses Society.

13th November. Flint Working by Mr. A. D. Lacaille ; this had the added interest of a film to illustrate how flint implements were fashioned.

These three lectures were held at The Centenary Hall, Chapel Street, Guildford.

11th December. At the New Bull Hotel, Leatherhead, Mr. A. W. G. Lowther, F.S.A., A.R.I.B.A., gave a talk on the Excavations at "The Mounts," Pachesham, near Leatherhead, in collaboration with the Leatherhead and District Local History Society. The talk was illustrated by an exhibition of finds from the site, plans and maps. The lecturer was followed by Mr. G. C. Dunning, F.S.A., who described the pottery found and its importance, and by Mr. J. H. Harvey, F.S.A., who spoke about the history of the site and its discovery, from early documents at the Public Record Office.

EXCAVATIONS.—*Farthing Down, Coulsdon,* in 1948. Generous financial support given by the Corporation of the City of London, the owners of Farthing Down, made it possible for Mr. Hope-Taylor to plan extensive excavations on this site, which were carried out on behalf of this Society during the month of June.

The chief objects of the excavations were :—

(1) To test the theory that a flat-grave Saxon cemetery lay on the Down, in addition to the burial mounds of that period which were excavated in 1871.

(2) To re-excavate certain of the barrows to obtain more information concerning their structure, and to find out how far the report on the 1871 digging (S.A.C. VI, pp. 109-117) was accurate and reliable, careful examination having disclosed strange discrepancies in it.

Both objects were achieved. A flat-grave cemetery was located, and six sample graves excavated (one of them disturbed). Finds included a small decorated pot (containing a small unworked piece of amber), two iron knives, an iron spear, beads and the wing bones of a goose, the last beside the left leg of an adult male Saxon. All the graves were orientated south-north. In one case there were slots in the grave-floor which had evidently housed wooden head-and-foot boards.

The other investigations proved that the **1871** excavations were carried out in a barbarous fashion and that the report is even more unreliable than superficial examination had indicated.

In addition a small mound of doubtful character (No. **13** on Grinsell's map, S.A.C. XLII, p. 46) was totally excavated. It proved to be a barrow and a grave-pit was located, but it would appear that no interment had ever taken place—the grave was empty and there was no indication that it had ever been disturbed.

It is hoped to continue the exploration of the flat-grave cemetery during **1949.**

Trial Excavations at Hambledon.—In his "County Book" on Surrey, Mr. Eric Parker describes the discovery of a large quantity of ancient pottery in his grounds, some thirty years ago. He expressed the wish that the site (on the "Tolt" near Hambledon) could be properly investigated, and showed the greatest courtesy to Mr. Hope-Taylor when the latter undertook trial investigations on the site (assisted by Mr. T. K. Walls).

Unfortunately the site proved to have been exhausted by the earlier unsystematic excavations, and the one undisturbed section that was located was only a few feet across—and that evidently not at the focus of the site. Nevertheless, sufficient evidence was found, in the shape of charcoal, stake-holes and pottery sherds, to suggest that this was a mediæval living site—probably no more than a hovel. The pottery previously found on the site (and now in Mr. Parker's collection at Feathercombe, Hambledon) was dated by Mr. Hope-Taylor to the **12th** and **13th** centuries : he intends, with Mr. Parker's permission, to make a fuller study of the collection and publish a note on it in a future volume of the *Collections.*

Old Malden.—Mr. L. W. Carpenter, Hon. Local Secretary for the area, is continuing the investigations of the interesting pre-Roman, Roman and Early Mediæval occupation site, first mentioned in the Annual Report for **1947.** The discovery of some ditches of Early Roman date (the finds from them include Samian Ware of the late **1st** century A.D., as well as coarse ware and a lead "plummet"—possibly from a surveyor's *groma*) is a new feature of the site. The mediæval period is represented by further rubbish pits and much late **12th** and **13th** century pottery, including a fine series of dishes and flagons. (A full account of the work is to appear in a future Research Paper. A preliminary note on some of the mediæval pottery is included in Volume L.)

"The Mounts," Pachesham, near Leatherhead.—The second season's work on the site of the Royal Manor of Pachenesham Magna was continued, jointly with the Leatherhead and District Local History Society, for a month during part of July and August.

The work was confined to the western third of the area contained by the moat, the latter having been investigated (at this western end of the site) during the previous season.

The trench dug across the site, from north to south, revealed a circular rubbish pit, 12 feet wide at the top and 6 feet 6 inches deep, and which proved to have been in use from about A.D. **1200** until about A.D. **1290** (as dated from the pottery thrown into it with bones and other refuse). About 1290 it was filled with building debris, including broken roof-tiles of the same type as those found in the lowest level in the moat, and proving conclusively that 1290 (not 1250 as suggested in the Interim Report[1]) was the approximate date both of the construction of the moat and of the first roofing of the buildings with tiles, both of which must have been carried out for Eustace de Haache (or de "Hatch"), who is known to have been doing work to his Manor (which he held as tenant of Walter de Thorp) in **1292/3**.

The earlier pottery forms a most important series, and some of the fragments are of types of ware of especial interest.

In addition to the rubbish pit, two walls and a rectangular pier of flint construction were found, and the following-up and planning of these structures will constitute the main work during the 1949 season.

The finds include : a piece of an applied ornament of bronze ; several iron objects, including a complete three-pronged (agricultural) fork dating (from the level in which it was found) from the latter part of the fourteenth century ; a spindle-whorl made of chalk ; pieces of a "mortar" made of Purbeck marble. Also (from the buildings) dressed blocks of sandstone (some with remains of carved mouldings) and a quantity of Roman tiles (brought to the site for use in the earlier walls). Pieces of an oven, apparently of Norman date, include some interesting "voussoir-shaped" bricks. A piece of a large, moulded, block of Purbeck marble must have been used in part of the structure—possibly the Chapel which is specifically mentioned as having been destroyed by William de Wymeldon.

The latest pottery found (from the uppermost level) is of about A.D. 1350/80, and includes pieces of highly ornamental glazed ware jugs and platters. With this pottery was much debris from the final (14th century) destruction of the buildings, including roof-tiles, nails and pieces of a green-glazed roof-finial, which appears to have consisted of a figure holding a (?hunting) horn, reminiscent of the two figures of "mounted knights" ("milites

[1] Transactions of the Leatherhead and District Local History Society, I, No. 1.

equitantes") ordered, for Banstead Manor, from the potteries at Cheam in 1372/3 (used for the roof of the hall).[1]

Finally, it seems clear that there was no Roman or pre-Roman occupation at this site (as conjectured in the Interim Report) and that the "calcined flints," of which many more were found this season in the rubbish-pit, are from hearths of late Norman date.

Tayles Hill, Ewell.—This site was selected to be the first of those explored with the aid of the Ewell Excavation Fund. Owing to its being found impossible to obtain any paid labour, work for this season was only carried out intermittently, and with a few voluntary helpers. On the northern side of the site a well-preserved Roman road, similar in construction to that found on the nearby Purberry Shot site, but running almost at right-angles to it, was encountered. Two trenches, about 20 feet apart, were dug across it, and it was found to be 21 feet wide between two small side ditches. The latter (as was the case with the road on the Purberry Shot site) had clearly served mainly as "setting-out" ditches when the road was constructed, and the gravel metalling, 1 foot in thickness at the crown of the road, had been allowed to spread into, and partially fill, them when deposited to form the road. Apart from some mesolithic flint implements from beneath the road, and a few scraps of Roman pottery on its surface, there were no "finds" from this work. Despite the absence of any dating evidence, the construction of the road can be presumed to be of late 2nd century date from its being of identical construction with that on the Purberry Shot site, and for which there was ample evidence as to its date (S.A.C. Vol. L, Purberry Shot Report). It seems probable that these roads formed part of a planned "grid" of roads (a suggestion which is supported by finds of pieces of roads and of ditches on other sites at Ewell), but they do not appear to have been in use for any great length of time.

The sections were measured up and photographs taken, and it is intended that further work be carried out at this site during 1949 as and when possible.

MUSEUM AND MUNIMENT ROOM.—*Library, Museum and Arts Committee of the Guildford Borough Council.* The Society's representative on this Committee continued to be Mr. Bernard Rackham C.B., F.S.A. On the Museum Sub-Committee, Mr. Rackham and Dr. W. B. Billinghurst. Sir Ralph Oakden and Miss Sumner were empowered to act as substitutes if one or both were unable to attend.

Loans to the Museum.—12th century pottery from Old Malden, on loan from Mr. L. W. Carpenter. Two pieces of Romano-British pottery from Old Malden, also on loan from Mr. Carpenter. 13th century tiles from Waverley Abbey, given by Mr. Chandler. Early Bronze Age beaker from Kew Gardens, given by Mrs. Wilkinson.

---

[1] *History of* Banstead, H. A. C. Lambert, (I) 1912, pp. 128, 357ff.

Deposits in the Muniment Room.—Four Pyrford Manorial documents, on loan from Lord Onslow. One Court Book, 1811-1923. One Rental and Customary, 13 Edward IV. One Rent Roll, 1666. One Abstract of Rolls 16th and 17th centuries. Documents relating to the parish of Cranleigh (16th to 19th centuries), given by Lady Bingley. Draft Court Book of the Manor of Woking, 1770-1871, given by Mrs. Lampson. In addition, two maps, one of Woking Manor, 1719, and one of Frensham Beale, 1705, formerly in the stockroom of the Society, have been placed in the Muniment Room.

Conditions and Hours of Opening.—The Museum has been open free from 11 a.m. to 5 p.m. every week-day since September. Special arrangements for parties will be made on request to the Curator.

Recent Excavations Case.—During the past year this case has contained objects from the Crohamhurst Romano-British occupation site ; from Old Malden ; from Romano-British kilns at Overwey, Tilford ; Romano-British and Mediæval sherds from Hascombe ; and Mediæval and 16th century pottery from Southwark.

Attendance at the Museum.—There were 11,340 visitors.

Museum Store.—At the instance of the Society, the Corporation had also rented and reconditioned the Old Mortuary, Mill Lane, for use as a Museum store ; this building is provided with heating and a sink, and can be used as a workroom if required.

Library.—Gifts to the Library include the following : TS. copy of the Egham Enclosure Act, 1814, given by T. A. Bryan ; *Some Surrey Manor Houses*, illustrated by Lord Hylton, given by Hon. Perdita Hylton ; *Rambles Round Guildford*, 1928, given by Miss Farewell Jones ; *Leaves of Southwell*, 1945, given by Miss Farewell Jones ; *London Illustrated*, no date, given by R. G. Adams ; *History of Busbridge*, by the Rev. H. M. Larner, 1947, given by the author ; *Ogilby's Road Map*, 1791, give by Mrs. Lloyd ; *History of Thorpe*, by Frederick Turner, 1924, given by Miss E. M. Turner ; *History of St. Mary's Church, Thorpe*, by E. A. Freeman, 1947, given by the author ; *Ewell and its Church*, by H. Veall, 1948, given by the author ; *Who's Who in Surrey*, 1936, given by Dr. Wilfrid Hooper, LL.D., F.S.A. ; *History of Edward Latymer and His Foundations*, by William Wheatley, M.A., 1936, given by the author ; *Short History of Ewell and Nonsuch*, by Cloudesley S. Willis, F.S.A., 1948, given by the author ; *Roman Ways in the Weald*, by I. D. Margary, F.S.A., 1948, given by the author ; *List of Rectors of Nutfield from* 1291, with notes compiled by the Rector, the Rev. E. C. Hyde, and given by him.

In addition to the above, volumes have been received from other Societies, in exchange. *Archæological News Letter* is received every month.

Maps.—C. *Smith's Map of Surrey*, dated 1804 ; *Travelling*

Chart ; The London-Brighton Railway, dated about 1860, given by Dr. Eric Gardner ; *Map of Tooting* (1856), given by E. R. Burder ; Seven Ordnance Maps of Surrey, 6 in., 1870 Survey, given by G. Mackenzie Trench ; Thirty Ordnance Maps of West Surrey, 25 in., 1870 Survey, given by Messrs. Messenger, Morgan and May, of Quarry Street, Guildford.

Paintings.—Portrait of John Evelyn after Kneller, dated 1687, by Cecil Parker. This has been lent to the Society by C. J. A. Evelyn, a Vice-President. Thirty Oil Paintings of Surrey Houses and Cottages, both exterior and interior, by Ernest Christie and given by Miss M. Christie. Drawings and water-colour drawings of Chipstead by Hassell, dated 1824-1831, given by Dr. Wilfrid Hooper. Two water-colours : Windmill near Croydon and Church at Barnes, painted by A.R.D., 1898, and given by Warren Dawson. Three photographs of Western Green Church, given by Mrs. Davey, of Esher.

Other Gifts.—Two prints of Richmond Palace, given by W. J. Pickering ; print of Old Merstam, given by Colonel C. E. Morris ; specification of Works Account of Fetcham, 1710, given by R. B. Benger ; deeds of Limpsfield, given by B. Crewdson ; antique alms box, given by G. V. Bridgewater.

COUNCIL.—The following members retire under Rule IV and are ineligible for re-election for one year : R. L. Atkinson, C.B.E., F.S.A., W. C. Berwick Sayers, W. J. Pickering, T. Gatton Swayne, C. E. Sexton. To fill these vacancies and that created by the resignation of Mr. C. D. Hawley, the following are the names of candidates in respect of whom a ballot will be held at the Annual General Meeting :—

Dr. Billinghurst : Nominated by Council.
F. E. Bray : Nominated by Council.
Philip Corder : Nominated by Council.
W. H. C. Frend : Nominated by J. Wilson-Haffenden ; seconded by W. G. D. Evans.
J. A. Frere (Bluemantle Pursuivant of Arms) : Nominated by L. R. Stevens ; seconded by Philip Corder.
Mrs. Gibson : Nominated by Council.
Arthur R. Laird : Nominated by J. Wilson-Haffenden ; seconded by Cloudesley S. Willis.
John Lee-Hunt : Nominated by W. C. Berwick Sayers ; seconded by L. R. Stevens.
Mrs. Doris May, J.P.: Nominated by J. Wilson-Haffenden ; seconded by W. G. D. Evans.
Commander R. D. Merriman, R.I.N. (Retd.) : Nominated by Major A. Talbot Smith ; seconded by Colonel C. E. Morris.
Major H. Patrick : Nominated by Council.
G. F. Sanger : Nominated by L. R. Stevens ; seconded by Mrs. A. Stevens.

Colonel H. W. Wagstaffe, C.S.I., M.C. : Nominated by L. R. Stevens, seconded by Mrs. A. Stevens.

Miss D. Weeding : Nominated by Council.

VICE-PRESIDENTS.—Lord Greene the Master of the Rolls has been elected a Vice-President of the Society, also I. D. Margary, F.S.A., author of the recent book *Roman Ways in the Weald*.

DEATHS.—The Council regrets to announce the death of the following members of the Society during 1948 : Edwin Frost, Major T. Lethaby, Miss E. M. Murray, Colonel W. A. Quennell, Miss A. M. Rosier, Duncan Tovey, Mrs. Prynne, E. J. Lake, Lord Farrer, Lionel Sproule, Major H. R. E. Rudkin, Miss J. B. Littlejohn, R. S. Morrish, Edwin Davies, Lieut.-Colonel J. S. Wilson, O.B.E., Charles Leveson-Gower, F. C. W. Hiley.

FINANCE.—The expenditure for the year exceeded the income by over £400, chiefly in consequence of the large outlay on publications. The sale of surplus stock of back volumes continues to be a most useful source of income and profit is still being derived from the "Reigate" volume.

Two generous contributions have been received for excavations, £200 from the Corporation of London for Farthing Down, and £100 from Mr. R. C. Sherriff, F.S.A., for exploration of Roman sites at Ewell.

More income is needed to enable the growing activities of the Society to be provided for and it would assist to this end if more members would enter into covenants for payment of their subscriptions.

There are still more than 300 members who have not yet complied with repeated requests that they pay their subscriptions by Banker's Order. It is apparently not sufficiently realized how much unnecessary labour and also expense in stationery and postage can be saved if this method is adopted.

MEMBERSHIP.—The increase continues, the total number of members at the end of the year having risen to 941. The Council have decided to discontinue Membership Cards in 1950, the advantages of their use not sufficiently justifying the additional labour and expense entailed by their issue.

SURREY ARCHÆOLOGICAL SOCIETY

Cash Account for Year ended 31st December, 1948

RECEIPTS

	£ s. d.	£ s. d.	£ s. d.
Balance as at 1st January, 1948		383 11 6	
Less Received in Advance:			
Entrance Fees	3 10 0		
Subscriptions	11 10 0	15 0 0	308 11 6
Subscriptions:			
Arrears, 1947	4 10 0		
Current, 1948	459 10 0		
In Advance, 1949	8 0 0		
In Advance, 1950	1 10 0		
In Advance, 1951	1 0 0	473 10 0	
Entrance Fees:			
Arrears, 1947	10 0 0		
Current, 1948	36 10 0		
In Advance, 1949	2 10 0		
Life Compositions: New		39 10 0	
Payments in Excess		48 0 0	
		6 3 0	567 3 0
Donations			118 15 1
Sale of Publications			74 14 2
Interest on Investments			
Income Tax recovered on Dividends and Covenants			93
"Reigate" Volume:			
Sales	25 1 0		
Less Royalty	4 9 3		
Sale of Rifle			20 11 9
Profit on Conversion of Defence Bonds			1 0 0
Contributions to Excavation Fund:			
Corporation of London re Farthing Down	200 0 0		
R. C. Sherriff, Esq., for Ewell Excavation	100 0 0		
Sundry	8 0 6	308 0 6	
		£1,525 3 3	

PAYMENTS

	£ s. d.	£ s. d.	£ s. d.
Castle Arch:			
Rent		12 0 0	
Insurance		7 0 4	
Librarian		156 0 0	
Caretaker		12 0 0	187 0 4
Printing and Stationery			54 7 4
Postages, Telephone and Petty Disbursements			50 13 5
Clerical Assistance and Typewriting			26 7 0
Visits and Lectures:			
Sundry Expenses			
Less Meeting Tickets and Registration Fees			
Annual Meeting Expenses			8 18 1
Excavation:			
Farthing Down		189 3 2	17 9 0
Sundry		180 5 1	
Contributions to Allied Societies			219 3 8
Publications:			10 3 6
Volume XLIX		547 12 9	
Volume L		103 13 8	
Research Paper No. 1	92 9 4		
Less Sales	2 1 8	90 7 8	801 41
Books and Maps Purchased			23 39
Typewriter			25 15 6
Photographs:			16 8 5
Tattersalls Map		15 18 2	
Oatlands Grotto		6 13 0	
Guildown Exhibits		2 10 0	
Southwark Documents Removal Expenses			
Balance as at 31st December, 1948:			
At Bank			25 1 2
			40 5 3
			£1,525 3 3

B

SURREY ARCHÆOLOGICAL SOCIETY

Statement of Liabilities and Assets at 31st December, 1948

LIABILITIES

	£ s. d.	£ s. d.
Entrance Fees and Subscriptions paid in advance ...		12 0 0
Excavation Fund:		
Ewell Excavation	100 0 0	
Sundry	131 15 7	231 15 7
Balance in favour of the Society:		
As at January 1st, 1948	2,989 12 2	
Deficit incurred during year ...	411 6 4	2,578 5 10
		£2,822 1 5

ASSETS

	£ s. d.	£ s. d.
Investments:		
£316 4s. 8d. 2½% Consols	300 0 0	
£21 2s. 0d. 3½% War Stock	20 0 0	
91 National Savings Certificates	72 16 0	
£415 0s. 0d. 3% Defence Bonds	415 0 0	
£500 0s. 0d. 2½% Defence Bonds (Conversion Issue)	500 0 0	
£400 0s. 0d. 3% Savings Bonds, 1975 ...	400 0 0	
£1,065 0s. 0d. 2½% Defence Bonds ...	1,065 0 0	2,772 16 0
(Market Value: £2,807 3s. 10d.)		
Cash:		
At Bank		49 5 5
		£2,822 1 5

L. R. STEVENS,
Hon. Treasurer.

Audited and found correct,
G. OGILVY JACKSON.
T. E. C. WALKER.

30th March, 1949.

The Library was valued at £650 in 1934. The Stock of Publications and the Society's Exhibits and Furniture are not valued. At 31st December, members whose subscriptions are in arrear number 13. There are 59 Life Members. During the year 17 members died, 36 resigned, 11 were removed, and 81 new members were elected.

SURREY ARCHÆOLOGICAL SOCIETY

Excavation Fund Account, 1948

RECEIPTS

	£ s. d.	£ s. d.
Balance in hand, 1st January, 1948 ...		142 18 4
Contributions :		
1 of £200 ...	200 0 0	
1 ,, 100 ...	100 0 0	
1 ,, 2 ...	2 0 0	
1 ,, 1 ...	1 0 0	
1 ,, 10 0 ...	10 0	
5 ,, 10 0 ...	2 10 0	
5 ,, 5 0 ...	1 5 0	
6 ,, 2 6 ...	15 0	
		308 0 6
		£450 18 10

PAYMENTS

	£ s. d.	£ s. d.
Excavations :		
Farthing Down ...	200 0 0	
The Mount, Leatherhead ...	10 0 0	
Thursley ...	9 3 3	
		219 3 3
Balance in hand, 31st December, 1948 :		
Ewell Fund ...	100 0 0	
Sundry ...	131 15 7	
		231 15 7
		£450 18 10

L. R. STEVENS,
Hon. Treasurer.

Audited and found correct,
    G. OGILVY JACKSON.
    T. E. C. WALKER.

30th March, 1949

SURREY ARCHÆOLOGICAL SOCIETY

CASTLE ARCH, GUILDFORD

Albury.—MISS O. M. HEATH, Albury House, Albury.

Aldershot.—J. H. GIBSON, M.D., The White House, Lansdowne Road, Aldershot.

Ashtead and Leatherhead.—A. W. G. LOWTHER, F.S.A., A.R.I.B.A., The Old Quarry, Ashtead.

Bagshot and Chobham.—G. C. B. POULTER, F.S.A.Scot., Hut 1, Collingwood Place, Camberley.

Bookhams.—J. H. HARVEY, Half Moon Cottage, Preston Cross, Little Bookham.

Camberley.—R. L. ATKINSON, C.B.E., F.S.A., Upper Portesbery, Camberley.

Chipstead.—MAJOR A. TALBOT SMITH, Flint Cottage, Chipstead.

Cobham.—T. E. C. WALKER, Spring Grove, Water Lane, Cobham.

Cranleigh.—H. G. EVANS, Wanborough Cottage, Wanborough Lane, Cranleigh.

Croydon.—W. C. BERWICK SAYERS, 52 Blenheim Crescent, S. Croydon.

Dorking.—E. L. SELLICK, Southmead, Westcott Road, Dorking.

Epsom.—D. A. BURL, 20 The Parade, Epsom.

Ewell.—CLOUDESLEY S. WILLIS, F.S.A., 9 High Street, Ewell.

Farnham.—W. F. RANKINE, F.S.A.Scot., Yew Tree Cottage, Wrecclesham.

Godalming.—J. F. NICHOLS, Ph.D., F.S.A., 15 Minster Road, Godalming.

Godstone.—MISS K. M. KENYON, M.A., F.S.A., Kirkstead, Godstone.

Haslemere.—G. R. ROLSTON, M.R.C.S., L.R.C.P., Crofts, Haslemere.

Horsell.—F. E. BRAY, Woodham Grange, Horsell, Woking.

East Horsley, West Horsley.—MISS D. ROSCOE, Tyrrellswood, West Horsley.

Kingston-on-Thames.—W. ST. L. FINNY, M.D., J.P., F.S.A., 41 Liverpool Road, Kingston Hill.

Kingswood.—J. WILSON-HAFFENDEN, Home Wood, Eyhurst Close, Kingswood, Surrey.

Old Malden.—L. W. CARPENTER, The School House, Church Road, Worcester Park.

Merstham.—COLONEL C. E. MORRIS, D.S.O., Merlebank, Church Hill, Merstham.

Reigate.—WILFRID HOOPER, LL.D., F.S.A., Loxwood, Ridgeway Road, Redhill.

Sanderstead.—B. HOPE-TAYLOR, 33 Purley Oaks Road, Sanderstead.

Seale and Runfold.—REV. T. F. GRIFFITH, Oak Hatch, Runfold, Farnham.

Shere, Peaslake and Gomshall.—A. E. P. COLLINS, Wayside, Wonham Way, Gomshall.

Surbiton.—S. WILLY, Ashbourne, Orchard Avenue, Thames Ditton.

Weybridge.—ERIC GARDNER, M.B., F.S.A., Portmore House, Weybridge.

Witley.—MISS M. HEWSON, St. Margaret's, Witley.

LIST OF MEMBERS

Corrected *to* 31*st* January, 1950.

Copies of Rules etc., may be had on application to the Honorary Secretary

----

Any Member intending to resign must signify this intention in writing before 1st January, otherwise he will be liable to pay his subscription for the current year.

It is particularly requested that speedy intimation of any change of residence, or errors in addresses, may be sent to the Honorary Secretary.

The date preceding each name indicates the year in which the name first appears in the List of Members.

1948 ABBEY, Miss Joan, Claremont, 74 *Chart Lane, Reigate.*

1943 Adams, R. G., *Kingsdown*, 10 *The Glebe, Worcester Park.*

1942 Allden, Miss M. E., *Headley Lodge, Ockford Road, Godalming.*

1949 Allen, Mrs. A., *Greenmead, Wood* Place *Lane,* Coulsdon.

1932 Allen, C. J., *Yew* Tree Cottage, Farley Green, *Albury.*

1948 Ames, E. F., *Holmesdale, Horseshoe Lane,* Merrow, *Guildford.*

1935 Angier, Mrs., *Hayburn, Church Grove, Hampton Wick.*

1939 Antrobus, P. K., *Prestbury, Oxted.*

1922 Armitage, N. C., M.A., *Hertslets,* Claygate.

1935 Armitage, Mrs. N. C., *Hertslets,* Claygate.

1927 Armitage Moore, C., *Winterfold House,* Cranleigh.

1949 Ashcombe, Lord, *Denbies, Dorking.*

1927 Asher, Mrs. W., *Round Oak, Weybridge.*

1912 Atkinson, R. L., O.B.E., M.C., M.A., F.S.A., *Upper Portesbery,* Camberley.

1931 Ayres, F. R., *Dunstable, The Mount, Guildford.*

1932 BACON, E., *La Boheme, Hurst Grove, Walton-on-Thames.*

1929 Bailey, Miss A., 33 *Park Town, Oxford.*

1943 Bailey, T. A., 12 *Anne Boleyn's Walk, Cheam.*

1943 Baily, G. D. P., *Eastlands,* near Billingshurst, *Sussex.*

1948 Baker, R. G. M., 50 *Hurst Lane, East Molesey.*

1949 Ball, R. Martin, 78 *Chaldon Way, Coulsdon.*

1925 Ballantyne, H., *Copt Hill* Court, *Copt Hill Lane,* Burgh Heath.

1943 Balthazar, Miss A., Princess *Court Hotel,* Victoria *Road, London, W.*8.

1918 Bamber, Mrs. B. C., *Clifton House, Castle Hill, Guildford.*

1929 Bamfield, Mrs. K. B., Purser's Piece, *Peaslake.*

1947 Banks, Mrs. R. H., *Beech Coppice, Woodland Way,* Kingswood.

1929 Bannerman, Capt. R. R. Bruce, M.C., F.S.A.Scot., British *Embassy, Washington* 8, *U.S.A.*

1923 Barclay, Lieut.-Col. R. W., J.P., D.L., *Bury Hill, Dorking.*

1942 Barford, Miss M. A., *The Park* Gate *Hotel,* 57 Bayswater *Road, London, W.*2.

1929 Bargman, D. C., *Handycot*, Calvert Road, Dorking.
1943 Barnes, Mrs. M., *Steepways*, Birches Close, Epsom.
1947 Barnes, Mrs. Mabel, *Pinehurst*, Hook Heath Avenue, Woking.
1947 Bartlett, Mrs. D. W., *4b The Grove*, Horley, Surrey.
1942 Barton, W. T., *Shepherd's Hurst*, Outwood.
1903 Bashall, J., M.A , *Carricknath, St. Mawes*, Cornwall.
1902 Bates, E., A.R.I.B.A., *46 Bath Hill Court, Bournemouth, Hants*.
1942 Bath, Miss E. J., *1 St. John's Road, Redhill*.
1944 Batstone, R. F. S., *1 Baskerville Road, Wandsworth Common, London, S.W.18*.
1891 Battersea Public Library, Lavender Hill, London, S.W.11.
1949 Battisombe, J. H., A.R.I.B.A., *Thrums, Epsom Road, Ewell*.
1933 Baxter, E. A., 39 Carlton Crescent, North Cheam.
1949 Beck, Miss N. E., *Swallowfield, Shere*.
1921 Beddington, Carshalton and Wallington Archæological Society (H. V. Molesworth Roberts, *Hon. Sec., 7 Mellows Road, Wallington*).
1936 Bee, A. R. W., *2 Marina, Tenby, S. Wales*.
1945 Behrens, Major E. Beddington, M.C., Ph.D., *99a Park Lane, London, W.1*.
1949 Belam, F. A., M.D., *Meadway, Beech Lawn, Guildford*.
1926 Bell, Mrs. M. C., *The Cottage, Lingfield*.
1902 Bell, W. A. Juxon, *Little Alces, Seaford, Sussex*.
1945 Bellis, Miss L. M. J., *Pearemount Cottage, Chilworth, Guildford*.
1936 Benger, R. B., *Burntwood, Headley Road, Leatherhead*.
1937 Benger, Mrs. E. M., *Burntwood, Headley Road, Leatherhead*.
1949 Bennet-Clark, Miss M. E., *Weylea, Wey Road, Weybridge*.
1936 Bermondsey Public Library, *Spa Road, Bermondsey, London, S.E.16*.
1903 Berry, F. J., *Limpsfield*.
1909 Bidder, Lieut.-Col. H. F., D.S.O., F.S.A., *The Malt House, Nettlebed, Henley-on-Thames, Oxon*.
1938 Billinghurst, W. B., M.A., 24 *The* Fairway, Merrow, Guildford.
1919 Binney, C. N., M.R.C.S., L.R.C.P., *Edgecombe, Walton-on-the-Hill*.
1949 Bird, Mrs. A. M., *Raglan Hotel, Reigate*.
1947 Bird, B. H., *Greystones, Bentley, Farnham*.
1947 Bird, Miss M. E., 39 *Gunnersby* Court, Bollo Lane, Acton, W.3.
1939 Birmingham Public Libraries, *Reference Library*, Birmingham, 1.
1944 Birmingham University Library, *Edmund* Street, Birmingham, 3.
1949 Bishop, J. S., 12 *The* Court, Berryfields, Guildford.
1944 Blackman, H., B.Sc., F.R.Econ.S., *Hadi, West Humble, Dorking*.
1943 Blackman, Mrs. I., *Hadi, West Humble, Dorking*.
1947 Blackwood, B. G. W., F.R.S.A., *Westmead, Chartway, Reigate*.
1949 Blake, F. M., *2 Worcester Close, Mitcham*.
1942 Blanchard, Mrs. A. A., *Holmbury, Station Road, Thames Ditton*.
1948 Blick, F. N., *24a Beaufort Road, Reigate*.
1925 Bloxam, R. N., *Ripley Court, Woking*.
1942 Bolsover, Miss E., *221 Commonside East, Mitcham*.
1948 Bond, R. M., *Beechwood, Betchworth*.
1936 Boorman, S., J.P., C.A., *Birchley, West Clandon*.
1945 Booth, Miss Anne, 20 *Church Hill, Aldershot, Hants*.

1936 Borelli, C. E., 35 & 36 *The* Borough, Farn*ham*.

1947 Bosanquet, Mrs. E. M., *Highcroft Hotel, Hindhead*.

1919 Boston Public Library, U.S.A , *per* Bernar*d Quaritch, Ltd.*, 11 Gra*fton* Street, *London, W.*1.

1948 Boucher, P. W., 22 *Fromondes Road, Cheam*.

1948 Bourdon Smith, P., For*ge Cottage, Hu*rst Green, O*x*ted.

1949 Bourke, D. E., *Fircone* Cottage, *Hart Hill, Hythe, Hants.*

1949 Bowen, H. C., 85 Farn*ham Road, Guildford*.

1944 Bowes, R. N., Par*k*side, *St. Mary's Road, Leatherhead*.

1924 Box, D. E. Hazel, 53, Farn*ham Road, Guildford*.

1926 Box, F. E., 4, *Christchurch Road, Winchester*.

1949 Boxall, A. L., *St. Margaret's, Cobham Road, Fetcham*.

1922 Boxall, Miss H., *Averill Lodge, Gloucester Road, Kingston Hill*.

1945 Boyling, N. D., 38 *Red Down Road, Coulsdon*.

1943 Brachi, R. M., Strath*more, Rydens Road, Walton-on-Thames*.

1943 Bradbury, Miss E. L., County *Hospital, Dorking*.

1941 Bradford, Miss W., 5 *Manor House, Station Road, Thames* Ditton.

1945 Brandon, Miss C., *Pearemount* Cottage, C*h*il*worth, Guildford*.

1949 Bray, C. A., *Woodham* Grange, Horsell, *Woking*.

1931 Bray, F. Edmund, K.C., *Trenchmore, Shere*.

1926 Bray, Francis E., *Woodham Grange, Horsell, Woking*.

1931 Bray, Mrs. Francis E., *Woodham Grange, Horsell, Woking*.

1949 Breen, Miss M. M., B.A., *Ashmead, Redhill*.

1945 Briant, Mrs. C., 18 *Morpeth Mansions, Westminster, S.W.*1.

1949 Bridges, T. E., Good*mans* Fur*ze, Headley, Epsom*.

1948 Bridgewater, G. V., *Lucas Green* Manor, *Chobham*.

1910 Brighton Public Library, Brig*hton*.

1949 Broadwood, Capt. E. H. T., M.C., C.C., J.P., *Lyne, Capel*.

1947 Bromley, Miss I. M., 2 *Little Stokely Farm, Bunch Lane, Haslemere*.

1947 Brookes-Smith, Mrs. M. G., Fern*hill, Hawley, Camberley*.

1947 Brounger, Miss M. G., *Orchard End, Churt, Farnham*.

1944 Brown, The Rev. C. K. F., M.A., B. Litt., D. Phil. (Oxon.) *Woolpit, Ewhurst*.

1945 Brown, Miss Jane, *Aldershot* County *High School for Girls, Aldershot, H*ants.

1948 Brown, J. F., 6 *Poyle Road, Guildford*.

1949 Browne, Mrs. P. M., *Glebefields*, Lower *Edgeborough Road, Guildford*

1943 Bruzaud, G. J., F.R.I.C.S., *Highfield End, West Byfleet*.

1943 Buck, A. G. Randle, *Dunkery House, Weare, Axbridge, Somerset.*

1949 Buckell, L. E., *The Hatch, Epsom Road, Leatherhead*.

1948 Burgess, S. L., 21 *Spencer Gardens, East Sheen, S.W.*14.

1920 Burl, D. A., 20 *The* Parade, *Epsom*.

1943 Burnham, R. H., 39 *Church Lane, Wallington*.

1946 Bushell, A. C., 2 *Albury Road, Merstham*.

1949 Butcher, D. J., LL.B., *Roselea, Springfield Meadows, Weybridge*.

1945 Butler, Miss E. M., 1 *A*lcon Court, *Earlsfield Road, Wandsworth Common, S.W.*18.

1892 Butler, Miss M., *The* Fis*hp*onds, Surbit*on H*ill.

1921 Butler, W., Lieut.-Col., *Percy House, West End, Esher*.

1949 CADMAN, A. L., 24 *Somers Road, Reigate.*
1945 California University Library, U.S.A., *per Stevens & Brown Ltd.*, 28-30 *Little Russell Street, London, W.C.*1.
1942 Campbell, Mrs. C. K., 102 *Longley Road, London, S.W.*17.
1947 Carpenter, L. W., *The School House, Church Road, Worcester Park.*
1942 Carrington, L. I., *The Grey Cottage, Chipstead.*
1941 Carruthers, F. G., B.A., F.S.A., 40 *Gloucester Road, Kew.*
1945 Carter, Miss J. M., 17 *Ardmore Avenue, Guildford.*
1948 Carter, W., C.B.E., M.A., *Intwood, Cobham Way, East Horsley.*
1946 Cartwright, Mrs. R. F., B.A., *St. Andrew's Vicarage, Surbiton.*
1944 Cash, Miss M. E., *Shepherd's Crown, The Avenue, Tadworth.*
1949 Castwood, H. W., *High Lanes, Grosvenor Road, Godalming.*
1943 Chadwick, V. R., M.I.Mech.E., 10 *Laurel Road, Barnes, S.W.*13.
1920 Chadwyck-Healey, Sir Gerald, Bart., *Balbeg, Straiton, Maybole, Ayrshire.*
1924 Chamberlain, J. A., B.Sc., 27 *Gilkes Crescent, London, S.E.*21.
1929 Chance, Miss M., *Meryon, Woodham Park Way, West Byfleet.*
1947 Chandler, G. E., 91 *High Street, Aldershot.*
1945 Chandler, H. J., F.L.A., *Public Library House, Finkle Street, Workington, Cumberland.*
1942 Chapman, H. C., 31 *York Street, London, W.*1.
1945 Charlwood, Mrs. S. E., 58 *Fengates Road, Redhill.*
1906 Charterhouse School Library, *Godalming.*
1945 Chater, Miss M., *Brendon, The Chase, Kingswood.*
1934 Cheesman, G. W., *Mark Merrow, Ridgeway, Guildford.*
1934 Cheesman, Mrs. G. W., *Mark Merrow, Ridgeway, Guildford.*
1947 Chesterton, Mrs. D. L., 15 *Elmhurst Court, St. Peters Road, Croydon.*
1915 Chicago, Ill., U.S.A., Newberry Library, *per B. F. Stevens & Brown, Ltd.*, 28-30 *Little Russell Street, London, W.C.*1.
1948 Child, M., F.R.S.A., *Gortraney, Horseshoe Lane, Merrow, Guildford.*
1947 Chiles, Mrs. R. K., 38 *Court Hill, Sanderstead.*
1946 Chipstead Residents' Association (Miss D. M. Bland, *Hon. Treas., Middleshaws, Walpole Avenue, Chipstead.*)
1949 Chisholm, J. D., 76 *Court Hill, Sanderstead.*
1944 Chivers, C. W., *Woodacre, Horsham Road, Cranleigh.*
1947 Christie, Miss M. G. C., 47 *Shaldon Road, Caterham-on-the-Hill.*
1919 Chubb, The Rev. H. P. B., *The Bungalow, High Street, Cobham, Surrey.*
1945 Clark, A. J., *Downderry, The Drive, Farnham Road, Guildford.*
1940 Clark, F. S., *The New Inn, Worplesdon.*
1945 Clark, Miss J. E., M.A., *Aldershot County High School for Girls, Aldershot, Hants.*
1949 Clark, Mrs. K. I., *Downderry, The Drive, Farnham Road, Guildford.*
1936 Clarke, F. J., *Gowdhurst, Chart Lane, Dorking.*
1946 Clarke, Miss H. K. B., 18a *Upper Green East, Mitcham.*
1947 Clarke, Miss M. A., *Gowdhurst, Chart Lane, Dorking.*
1948 Clarke-Williams, A. R., M.A., LL.B., F.R.H.S., F.Z.S., *Woodville, Ongar Hill, Addlestone.*
1921 Clay, Lt.-Col. E. C., C.B.E., *Berry Hall, Great Walsingham, Norfolk.*
1928 Cleveland Public Library, 325 *Superior Avenue, Ohio, U.S.A., per Hy. Sotheran Ltd.*, 43 Piccadilly, *London, W.*1.

1932 Coggin, Mrs. M., *Darenth, Deepdene Drive, Dorking.*
1930 Coggin, Capt. T. G. C., *Darenth, Deepdene Drive, Dorking.*
1949 Coleman, F., *Lockner Holt, Chilworth.*
1935 Collins, A. E. P., *Wayside, Wonham Way, Gomshall.*
1949 Collins, F. J., *The Caravan, Station Road, Effingham.*
1936 Collison-Morley, L., *Nostra, Shamley Green, Guildford.*
1937 Colyer, H. G., *Brendon, Chesham Road, Guildford.*
1946 Combe, A. C., *Amulree, Eyhurst Close, Kingswood.*
1931 Combridge, J. T., M.A., *15 Campden Grove, London, W.8.*
1912 Constitutional Club, *Northumberland Avenue, London, W.C.2.*
1947 Cook, Miss E., B.A., *Newlands, Chipstead.*
1947 Cook, J. B., M.D., B.Ch., D.P.H., M.R.C.S., L.R.C.P., *2 Pembroke Villas, The Green, Richmond.*
1927 Cooke, B. Campbell, *9 Heath Rise, Putney Hill, London, S.W.15.*
1930 Cooksey, The Rev. Canon W., P.P., H.C.F., *The Presbytery, Caterham.*
1947 Cooper, Mrs. D. N., *Kingsweir, Heath Drive, Tadworth*
1946 Cooper, Miss J. M., J.P., *Ramster Gate House, Chiddingfold.*
1903 Cooper, W. V., *42 Gloucester Place, London, W.1.*
1926 Copenhagen Royal Library, *per Francis Edwards Ltd., 83a High Street, Marylebone, W.1.*
1944 Corder, P., M.A., *108 Riddlesdown Road, Purley.*
1925 Corfield, Dr. C., *Broadmark Place, Rustington, Sussex.*
1919 Cornell University Library, U.S.A., *per Messrs. E. G. Allen & Son, Ltd., 14 Grape Street, London, W.C.2.*
1949 Cornish, F., *Lonsdale, 63 Cheam Road, Ewell East.*
1949 Costar, N. E., *9 Margaretta Terrace, Chelsea, S.W.3.*
1947 Cotton, A. F. S., *Ebbisham, Walton-on-the-Hill.*
1926 Cotton, A. R., M.B.E., F.S.A., *Inward Shaw, Park Lane, Ashstead.*
1930 Cotton, Mrs. A. R., *Inward Shaw, Park Lane, Ashstead.*
1946 Cotton, Mrs. E., *Ebbisham, Walton-on-the-Hill.*
1927 Cottrell, Mrs. F. M., *Dunedin, Giggs Hill, Thames Ditton.*
1948 Coulsdon and Purley Public Libraries, *Central Library, Banstead Road, Purley.*
1942 Couzens, Mrs. D. L., *Tepestede, Chipstead.*
1948 Covell, Maj.-Gen. Sir Gordon, C.I.E., *Sunridge, Fairoak Lane, Oxshott.*
1942 Cox, Miss D., *Westholme, Chestnut Avenue, Esher.*
1942 Cox, Miss H. M., *Westholme, Chestnut Avenue, Esher.*
1942 Crandell, Miss E. G., *15 Balfour Road, Ilford, Essex.*
1945 Crandell, Mrs. F. K., *15 Balfour Road, Ilford, Essex.*
1935 Cranleigh School Archæological Society, *Cranleigh School, Cranleigh.*
1926 Crawley, J. P., *The Holt, Canon's Hill, Old Coulsdon.*
1943 Creasy, F. J. R., *Clevelands, Star Lane, Chipstead.*
1940 Cresswell, The Rev. C. L., C.V.O., M.A., F.S.A., *Three Barrows Place, Elstead, Surrey.*
1938 Crewdson, B., *Red Lane Farm, Limpsfield.*
1937 Croke, Dr. A. E., *Sussex House, High Street, Guildford.*
1948 Crosbie-Walsh, T., F.R.I.C., F.C.S., *44 Woodcrest Road, Purley.*
1926 Crosfield, Miss M. C., F.G.S., *Greensand, 78 Doods Road, Reigate.*
1927 Cross, Miss D. L., *Windlecote, Worplesdon Hill, Woking.*

1946 Cross, F. T., *Southern Wood, West Humble, Dorking.*
1945 Cross, John, *Windlecote, Worplesdon Hill, Woking.*
1946 Cross, Mrs. M. A. W., *Southern Wood, West Humble, Dorking.*
1907 Crosse, Miss K. M., Caterham Hotel, Caterham Valley.
1943 Croydon Natural History Society, *Hon. Sec.* W. Benians, F.A.I., M.R.San.I., 34 *Raleigh Avenue, Wallington,* Surrey.
1892 Croydon Public Library, Croydon.
1942 Cruickshank, Mrs. D. M., *Little Orchard,* Great Bookham.
1914 Currie, L. C. E., *Pardons, Warwicks Bench, Guildford.*

1942 Dadswell, Miss I. M., 38 *Greenhill, Sutton,* Surrey.
1932 Dalley, Mrs. M. W., 24 *Lansdowne Road, Aldershot, Hants.*
1947 Dance, Miss E. M., M.A., Ph.D., *The Museum,* Castle *Arch, Guildford*
1949 Dane, Mrs. S., *Wychanger* Fields, *Shere.*
1942 Davey, H. J., Grantley *Villa, Cranleigh.*
1943 Davies, M. R., F.C.A., *Cartref, Ladyegate Road, Dorking.*
1940 Davies, W. E., 7 *Whitethorn Gardens, East* Croydon.
1943 Dawkins, A. R., *Pendennis, Fairmile Lane, Cobham,* Surrey.
1949 Dawson, P. A., 1 Tanners Lane, *Haslemere.*
1949 Dawson, Mrs. R. M., 3 *Boxgrove* Court, Guildford.
1946 Deanesley, Professor Margaret, *Roval Holloway College, Englefield Green.*
1941 de Castro, Gaston, 127 *Whitehall Court,* S.W.1.
1947 de Roemer, Major C. W., J.P., *Overwey,* Tilford, Farnham.
1945 Deeping, G. Warwick, Eastlands, *Weybridge.*
1949 Denniss, Mrs. V. L., *Redwood, Limpsfield.*
1915 Detroit Public Library, *per* B. F. *Stevens &* Brown, *Ltd.,* 28-30 *Little Russell Street, London,* W.C.1.
1946 Devereux, Miss K., 18a *Upper* Green East, *Mitcham.*
1945 Devonshire Club, *St. James's, London,* S.W.1.
1946 Dewar, Miss C. B. V., *The Shieling, Kingswood Warren,* Tadworth.
1946 Dewar, W. G. F., B.A., *The Shieling,* Kingswood *Warren,* Tadworth.
1948 Dickinson, W. L., Laurel Bank, 38 *Manor Road, Wallington.*
1946 Disney, A. A., *Plain Cottage, Dockenfield,* Farnham.
1946 Dixon, A. H., *Gincox* Farm, *Oxted.*
1944 Dixon, Mrs. M., *Gincox* Farm, *Oxted.*
1938 Dobson, C. G., 47 *Anne Boleyn's Walk, Cheam.*
1935 Dolby, Mrs. E., *Sandiacre, Lower Bourne, Farnham.*
1947 Dopson, L. H., *Wildwood,* Broad *Lane, Newdigate.*
1941 Dowson, Lady Evelyn T., *The Cobbles, Walton-on-the-Hill.*
1948 Draper, J. G. B., *Rowley Cottage, Epsom Road, Guildford.*
1949 Drewitt, F. Drayton, *Wanborough House, Cranleigh.*
1945 Duke University Library, *Durham, North* Carolina, *U.S.A., per Stevens & Brown, Ltd.,* 28-30 *Little Russell* Street, London, W.C.1.
1932 Duncan, C. M., J.P., *Green Loaning, The Chase, Reigate.*
1942 Durrant, T. V. S., 14 *Chelsea Square, London,* S.W.3.

1940 EARL, E. A., 7 *Somers Road, Reigate.*
1925 Eason, E. W., 20 *The Green, Kew.*
1944 Easton, Mrs. D., *Hunters Hall,* Tadworth.

1922 Ebbisham, Lord, G.B.E., F.S.A., 41 *Upp*er *Brook* Street, *London, W*.1.

1946 Edgley, Mrs. *G. A.*, 26 *Foxglove Avenue, Beckenham, K*ent.

1939 Edwards, H. L., 65 *Church* Street, *Epsom.*

1949 Edwards, Miss M. B., 4 Ban*don Rise, Wallington.*

1948 Edwards, Mrs. Trevor, 115 Coulsdon *Road, Old* Coulsdon.

1930 Egerton, Major G. W., *Godstone* Place, *Godstone.*

1946 Eiger, L. C., M.I.Mech.E., Cedar *Cot, K*ings *Road,* Fleet, *H*ants.

1943 Elliot, F. H., J.P., C.A., *The* L*arches, Woldingham.*

1949 Elliott, R. F., A.R.I.B.A., Bri*dge* Cottage, *Dorking Road, Leatherhead.*

1949 Ellis, J. C., 38 *Highlands Road, Leatherhead.*

1906 Ellis, Stanley, 58 *Chertsey* Street, *Guildford.*

1943 Ellwood, Mrs. A., *Highlands, Warwicks* Bench*, Guildford.*

1941 Ellwood, L. A., M.A., LL.B., *Highlands,* Warwick*s* Bench*, Guildford.*

1943 Ely, Alan, 3 *Undercroft, Raglan Road, Reigate.*

1943 Ely, Mrs. Helen, 3 *U*ndercroft, *Raglan Road, Reigate.*

1932 Ely, M., *Highlands,* Brigh*ton Road,* Sutton, *Surrey.*

1939 English, E. E., *Caterham Hotel, Harestone Valley Road, Caterham.*

1939 Epsom & Ewell Borough Council, *c/o The* Librarian, *Public Library, Ewell* Court, *Ewell.*

1949 Etherington, Miss M. M., *Anadana, Mount Park*, Car*sh*alton.

1928 Evans, Miss B. R., *Holly House, Rose Hill, Dorking.*

1946 Evans, D. J., *White Heather, The Riding, Woodham, Woking.*

1939 Evans, Miss E. M., *Wanborough* Cottage, *Cranleigh.*

1937 Evans, H. G., *W*anborough Cottage, *Cranleigh.*

1945 Evans, Maurice, 17 *Madrid Road, Guildford.*

1938 Evans, Miss Mildred, *Little Gables, Ewhurst Road, Cranleigh.*

1943 Evelyn, C. J. A., *St James*'s Club, Piccadilly, *W.* 1.

1941 Everard, H. V. H., B.Sc., 63 *Summerville* Gard*ens, Cheam.*

1932 Evershed, W. L., F.S.I., 36 *Ancton Way West, Elmer Sands, Bognor Regis, Sussex.*

1931 FAGG, C. C., *Juniper Hall, Mickleham.*

1948 Fairer, T. J., F.R.I.C.S., L.R.I.B.A., *Quenington, Hawks Hill, Leather-head.*

1931 Falkner, V. M., 63 *Elmfield Avenue,* Teddington, *Middlesex.*

1937 Fanshawe, Brigadier L. A., C.B.E. D.S.O., *Newnhams, West End* Grove, *Farnham.*

1939 Farmer, James A., *C.C., White Lodge, Leatherhead.*

1941 Farnham Field Club (*Hon. Sec.,* G. H. Bacon, B.A., *A*lba*r,* 40 *Ridg*way *Road, Farnham).*

1942 Farrer, The Dowager Lady, 1 *Upp*er *Phillimore* Gardens, *W*.8.

1942 Farwell, C. W., 1 Furn*ess Lodge, Derby Road, East Sheen, London, S.W*.14.

1943 Fawcett, Walter, *Pond* Cottage, *Walton-on-the-H*ill.

1938 Fearon, Mrs. E. G., *Clear Down, Westc*ott, *Dorking.*

1912 Fearon, J. G., *Clear Down, Westcott, Dorking.*

1931 Fearon, Major P. V., *Danesway, High* Trees *Road, Reigate.*

1945 Fielder, G. H., A.R.I.B.A., *Meadowsweet, East Lane, East Horsley.*

1932 Finny, Mrs. E. A. St. Lawrence, J.P., 41 *Liverpool Road, Kingston H*ill.

1892 Finny, W. E. St. Lawrence, M.D., J.P., F.S.A., **41** *Liverpool Road,*
Kingston Hill.
1949 Flint, M. F., 108 *Cornwall Road, Cheam.*
1933 Forge, J. W. L., Green Gables, Cavendish Road, Weybridge.
1946 Fortescue, A. E. M., *Pond Meadow,* Preston Cross, Great Bookham.
1946 Fortescue, Mrs. Beatrice, *Pond Meadow,* Preston Cross, Great Bookham.
1946 Fortescue, S. E. D., *Pond Meadow, Preston Cross, Great Bookham.*
1949 Francis, Mrs. D. L., 10 *Wodeland Avenue, Guildford.*
1943 Francis, T. R., 23 Bavant Road, Norbury, S.W.16.
1948 Fraser, E. McL., **8** *Biddulph Road, Maida Vale,* W.9.
1944 Freeman, E. A., *The Stores, Village Road,* Thorpe.
1943 Freeman, P. J., *Stonewall, Wolf's Row, Limpsfield.*
1942 Freeth, Miss C. M., Pursers Piece, Peaslake.
1947 Frend, W. H. C., D.Phil., *Copp Cottage, Hindhead.*
1943 Frere, J. A., Bluemantle Pursuivant of Arms, *College of Arms, Queen*
Victoria Street, London, E.C.4.
1938 Frere, S. S., F.S.A., *Lancing College, Shoreham-by-Sea,* Sussex.
1948 Frewin, Miss B. C., Crossways, *Windmill Lane, Ewell.*
1943 Fulk, E. T., 3 *Avonmore Avenue, Guildford.*
1948 Fuller-Clark, H. H., *Ingoldsby, Dene Road, Ashtead.*

1909 GARDNER, E., M.B., F.S.A., Portmore House, *Weybridge.*
1919 Gardner, Mrs. D. C., *Portmore House, Weybridge.*
1934 Gardner, Mrs. S. E. M., *St. Aubyns,* Ottershaw.
1936 Garmonsway, G. N., M.A., *Abermaid, The* Green, *Ewell.*
1948 Gaywood, Major L. R., **17** *Nightingale Road,* Carshalton.
1949 Gibb, Mrs. M. E., *Canehill Hospital,* Coulsdon.
1927 Gibson, E. Morris, Great Halfpenny, *Cheam.*
1911 Gibson, J. H., M.D., *The White House, Aldershot, Hants.*
1932 Gibson, Mrs. M. F., J.P., *The White House, Aldershot, Hants.*
1943 Giles, W. A., *St.* George's Cottage, *Highfield, West Byfleet.*
1936 Gill, R C., LL.B., *The* Cottage, *Yardley Hastings, Northampton.*
1937 Giuseppi, J. A., F.S.A., Cahir House, Station Road, *Thames Ditton.*
1896 Giuseppi, M. S., I.S.O., F.S.A., **72** Burlington *Avenue, Kew* Gardens
1932 Giuseppi, Miss M., **72** Burlington *Avenue, Kew Gardens.*
1947 Glogg, F. H., **112** Chaldon *Way,* Coulsdon.
1942 Glover, Major J. H., *Catbells, West Humble, Dorking.*
1948 Gluckstein, K. M., *Cobdens* Farm, *Alfold.*
1943 Godalming Museum, 35 Bridge Street, Godalming.
1935 Goldsmiths Librarian, *University of London Library,* Bloomsbury,
London, *W.C.*1.
1937 Goodchild, Capt. R. G., *Woodlands, The* Great Quarry, *Guildford.*
1945 Goodhart-Rendel, H. S., P.P.R.I.B.A., *Hatchlands,* East Clandon,
Guildford.
1937 Gordon, Major The Lord Adam, Fulbrook House, *Elstead, Surrey.*
1945 Gostling, Mrs. C. M., *Glenshee Lodge,* Maori Road, Guildford.
1948 Gough, E. S. E. Wyatt, 14 *Mead Road, Guildford.*
1947 Goulding, R. V., 15 *Albury Road, Guildford.*
1930 Graham, J., C.B.E., *Heathside, Limpsfield.*

1945 Graham, Miss M. I., *Heathside, Limpsfield.*

1944 Grant, Miss M., 1 *Catherine Villas, Copse Hill, Wimbledon, S.W.20.*

1945 Gravett, Mrs. D., 85 *Seaforth Avenue, New Malden.*

1944 Gravett, K. W. E., 85 *Seaforth Avenue, New Malden.*

1932 Gray, H. E. C., *Marsham, Leatherhead Road, Ashtead.*

1938 Gray, Mrs. R., *Tudor House, High Street, Henfield, Sussex.*

1937 Green, A. Case, *Toftrees, Heathfield Drive, Redhill.*

1947 Green, A. J. B., M.A., 13 *Pewley Hill, Guildford.*

1945 Green, Mrs. A. M., *Rookery Cottage, Hazelwood Lane, Chipstead.*

1942 Green, Col. C. R. M., M.D., F.R.C.S., *Glenshee Lodge, Maori Road, Guildford.*

1945 Green, E., *Rookery Cottage, Hazelwood Lane, Chipstead.*

1947 Green, Mrs. J. K., M.A., 13 *Pewley Hill, Guildford.*

1947 Greene, Lord, P.C., O.B.E., M.C., F.S.A., *The Wilderness, Holmbury St. Mary.*

1926 Grenside, Mrs. D., *Lobs Wood, Weybridge.*

1945 Gribble, Mrs. M. M., 114 *Gloucester Court, Kew Road, Kew.*

1941 Griffith, The Rev. T. F., *Oak Hatch, Runfold, Farnham.*

1949 Griffiths, T. L., *Barfield Boys School, Runfold.*

1924 Grisdale, Miss K. P., *Esgairs, Horsell, Woking.*

1945 Grosvenor, G. R., *Little Pyrford, Old Woking Road, Pyrford.*

1945 Grosvenor, Mrs. I. M., *Little Pyrford, Old Woking Road, Pyrford.*

1946 Groves, Miss A., *Sandway, Upper Rose Hill, Dorking.*

1944 Guildford Corporation, *Public Library, Guildford House, 10a High Street, Guildford.*

1898 Guildford Institute, *Ward Street, Guildford.*

1945 Gull, E. M., 54 *Warren Road, Guildford.*

1947 Guthrie, Miss W. C. A., 43 *Shortheath Road, Farnham.*

1949 Gwyn, C., *Grove Heath Road, Ripley, Woking.*

1949 Gwynne, Miss J. M., M.A., 36 *Sydney Road, Guildford.*

1949 HAINING, Sir Robert H., K.C.B., D.S.O., J.P., *Chart House, Ash Vale.*

1949 Hale, Mrs. E. L., *Four Wents, Cobham.*

1944 Haler, David, M.B., B.S.(Lond.), D.C.P.(Lond.), 29 *The Oaks, Pyrford Road, West Byfleet.*

1944 Haler, Mrs. D., 29 *The Oaks, Pyrford Road, West Byfleet.*

1944 Hall, W. A., *Arthur's Seat, Whitehill, Caterham.*

1903 Hammersmith Public Libraries, *Carnegie (Central) Library, Hammersmith, W.6.*

1935 Hanham, L. L., M.R.C.S., L.R.C.P., *Holmwood, The Crescent, Sidcup.*

1944 Hanscomb, C. E., F.R.I.B.A., *Marlow, Eastwick Road, Great Bookham.*

1944 Hanscomb, Mrs. M., B.A., *Marlow, Eastwick Road, Great Bookham.*

1909 Harding, Sir Edward J., M.A., *Greenacre, Peaslake.*

1949 Harding, Miss J. M., 20 *Horsham Road, Dorking.*

1944 Harman, Mrs. M. A., *Priests House, Leigh, Reigate.*

1948 Harries, Miss J. M., B.A., F.L.A., *Copsley, Shere Road, West Horsley.*

1944 Harris, Lady Alice S., *Lockner Holt, Chilworth.*

1947 Harrison, David, LL.D., 27 *St. Lawrence Drive, Eastcote, Middlesex.*

1922 Hart, J. H., *Vine Cottage, Vine Place, Brighton, Sussex.*

C

1942 Hart, P. D., 29 *Addiscombe* Grove, Croydon.

1916 Harvard College Library, U.S.A., *per Edward G. Allen & Son, Ltd.*, 14 Grape Street, London, W.C.2.

1943 Harvey, Miss D. E., B.Sc., F.R.G.S., 33 *De Vere Gardens, London, W.8.*

1944 Harvey, J. H., F.S.A., *Half Moon Cottage, Little Bookham.*

1943 Haslam, R. H., *Mill House, Wonersh.*

1917 Haslemere Natural History Society (John Clegg, Curator), *Educational Museum, Haslemere.*

1947 Hatch, Miss E. M. B., *Ockford Hill, Godalming.*

1919 Hawkins, L. M., M.A., Flat 2, 3 Palmeira *Square, Hove, Sussex.*

1947 Hayes, Capt. C. A., *Old Manor Hotel, Witley.*

1933 Hazeldine, F. J.

1946 Headley, Miss D. E., *Peebles,* 37 *Albany Park Road,* Kingston-upon-Thames.

1912 Heath, Miss O. M., *Albury House, Albury.*

1948 Hemphrey, M. B. K., *Tabora, Lynchford Road,* Farnborough, Hants.

1948 Henderson, Miss M. E., *Brackenside, Peaslake.*

1942 Henri, Mrs. L. R., *Warren Lodge,* Brighton *Road, Kingswood.*

1936 Hewson, Miss Margaret, *St. Margaret's, Witley.*

1947 Hicks, M. A., 24 *Lakers Rise, Woodmansterne,* Banstead.

1946 Hicks, Mrs. M. A., M.A., *The Alton, Alma Road, Reigate.*

1946 Higginson, J. A., 8 *Chesterfield Drive, Esher.*

1947 Hill, Mrs. E. E., M.A., *Woodside, St. John's Road,* Cove, Farnborough, Hants.

1930 Hill, F. Rowland, 182 Gray's *Inn Road, London, W.C.1.*

1949 Hills, Miss B. C. F., 8 *St. Martin's Avenue, Epsom.*

1948 Hills, W. C., 120 *Downs Road,* Coulsdon.

1943 Hind, Capt. H. W., D.S.O., M.C., F.A.L.P.A., 32 *High* Street, Sutton, Surrey.

1944 Hipkins, W. S., 9 *The Drive,* Banstead.

1944 Historical Association, The (Mid-Surrey Branch) (*Hon. Sec.*, A. Trubshawe, M.A., 143 *Stanley Park Road,* Carshalton.)

1946 Historical Society, Cooper's Hill College, *Englefield* Green, *Egham.*

1935 Hodgins, R. C., 39 *High* Street, Godalming.

1945 Hodgson, K. W., M.A.

1935 Hogg, A. H. A., 116 Barton *Road, Cambridge.*

1946 Hogg, Lt.-Col. W. L., D.S.O., *Harlyn, Sandy Way, Cobham,* Surrey.

1936 Holmes, J. M., *Rose Cottage, Hay* Street, *Braughing, Herts.*

1948 Holt, Mrs. E. M., 9 Lansdowne *Road, Aldershot, Hants.*

1939 Home, Major Gordon, *Lessudden House, St.* Boswells, *Roxburghshire.*

1933 Hooper, Miss Hilda J., 97 *Gleneldon Road,* Streatham, S.W.16.

1912 Hooper, L. J. E., *Chiddingfold House, Chiddingfold.*

1932 Hooper, Miss M., *Loxwood, Redhill.*

1921 Hooper, Wilfred, LL.D., F.S.A., *Loxwood, Redhill.*

1949 Hope, M. St. John, 17 *Holman Court, Ewell.*

1949 Hope, Mrs. V. C., 17 *Holman Court, Ewell.*

1942 Hope-Taylor, B., 33 *Purley Oaks Road,* Sanderstead.

1947 Horsley-Smith, The Rev. C. J., *The Hermitage, South Holmwood, Dorking.*

1944 How, S. T. G., 4 *Cedar Court, Portsmouth Road, Long Ditton.*

1941 Howard, J., 177 Banstead Road, Carshalton.

1944 Howard, Miss M. Maitland, 36 *Mulgrave Road*, Sutton, Surrey.

1947 Howard, Mrs. S. D., M.B.E., J.P., *Moy*, Esher.

1946 Huddart, Mrs. E. G., B.Sc., *c/o Ordnance Factories Directorate*, 6 *Esplanade East, Calcutta*.

1943 Hudson, Miss W. M., *Highlands, Gomshall*.

1915 Hughes, A. E., J.P., F.R.I.B.A., Farleigh, Claremont Lane, Esher.

1946 Hutcheson, Mrs. A., M.A., 40 *Wolsey Road*, Esher.

1947 Hutchings, G. E., F.R.G.S., F.G.S., *Juniper Hall, Mickleham*.

1949 Hutchings, Miss M. St. A., 51 *Thrale Road*, Streatham, S.W.16.

1949 Hutchings, Miss R. St. M., 51 *Thrale Road*, Streatham, S.W.16.

1949 Hyde, A. R., *Ridgecote, Deepdene Wood, Dorking*. ·

1938 ILLINOIS, University of, Library, Urbana, *Illinois, U.S.A*.

1935 Institute of Historical Research, Senate House, University of London, *W.C.1*.

1949 Iowa, State University of, Library, Iowa City, Iowa, *U.S.A*. *Per B. H. Blackwell Ltd*., 48-51 Broad Street, Oxford.

1948 Irving, A. H., 128 *Bedonwell Road, Bexley Heath*, Kent.

1909 Iveagh, The Earl of, C.M.G., Pyrford Court, *Woking*.

1933 JABEZ-SMITH, J., *Winshields, Ashley Road, Walton-on-Thames*.

1940 Jackson, G. O., Broadacre, *Oxshott*.

1941 Jacobs, S., Ennis Cottage, 26a *Ennismore* Gardens Mews, S.W.7.

1949 Jameson, Mrs. M. G. E., *Woodland Cottage, Downswood, Epsom Downs*.

1944 Jarman, Miss M., 33 *De Vere Gardens*, London, *W*.8.

1943 Jarvis, R. C., 31 *Hitherfield Road*, Streatham, S.W.16.

1949 Jasper, R. H., 2a *Lower Hill Road, Epsom*.

1939 Jeal, E. G., *Uplands, Trevennan, St. Teath, Bodmin*.

1948 Jeffrey, Miss P. C., *Wyndley, Deepdene Park Road, Dorking*.

1924 Jell, G. C., Broome Park, Canterbury, Kent.

1908 Jenkinson, Hilary, Sir, C.B.E., M.A., F.S.A., *Arun House, Horsham, Sussex*.

1919 Jennings, R. A. U., M.A., F.S.A., *Littlefield, Marlborough*, Wilts.

1949 Jobson, P. A., 4 *Louis Fields*, Fairlands Estate, *Worplesdon*, Guildford.

1942 Johnson, H. B., M.R.I., 33 Cornhill, London, *E.C.3*.

1925 Johnston, G. D., 10 *Old Square*, Lincoln's *Inn*, London, *W.C.2*.

1949 Johnston, G. K., *Ann's Cottage, Trodds Lane, Guildford*.

1945 Jolly, L. B., *Sherwood, Warwicks Bench Road*, Guildford.

1946 Jones, Mrs. A. Tarran, 40 Broadhurst Gardens, Reigate.

1940 Jones, E. H. Landel, LL.D., *Ways End, Torrells Corner, Peaslake*.

1922 Jones, Miss M. Farewell, *Highfield, Sidmouth, Devon*.

1949 Joules, Miss M., 13 *St. Omer Road, Guildford*

1949 Jupe, M. L., *The Well House*, Thursley, Godalming.

1930 Jupp, C. Stedman, *Netherbury, Cobham*, Surrey.

1942 KEE, Mrs. H. M., 17 *Oakeshott Avenue*, London, N.6.

1944 Keeley, Mrs. B., *Appletrees*, Lords Hill, Shamley Green, Guildford.

1912 Kelly, A. L., *Hockley Lands, Worplesdon*.

1943 Kemp, Sir Joseph H., C.B.E., 41 *Langley Park Road, Sutton*, Surrey.

1946 Kemp, Miss Mona E., 18 Tritton Avenue, Beddington, Croydon.
1930 Kempster, Mrs. J. W., Chalk Hill, Guildown, Guildford.
1946 Kennaway, Mrs. F. L., Annfield, Maori Road, Guildford.
1944 Kennedy, Lady Dorothy, Woodstock, Shalford.
1911 Kensington Public Library, Kensington High Street, London, W.8.
1947 Kent, A. B., 28 Fengates Road, Redhill.
1944 Kenyon, Sir Frederic G., G.B.E., K.C.B., F.S.A., Kirkstead, Godstone.
1934 Kenyon, Miss K. M., M.A., F.S.A., Kirkstead, Godstone.
1948 Keogh, F. R., 191 Wiltington Road, Whalley Range, Manchester 16.
1938 Kernahan, Mrs. J., Milestone Cottage, Coldharbour Lane, Pyrford, Woking.
1901 Kingston-upon-Thames Public Library, Kingston-upon-Thames.
1949 Kitchener, D. H., 8 Lovelace Road, Surbiton.
1943 Knox, General Sir Harry H. S., K.C.B., D.S.O., The Old Lodge, Byfleet.

1942 LAMBERT, Capt. G. A., 8 Graywood, East Hoathly, Lewes, Sussex.
1932 Lambert, H. Uvedale, South Park Farm, Blechingley.
1949 Lanaway, Miss B., 5 Wheatsheaf Close, Horsell, Woking.
1948 Lane, Mrs. E. A. C., Lomond, Horley.
1939 Langham, E. W., Over Compton, Waverley Lane, Farnham.
1944 Lavender, R. T., 56 Woodfield Avenue, Streatham, S.W.16.
1945 Law, Miss M. D., 19 Fengates Road, Redhill.
1936 Lawrence, Mrs. E. A., Woodcroft, Merrow, Guildford.
1949 Lawrence, Iris, Lady, Frog Grove, Wood Street, Guildford.
1923 Lawson, H. P., Lynbrook, Knaphill, Woking.
1947 Lawson, Peter H., The Mount, Chobham.
1943 Layton, E. S., The Grey Cottage, The Green, Esher.
1929 Leaning, Mrs. F. E., 51 Brockwell Court, Effra Road, Brixton, S.W.2.
1945 Lee, A. Knyvett, Cutmill Platts, Shackleford, Godalming.
1948 Lee-Hunt, Mrs. I. M., 2 Ederline Avenue, Norbury, S.W.16.
1948 Lee-Hunt, J., 2 Ederline Avenue, Norbury, S.W.16.
1948 Leechman, Miss E. M. B., Hill View Cottage, Lingfield.
1925 Lees, Miss E. M. L., 26 Cecil Road, Cheam.
1949 Le Feuvre, M., Little Mede, Blundell Lane, Cobham.
1945 Leighton, R. B., F.R.G.S., 53 Farnham Road, Guildford.
1947 Leleux, V., A.C.I.S., Ladywood, Green Lane, Shortheath, Farnham.
1919 le Marchant, H. C., Norney Grange, Fashing, Godalming.
1927 Leveson Gower, R. H. G., Titsey Place, Limpsfield.
1946 Lewarne, J. G. W., Feock, Cobham Road, Fetcham, Leatherhead.
1946 Lewington, D. C., Avalon, Smallfield, Horley.
1946 Lieberg, H. M., Nightingale Lodge, Nightingale Road, Godalming.
1942 Liggett, Miss M. D., B.A. (Chief Librarian, Guildford Public Libraries),
        Guildford House, 10a High Street, Guildford.
1938 Lightfoot, Miss F. M., Hartford House, Blackwater, Camberley.
1949 Lillie, Rev. H. W. R., 114 Mount Street, London, W.1.
1938 Lindner, A. F. H., M.A., 140 Copse Hill, Wimbledon, S.W.20.
1940 Lindner, Mrs. G. A., 140 Copse Hill, Wimbledon, S.W.20.
1920 List, Mrs A. M., North Lodge, Portsmouth Road, Guildford.
1939 Lloyd, Major C. W., R.A., White Lodge, Baldwin Avenue, Eastbourne,
        Sussex.

1948 Lloyd-Jones, C. W., C.I.E., *Round Hay, Pit* Farm *Road, Guildford.*

1949 Lloyd-Jones, Mrs. E. K., 3 *Pit* Farm *Road, Guildford.*

1945 Lloyd-Jones, Miss J. K., *Round Hay, Pit* Farm *Road, Guildford.*

1928 Lloyds Bank Ltd., *Guildford.*

1948 London County Council Members' Library, County *Hall, Westminster* Bri*dge, S.E.*1.

1865 London, The Corporation of, *Guildhall Library, London, E.C.*2.

1891 London Library, *St. James's Square, S.W.*1.

1948 Loosely, Miss B., 13 *Pennard Mansions, W.*12.

1948 Loosely, Miss N., 13 Pennar*d Mansions, W.*12.

1949 Lowe, Miss L. D., 2 *Oakhill Road, Surbiton.*

1943 Lowndes, Mrs. D. R., *Dene Ridge, Deepdene Gardens, Dorking.*

1949 Lowndes, William G., *Dene Ridge, Deepdene Gardens, Dorking.*

1927 Lowther, A. W. G., F.S.A., A.R.I.B.A., *The Old* Quarry, *Ashtead.*

1949 Lucas, Mrs. A. M., B.A., 33 *Manor Way, Onslow Village, Guildford.*

1947 Lucy, R. M. H., 58 *Northwood Avenue, Purley.*

1949 Ludford, J. H., B.A., LL.B., 3 *Poplar Road, Leatherhead.*

1936 Lund University Library, *Lund, Sweden.*

1945 Lygon, The Hon. Mrs. C. A., Greyfriars, *Castle Hill, Guildford.*

1938 MACANDREW, A. G., 185 *Coombe Lane, S.W.*20.

1944 MacAndrew, Mrs. M., Beeches, *Peastake.*

1912 MacAndrew, Miss, *The Innerfold,* Park *Road, Rottingdean, Brighton.*

1941 Macgregor, J. E. M. F.R.I.B.A., *The Mill, Shalford, Guildford.*

1942 MacLean, Dr. I. M. M, F.R.S.A.I., 9 *Abbey Gardens, N.W.*8.

1943 Malden and Coombe Public Library, *Kingston Road, New Malden.*

1910 Manchester, John Rylands Library.

1949 Mann, S. E., LL.B., *Hill House, Upper Deepdene Drive, Dorking.*

1948 Manners, Miss A., *Little Gate House, Cobham, Surrey.*

1949 Manning, F. E., M.A., 50 *Latchmere Road, Kingston-upon-Thames.*

1945 Maplesden, Mrs. G. E., 2 *Glenside, South* Terrace, *Dorking.*

1927 Margary, I. D., M.A., F.S.A., *Yew Lodge, East Grinstead, Sussex.*

1938 Marks, Julian D., *Snoxhall, Cranleigh.*

1944 Marsden, W. J. M., M.A., 29 *Fairway, Merrow, Guildford.*

1932 Marsh, Miss F., *Anderida, South Holmwood, Dorking.*

1912 Marshall, Mrs. Dendy, *Chinthurst Lodge, Guildford.*

1936 Marshall, Sir John, K.C.I.E., Litt.D., *Avondale, Sydney Road, Guildford.*

1928 Marson, Miss K. M., *Innisfree, Albury Road, Guildford.*

1939 Martin, Major-Gen. J. F., C.B., C.M.G., C.B.E., *Waverley Cottage,* Fleet, *Hants.*

1949 Martin, Miss E. M., 31 *Union Street, Aldershot, Hants.*

1945 Martin, Miss M. M. A., B.A., 31 *Union Street, Aldershot, Hants.*

1928 Mason, Arthur J., F.R.S.A., *Rocklea,* 112 *Drakefield Road, Tooting, S.W.*17.

1935 Master, Capt. C. E., Hoskins, Barrow *Green Court, Oxted.*

1935 Master, Mrs. Hoskins, Barrow *Green Court, Oxted.*

1946 Matthew, Miss M. S. M., B.A., 12 *Westbury Avenue, Claygate.*

1944 Matthews, Miss C. R., 71 *Ladbroke Road, Redhill.*

1948 Maude, Sir John, K.C.B., *The Copse, Oxted.*

1944 May, Mrs. Doris, J.P., 4 *Beechwood Road, Sanderstead.*

1948 May, S. G. W., 4 *Beechwood Road, Sanderstead.*
1945 McLaren, Miss A. M. D., *Wonicombe,* Furze *Hill,* Kingswood.
1925 Mellersh, Miss E. M., *Matteryes, Hambledon, Godalming.*
1945 Merriman, Mrs. L., *Somerdown,* 26 *Somers Road, Reigate.*
1945 Merriman, Commander R. D., R.I.N. (Retd.), *Somerdown,* **26** *Somers Road, Reigate.*
1930 Michigan, University of, General Library, *Ann Arbor, Michigan, U.S.A., per Hy. Sotheran Ltd.,* 43 Piccadilly, London, *W.*1.
1947 Miles, Capt. E. C., 27 *Meadway, Coulsdon.*
1936 Miller, H. Eric, *Old House, Ewhurst Green.*
1930 Millett, Lt.-Col. S. C., *Perivale,* Pine Plains, *New York City, U.S.A.*
1906 Milne, J. G., 23 *Belsyce* Court, *Woodstock Road, Oxford.*
1947 Milner, Harold, 49 *Anne Boleyn's Walk, Cheam.*
1949 Mimmack, J. M. H., *Broadfield, Peaslake, Guildford.*
1891 Minet Public Library, *Knatchbull Road,* Camberwell, *S.E.*5.
1944 Monckton, Mrs. A., 83 *Ember Lane, Esher.*
1944 Monckton, M. G., 83 *Ember Lane, Esher.*
1937 Money, E. D., *Buckstone Farm, Chobham.*
1949 Moody, S. S. (H.M.I.), 5 *Revell Road, Cheam.*
1947 Moore, A. H. W., F.S.A., 5 Grosvenor Crescent, London, *S.W.*1.
1944 Moore, H., *Hawthorn Cottage, Ashtead.*
1945 Moore, Mrs. I. F., *The Dell, Send Hill, Woking.*
1943 Moore, T. G., 105 *Southbourne Grove, West Southbourne,* Bournemouth, *Hants.*
1933 Morley, E. L., *Glebe, Crossfield* Place, *Weybridge.*
1947 Morris, Col. C. E., D.S.O., *Merlebank, Church Hill, Merstham.*
1912 Morris, J. E., B.A., *Mount Pleasant, Totnes, Devon.*
1930 Morrish, Mrs. C. L., *Clear Down, Westcott, Dorking.*
1922 Morrish, H. G., *Langhurst, Derby Road, Haslemere.*
1937 Morrish, H. J., *Wayside Cottage, Kintbury, Berks.*
1947 Mosse, Capt. H. T., R.N. (Retd.), 25b *The Fairfield,* Farnham, Surrey.
1947 Mosse, Mrs. V., 25b *The Fairfield,* Farnham, *Surrey.*
1910 Moysey, Miss E. L., 223 *Worplesdon Road, Stoughton, Guildford.*
1948 Munk, H. W., *Two Magpies, Wood Lane,* Fleet, *Hants.*
1914 Musgrave, Miss Frances, *Olivers, Hascombe, Godalming.*

1936 NATION, N., *Clevedon, St. Omer Road, Guildford.*
1928 Nevill, Humphry, 69 *Te Awe Awe* Street, *Palmerston North, New Zealand.*
1948 Nevill, Lt.-Col. S. S., O.B.E., 34 *Hatherley Grove, London, W.*2.
1933 Nevill, W. Howard, Courtleet, Burwood *Park, Walton-on-Thames.*
1928 Nevinson, J. L., 18 *Hyde Park* Place, London, *W.*2.
1939 New England, Library of Historical Genealogical Society, Boston, Mass., U.S.A., *per* B. F. Stevens & *Brown Ltd.,* 28-30 *Little Russell Street, W.C.*1.
1917 Newill, The Ven. Archdeacon E. J., Trevelyan, Cranley Road, Guildford.
1941 Newson, J., *Hasketon, High* Trees *Road, Reigate.*
1915 New York Public Library, *per* B. F. Stevens & Brown, *Ltd.,* 28-30 *Little Russell Street, W.C.*1.

1926 Nichols, J. F., M.C., M.A., Ph.D., F.S.A., F.R.Hist.S., 15 Minster Road, Godalming.
1938 Nicholson, R. P., C.M.G., C.B.E., Tallboys, Abinger Hammer, Dorking.
1936 Nightingale, Mrs. J. L., 31 West Street, Reigate.
1943 Nightingale, T., 31 West Street, Reigate.
1948 Nonsuch Society, The (Hon. Sec. A. R. Laird, Ivy Cottage, London Road, Ewell).
1938 Norman, W. H., M.B.E., Witley, Salisbury Avenue, Cheam.
1935 Norton, J. G., Stonards Cottage, Shamley Green, Guildford.

1936 OAKDEN, Sir Ralph, C.S.I., O.B.E., Stowford House, Pit Farm Road, Guildford.
1949 Oakeshott, R. E., 103 Downs Court Road, Purley.
1949 Oates, R. W., Durrant House, Western Road, Branksome Park, Bournemouth, Hants.
1930 Oddy, A. E., 21 Upper Wimpole Street, London, W.1.
1949 Offor, R., B.A., Ph.D., 24 Tangier Road, Guildford.
1941 Ogburn, Mrs. E. E., 28 Fernhill Gardens, Kingston-upon-Thames.
1947 Oliver, V. F. M., B.A., A.M.I.Mech.E., Hillside, Bagshot.
1938 Ollive, Miss W., Maycot, Woodlands Way, Kingswood.
1921 Onslow, The Dowager Countess of, Dippenhall Meads, Farnham.
1943 Orbell-Durrant, Mrs. D., Dene End, Tilford, Farnham
1947 Ordnance Survey Office, Archæology Branch, Leatherhead Road, Chessington.
1944 Orvis, S. M., 48 Warnham Court Road, Carshalton.
1924 Owen, Mrs. D., Millhouse, Boxford, Newbury, Berks.
1932 Oxted and Limpsfield Amenities Association, 2 Plaza Chambers, Oxted.
1946 Oxted and Limpsfield Central Library, Gresham Road, Oxted.
1949 Ozanne, P. C., 27 Trafford Road, Thornton Heath.

1898 PAGE, G. F., J.P., F.S.I., F.A.I., Coombe Barton, Kingston-upon-Thames.
1940 Paget, C. G., 88 George V Avenue, Worthing, Sussex.
1940 Parker, Miss A. C., 30 Museum Chambers, W.C.1.
1945 Parker, Eric, Feathercombe, Hambledon, Godalming.
1924 Parkes, Miss Joan, Preyste House, Petworth, Sussex.
1948 Parkinson, H., B.A., B.Com., Pines Crest, Pelhams Walk, Esher.
1948 Parkinson, K., Pines Crest, Pelhams Walk, Esher.
1948 Parrish, E. J., Killasser, Tadworth.
1943 Parsloe, G., B.A., F.R.Hist.S., 1 Leopold Avenue, Wimbledon, S.W.19
1943 Parsons, The Rev. Canon R. E., Wotton Rectory, Dorking.
1949 Pater, J. E., 157 Coombe Road, Croydon.
1949 Paterson, Lt.-Col. T., 20 Pitfarm Road, Guildford.
1949 Paterson, Mrs. G. R., 20 Pitfarm Road, Guildford.
1938 Patrick, Major H. C., Gwanda, Compton Lane, Farnham.
1907 Patrick, W. T., J.P., Treverward, Nightingale Road, Guildford.
1937 Patterson, J. A., 134 Salisbury Road, Totton, Hants.
1943 Peck, A. B., Branksome, Eversfield Road, Reigate.
1943 Peck, Mrs. E. F., Branksome, Eversfield Road, Reigate.
1949 Penty, Miss D. H., 3 Pitfarm Road, Guildford.

1949 Perkins, K. L., M.A., *Hydon Heath Camp School, Godalming.*
1949 Perry, A. L. H., B.Sc., F.I.M., *22 Raymond Road, Wimbledon, S.W.19*
1948 Petree, J. F., M.I.Mech.E., *36 Mayfield Road, Sutton.*
1948 Pfeffer, J. A., *165 Heythorp Street, Southfields, S.W.18.*
1918 Phillips, W. H., *141 South Croxted Road, West Dulwich, S.E.21.*
1949 Philpott, R. F., *18 Cleardene, Dorking.*
1946 Physick, J. F., *15 Selsdon Road, West Norwood, S.E.27.*
1931 Pickering, W. J., *9 Heathcote Road, Epsom.*
1931 Pierce, E. A., *Knowle Hill Cottage, Cobham, Surrey.*
1948 Pilditch, Sir Frederick, *Heronsbrook, Old Deer Park, Wonersh, Guildford.*
1948 Pilditch, Lady, *Heronsbrook, Old Deer Park, Wonersh, Guildford.*
1941 Pinches, Mrs. N., M.B.E., *Warren Hill Cottage, Beachy Head Road, Eastbourne, Sussex.*
1904 Pinckard, G. H., J.P., M.A., *Queenshill, Sunningdale, Berks.*
1945 Pirrie, H. G., *Silverdale, Heathside Road, Woking.*
1949 Pizzey, C. J., *1 Godstone Road, Caterham.*
1941 Plaistowe, Cuthbert, *Mansfield, Elgin Road, Weybridge.*
1938 Plant, Chas., *13 Wharfedale Gardens, Thornton Heath.*
1948 Plant, Mrs. H. C., *13 Wharfedale Gardens, Thornton Heath.*
1942 Plant, Miss R., *1 Cotmandene, Dorking.*
1939 Plummer, S. H., *Longmead, The Hildens, Westcott, Dorking.*
1936 Pointer, H. W., M.A., *Woodlands, Grosvenor Road, Godalming.*
1947 Pope, Mrs. S. R., *Chart Croft, Limpsfield.*
1946 Popplewell, F., *Kilspindie, Wonersh Park, Guildford.*
1946 Popplewell, Mrs. N. S., *Kilspindie, Wonersh Park, Guildford.*
1948 Portch, Miss K. M. C., *Sapperton, Peaslake.*
1933 Potter, Mrs. Grayson, *Pleasaunce, Mark Way, Godalming.*
1942 Poulter, C. G. B., *M.Y. Witch o' the Wey, c/o Walsham Lock, Pyrford, Woking.*
1938 Poulter, G. C. B., F.S.A.Scot., F.R.S.A.I., *Hut 1, Collingwood Place, Camberley.*
1944 Powell, L., M.C., *The Weir House, Guildford.*
1948 Prest, J. M., *21 Tower Road, Tadworth.*
1945 Preston, Mrs. D. W., *Deganwy, Warren Drive, Kingswood.*
1945 Preston, R. H., *Deganwy, Warren Drive, Kingswood.*
1943 Price, Sir Keith W., *Wintershall, Bramley.*
1932 Price-Hughes, Miss C., *Redlands, Shalford.*
1928 Prickett, F. F., *Junior Carlton Club, Pall Mall, London, S.W.1.*

1945 QUARE, Mrs. M., *Chantry Cottage, Leigh, Reigate.*
1944 Quekett, Miss E. M. T., *Ridgefield, Horsell Park, Woking.*
1933 Quekett, Mrs. M. A. W., *Ridgefield, Horsell Park, Woking.*
1947 Quinton, C. L., *3 Langley Park Road, Sutton, Surrey.*

1938 RACKHAM, Bernard, C.B., F.S.A., *9 Poyle Road, Guildford.*
1947 Raes, P. E., *7 Carroll Avenue, Merrow, Guildford.*
1938 Rahbula, E. A. R., O.B.E., M.C., F.S.A., *Atholl Lodge, 74 Storeys Way, Cambridge.*
1947 Rainier, Mrs. G. M., M.B.E., *44 Ewell Downs Road, Ewell.*

1945 Raison, C. E., Barnet Cottage, Westcott, Dorking.
1935 Rankine, W. F., F.S.A.Scot., Yew Tree Cottage, Wrecclesham.
1947 Rankine, Mrs. W. M., Yew Tree Cottage, Wrecclesham.
1944 Rathbone, Mrs. D., Oldberrow, Clockhouse Mead, Oxshott.
1948 Rawling, Mrs. H. M., 35 Peaks Hill, Purley.
1932 Readhead, Mrs. T. F. L., Great House, Hambledon, Surrey.
1915 Reading Public Libraries, Central Library, Reading.
1942 Reece, C. D. S., 6 Burntwood Lane, Caterham.
1949 Remnant, E. A., T.D., F.R.I.B.A., 15 Fernshaw Road, Chelsea, S.W.10
1941 Rich, T., O.B.E., Didmarton Cottage, Woldingham.
1920 Richards, F. L., Penryn, 10 Kingsway, Woking.
1924 Richardson, Mrs. A. M. Baird, The Rectory, Kingham, Oxford.
1936 Richardson, E. F., The Lodge, Maids Moreton, Buckingham.
1891 Richmond Public Library, Richmond, Surrey.
1944 Riley, Major-Gen. Sir Guy, K.B.E., C.B., Gatton, 26 Nightingale Road, Guildford.
1939 Ritson, T., Wykeham Park House, Frimley Green, Aldershot.
1936 Ritson, Mrs. W. A., Wykeham Park House, Frimley Green, Aldershot.
1949 Roberts, Mrs. C. E., 52 Chestnut Avenue, Esher.
1949 Roberts, T. C., 52 Chestnut Avenue, Esher.
1933 Robo, The Rev. E., Catholic Church, Farnham.
1906 Robson, P. A., F.R.I.B.A., Percival House, Dartmouth Row, S.E.10.
1924 Rogers, H. Mordaunt, P.P.A.I., F.S.I., The Manor House, Upper Hardres, Canterbury.
1932 Rolston, G. R., M.R.C.S., L.R.C.P., Crofts, Haslemere.
1948 Rolston, Dr. Mary E., Crofts, Haslemere.
1899 Roscoe, Miss Dora, Tyrrellswood, West Horsley.
1946 Rose, Mrs. M. J., Pleasants Cottage, Wisley, Ripley.
1948 Rossiter, F. C., 7 Coulsdon Rise, Coulsdon.
1948 Rossiter, S., Farringford, Stoneyfield Road, Cheam.
1949 Ruby, A. T., M.B.E., 53 Nutcroft Grove, Fetcham.
1946 Ruff, Mrs. K. L., Westcott, Buckland Road, Lower Kingswood.
1948 Rumbold, R., 50 Coombe Road, Croydon.
1949 Russ, Miss D. K., 14 Rectory Close, Long Ditton.
1949 Russ, Miss P. M., 14 Rectory Close, Long Ditton.
1938 Ruston, E. T., M.B., 28a South Molton Lane, W.1.
1946 Rutherford, Mrs. B. O., Chesterton, Parkwood Avenue, Esher.
1938 Ryde, E. H. N., Poundfield House, Old Woking.

1945 SALE, J. F., Hillcrest, Guildown, Guildford.
1942 Salmon, J., 61 Kensington Court, W.8.
1943 Sanders, A. E., 75 Broadhurst, Ashtead.
1938 Sanderson, C., West Garth, High Trees Road, Reigate.
1943 Sanderson, The Rev. Finlay, Denham, Deepdene Park Road, Dorking.
1947 Sanford, J. C., Fir Lodge, Hollyme Oak Road, Coulsdon.
1943 Sanger, G. F., Willingham Cottage, Send.
1923 Saunders, W., J.P., Manor Hotel, Hanger Hill, Weybridge.
1938 Savill, A. G., 66 Winifred Road, Coulsdon.
1949 Sawtell, E. J., Woodbury, Castle Road, Horsell, Woking.

1927 Sayers, W. C. Berwick, F.L.A., 52 Blenheim Crescent, South Croydon
1931 Scears, E., *Heath Bank, White Post Hill, Redhill.*
1938 Scott, A. A., *Laneside, Westfield, Hoe Lane, Abinger.*
1935 Scott, Miss A. M., *3 Hawley Grange, Hawley, Camberley.*
1949 Scott, Miss J., *Morholme, Guildford Road, Woking.*
1927 Scott, R. B., *6 Alan Road, Wimbledon, S.W.19.*
1942 Scott-Willey, H. H. S., F.R.I.B.A., *Homewood, Chipstead.*
1949 Searle, E. W., *10 Dowanhill Road, Catford, S.E.6.*
1946 Searle, Miss K. M., *Basildon, West Byfleet.*
1920 Secretan, Spencer D., *Swaines, Rudgwick, Horsham, Sussex.*
1936 Sellick, E. L., *Southmead, Westcott Road, Dorking.*
1944 Seth-Smith, David, *7 Poyle Road, Guildford.*
1939 Seward, R. W., *Fairview, Northdown Road, Woldingham.*
1947 Sewill, Mrs. R., *Staggers Avon, Charlwood.*
1940 Sexton, C. E., *Cofield, London Road, Redhill.*
1941 Sexton, Miss L., *Cofield, London Road, Redhill.*
1949 Seyler, C. A., D.Sc., *3 Rodney Road, New Malden.*
1910 Shallcrass, J., *Kifrı, Tadworth Street, Tadworth.*
1945 Shaw, R. B., *Colinton, Deans Road, Merstham.*
1936 Shearman, Capt. P., *46 The Glade, Stoneleigh, Ewell.*
1941 Shepherd, Miss O. A., *Rose Bungalow, Norbury Park, Dorking.*
1948 Sherriff, R. C., F.S.A., *Rosebriars, Esher.*
1942 Shirley, T. F., *White Cottage, Grayshott, Hants.*
1945 Shrewsbury, F. R., *The Spinney, Beech Drive, Kingswood.*
1948 Shrimpton, Mrs. P., *64 Salter's Hill, Upper Norwood, S.E.19.*
1947 Simms, R. S., M.A., *Bedruthan, Carlton Road, Redhill.*
1944 Simpson, Miss C. A., *St. Margaret's, Barnet Lane, Wonersh, Guildford.*
1944 Simpson, W. A., *Rannoch, Brockham Lane, Betchworth.*
1942 Skene, The Rev. Canon F. N., M.A., R.D., *The Vicarage, Banstead.*
1932 Skinner, Mrs. M. Montagu, *Inglewood, Bramley, Guildford.*
1930 Slingsby, F. Hugh, M.C., B.A., *12 Tennyson Road, Worthing, Sussex.*
1946 Slyfield, G. N., *47 North Parade, Horsham, Sussex.*
1934 Smallpeice, F. W., *Manor House, Puttenham.*
1942 Smeaton, Mrs. M., *Beauchief, Parkwood Avenue, Esher.*
1945 Smith, Miss A. M. Hamilton, *The Haven, Warren Road, Reigate.*
1921 Smith, Miss B. I., *37 St. James Road, Surbiton.*
1922 Smith, C. W., LL.M., *11 Claremont Gardens, Tunbridge Wells, Kent.*
1944 Smith, E. E. F., *49 Mayford Road, Wandsworth Common, S.W.12.*
1949 Smith, F. J., F.R.I.C.S., *Fivewents House, Swanley, Kent.*
1945 Smith, G. H., *Rose Lawn, Leatherhead Road, Ashtead.*
1945 Smith, Miss Mary, *County High School for Girls, Aldershot.*
1946 Smith, Group Capt. Sidney, D.S.O., A.F.C., *20 Castle Street, Farnham.*
1946 Smith, Mrs. W. Sidney, *20 Castle Street, Farnham.*
1938 Smither, H. C., *42 Downing Street, Farnham.*
1939 South-Eastern Society of Architects (G. M. Kingsford, A.R.I.B.A., *Hon.
        Sec., Littlewood, Echo Pit Road, Guildford.)*
1937 Southwark Library, *Town Hall, Walworth Road, London, S.E.17.*
1949 Sowden, Miss D. E., *The White Cottage, Hoe Lane, Abinger Hammer,
        Dorking.*

1943 Sowden, Miss M. E., M.A., *The White Cottage, Hoe Lane, Abinger Hammer, Dorking.*

1927 Sowerbutts, J. A., M.C., Mus.B., F.R.A.M., F.R.C.O., 2 *Annandale Road, Guildford.*

1926 Spens, Miss E. M., *Hornbeams, Worplesdon.*

1948 Spreckley, W., *Pilgrim Cottage,* Buckland, *Betchworth.*

1942 Sproule, Mrs. A., *Hill Crest, New Road,* Tadworth.

1945 Spurling, Miss J., *Tudor House, Walton-on-the-Hill.*

1945 Squire, A. Pepys, *Farley, Chart Sutton, Maidstone,* Kent.

1944 Squire, Miss D., *Farley, Chart Sutton, Maidstone,* Kent.

1947 Squire, Miss O. F., *Brédune, Kenley.*

1937 Stafford, Mrs. V. L., 1 *William Street House, William* Street, Knightsbridge, *S.W.*1.

1939 Stallard, Lieut.-Col. H. G. F., *Redhearn, Churt, Farnham.*

1901 Stebbing, W. P. D., J.P., F.S.A., *Five Ways, Upper Deal,* Kent.

1945 Stevens, Mrs. A. B., 64 *Scarsdale Villas, Kensington, W.*8.

1948 Stevens, A. J., B.A., F.R.G.S., *Burton Cottage, Wings Road, Upper Hale, Farnham.*

1947 Stevens, Mrs. E. C., M.B., *St. Pauls Vicarage, Augustus Road, Wimbledon Park, S.W.*19.

1948 Stevens, F. I., *Longhill,* 49 *Marlpit Lane,* Coulsdon.

1939 Stevens, Miss K. C., *Burton Cottage, Wings Road, Upper Hale, Farnham.*

1918 Stevens, L. R., F.S.A., F.C.A., 64 *Scarsdale Villas, Kensington; W.*8.

1943 Stevens, The Rev. Canon T. P., R.D., *St. Paul's Vicarage, Augustus Road, Wimbledon Park, S.W.*19.

1941 Steventon, A. A., 20 *Arundel Avenue, Ewell.*

1941 Steventon, Mrs. A, 20 *Arundel Avenue, Ewell.*

1946 Stewart-Smith, G., *The Pantiles, Oakfield Glade, Weybridge.*

1943 Stone, Mrs. G. E., 11 *The Drive, Wells Road, Epsom.*

1939 Strange, F. W., F.R.S.A.I., 122 *Lexham Gardens, Kensington, W.*8

1945 Stratton, Mrs. E. E., *Northcote, Reigate.*

1937 Streatham Antiquarian and Natural History Society, 106 *Heybridge Avenue, Streatham, S.W.*16.

1902 Streatham Public Library, *High Street, S.W.*16.

1943 Strickland, Mrs. Vera, 137 *Ember Lane, Esher.*

1945 Stuart, P. R., *Wyncote, Dunsdon Avenue, Guildford.*

1947 Stuart, Miss S. E., 1 *Darjeeling, Jenner Road, Guildford.*

1945 Stubbs, Mrs. M. B., *Bell Cottage, Fetcham, Leatherhead.*

1942 Stubbs, S. G., M.B.E., *Bell Cottage, Fetcham, Leatherhead.*

1947 Summers, M. D., *Fenhay, Poughill, Crediton, Devon.*

1934 Summers, R. F. H., *P.O. Box* 240, *Bulawayo, Southern Rhodesia.*

1944 Sumner, Miss D. M., 4 *Grangefields, Stringers Common, Guildford.*

1946 Surbiton Corporation, *Council Offices, Ewell Road, Surbiton.*

1928 Surrey County Council, *County Hall, Kingston-upon-Thames.*

1927 Surrey County Library, 140 *High* Street, *Esher.*

1922 Sutherland, The Duke of, K.T., P.C., *Sutton Place, Guildford.*

1942 Sutton and Cheam Central Public Library, *Manor Park Road, Sutton,* Surrey.

1946 Swayne, Geoffrey O., 15 *Waterden Road, Guildford.*

1920 Swayne, T. Gatton, *North Down, Warwicks Bench, Guildford.*
1947 Swayne, T. R. G., *14 York Road, Guildford.*
1942 Sykes, Mrs. A. E., *Sandway, Upper Rose Hill, Dorking.*
1949 Sykes, Mrs. O. B., *Elthorpe, Ballards, Limpsfield.*
1931 Sykes, P. D., *Sandway, Upper Rose Hill, Dorking.*
1947 Syrett, C. G., *Waterslade, Shaws Corner, Redhill.*

1943 TADGELL, Mrs. E., *Collingdon, Grove Road, Cranleigh.*
1942 Tadgell, H. R., *Collingdon, Grove Road, Cranleigh.*
1929 Talbot Smith, Major A., *Flint Cottage, Chipstead.*
1945 Talbot Smith, Mrs. M. E., *Flint Cottage, Chipstead.*
1946 Tarrant, P. E., *Wistaria Cottage, High Road, Byfleet.*
1934 Tassie, J. A., *Compton, West Byfleet.*
1947 Tattersall, J. U., *Lynn, Downs Court Road, Purley, Surrey.*
1941 Tattersall, Mrs. V. M., *Lynn, Downs Court Road, Purley, Surrey.*
1948 Taylor, F. O. M., *Royal Oak, Crondall, Farnham.*
1942 Thomas, Miss J., *Matton, Windsor Road, Chobham*
1947 Thompson, D. W., *Sandy, Bluehouse Lane, Limpsfield.*
1949 Thompson, E. de B., *12 The Ridgway, Sanderstead.*
1938 Thompson, Mrs. K., *Wheeler's Farm, Pyrford, Woking.*
1931 Thorp, Thomas, *149 High Street, Guildford.*
1941 Thorpe, Miss M., *19 Fengates Road, Redhill.*
1946 Tiltman, R. F., *Woodside Cottage, Crampshaw Lane, Ashtead.*
1941 Tinkler, Miss E. G. Fane, *Jericho, Ridgeway Road, Dorking.*
1942 Todd, Mrs. A. M., *Chanctonbury, Croydon Road, Reigate.*
1942 Todd, Miss E. F., *Chanctonbury, Croydon Road, Reigate.*
1949 Todd, Cdr. K. R. U., R.N., F.R.A.I., *Three Beeches, Greendene, East Horsley.*
1948 Toosey, Miss C. B., *Gate End, Guildown Road, Guildford.*
1944 Topping, Mrs. J., Ph.D., *An Groban, Fir Tree Road, Leatherhead.*
1942 Toy, Sidney, F.S.A., F.R.I.B.A., *62 Church Road, Epsom.*
1948 Traylen, C. W., *87 North Street, Guildford.*
1943 Tricker, E. S., *64 Ember Lane, Esher.*
1934 Tringham, S. W. G., *Chobham Ridges, The Maultway, West Camberley.*
1931 Tringham, Miss D. S., *Chobham Ridges, The Maultway, West Camberley.*
1931 Tringham, The Rev. Canon H. J. F., *Longcross Vicarage, Chertsey.*
1945 Trinick, G. E. M., *Mead House, Redhill.*
1948 Turner, Dr. A. G., *17 Alexandra Road, Farnborough, Hants.*
1948 Turner, Mrs. M. M., *17 Alexandra Road, Farnborough, Hants.*
1948 Turner, D. J., *60 Harcourt Road, Thornton Heath.*
1948 Turner, Miss E. M., *c/o Lloyds Bank Ltd., 50, Notting Hill Gate, London, W.11.*
1947 Turner, L. A., *36 Court Farm Avenue, Ewell.*
1943 Turner, S. R., F.R.I.B.A., *Rosegarth, 27 West Drive, Cheam.*
1945 Tyler, B., *Heston, 7 Hartswood Avenue, Reigate.*

1945 UTAH, The Genealogical Society of, *80 North Main Street, Salt Lake City, Utah, U.S.A.,*

1926 VAN LESSEN, Mrs. D. M., *East Manor, Bramley, Guildford.*

1923 Vawdrey, R. W., *The* Crossways, *Limpsfield*.
1946 Veall, H., 63 *Gayfere Road, Ewell*.
1945 Veitch, Mrs. A. K., *Westcott, Buckland Road, Lower Kingswood*.
1945 Veitch, L. H., *Westcott, Buckland Road, Lower Kingswood*.
1943 Venning, C. W., B.Sc., *Lullington, Pilgrim's Close, West Humble, Dorking*.
1947 Venning, Mrs. J., *Lullington, Pilgrim's Close, West Humble, Dorking*.
1916 Victoria and Albert Museum Library, *South* Kensington, *S.W.7*.
1916 Victoria Public Library, *Melbourne, Australia, per W. H. Smith & Son, Ltd., Strand House, London, W.C.2*.
1945 Vinter, Mrs. E. T., *Brackendene, Clock House Close, Byfleet*.

1937 WADE, Major A. G., M.C., *Ash* Cottage, Bentley, Hants.
1948 Wagner, Mrs. D., 73 *Addiscombe Road*, Croydon.
1947 Wagstaff, Col. H. W., C.S.I., M.C., *Hereward, London Road, Guildford*.
1949 Wainwright, Lt.-Col. J. G. (I.A. retd.), Field View, Southerns Lane, *Chipstead*.
1903 Walford Bros., 69 *Southampton Row, London, W.C.1*.
1926 Walker, T. E. C., *Spring Grove, Cobham, Surrey*.
1942 Wallis, B. J., *Holman House, Epsom* College.
1946 Walls, Tom K., *The Looe, Reigate Road, Ewell*.
1948 Walsh, A., 149 *Eastworth* Road, Chertsey.
1913 Walton, Frank W., *Lime Cottage, The Avenue, Claygate*.
1889 Wandsworth Public Library, *West Hill, S.W.18*.
1946 Warburton, Mrs. I., *Arley, Rydens Road, Walton-on-Thames*.
1946 Warburton, J. R., F.S.A., *Arley, Rydens Road, Walton-on-Thames*.
1946 Ward, Miss E., *Tilway*, Tilford Road, Farnham.
1944 Ward, L. J., *Jenkins Barn, Cranleigh*.
1943 Ward, V. G., M.D., *The* Tiled House, *West Byfleet*.
1920 Ward, W. E., 9 Grove Park, *Denmark Hill, S.E.5*.
1945 Ware, Mrs. R. E., *The Vicarage, North Holmwood, Dorking*.
1943 Ware, The Rev. R. M., M.A., *The* Vicarage, North Holmwood, Dorking.
1947 Warman, Miss F. E., 22 *Coveham* Crescent, *Cobham*.
1941 Warren, Miss E. A., *Oak* Cottage, *Burscombe* Lane, *Sidford*, Devon.
1946 Warren, Miss R. L. M., *Coombe End, Shere*.
1947 Waterhouse, Sir Nicholas E., K.B.E., M.A., F.C.A., Norwood Farm, *Effingham*.
1948 Wates, N. E., *Elmore, Chipstead*.
1943 Watkin, Miss C. M., Fairmead, *Chichester Road, Dorking*.
1943 Watkin, Mrs. Helena, Fairmead, *Chichester Road, Dorking*.
1946 Watkin, Miss Magdalen, Fairmead, *Chichester Road, Dorking*.
1936 Watkins, H. F., *Newnham, Horsell Park, Woking*.
1948 Watson, G. I., M.D., M.R.C.S., *Covan, Peaslake*.
1945 Watson, Miss Maud J., *Tanglewood, Sole Farm Road, Great Bookham*.
1944 Watson, Miss M. T., *The* Quest, *St. Paul's Road, Dorking*.
1946 Watts, Miss B. M., 41 *Chisholm Road, East Croydon*.
1949 Watts, H. S. F., 100 *Kingsdown Avenue, South* Croydon.
1941 Waymont, R., c/o Mrs. *Edge,* Council House, *Big Arrowery, Hanmer, Whitchurch, Salop*.
1942 Webb, Miss I. C., *Rayleigh, 79 Ember Lane, Esher*.

1946 Webber, J. V., 41 *Hawke Road*, London, *S.E.*19.
1944 Wedgwood, Miss A., 14 *Kings Road, Wimbledon, S.W.*19.
1946 Wedgwood, Sir Ralph, Bart., C.B., *Leith Hill* Place, *Dorking.*
1937 Weeding, Miss D., Tatton, *Hook Heath, Woking.*
1946 Weeding, Miss E. Maude, Tatton, *Hook Heath, Woking.*
1930 Weekes, Miss E. H., *Woodmancourt, Godalming.*
1942 Westminster, City of, Public Libraries, *Administration Department, St. Martin's* Street, *W.C.*2.
1934 Wheatley, W., M.A., 4 Castle Gate, *Richmond,* Surrey.
1947 Wheeler, J. C., *Headley, White Lane, Guildford.*
1947 Wheeler, Mrs. V. H., *Headley, White Lane, Guildford.*
1944 Whitaker, Mrs. M. G., *Redroof,* Sandown *Road, Esher.*
1938 Whitaker, R. E., *Redroof,* Sandown *Road, Esher.*
1945 Whitbourne, Mrs. A. M., *Ridgeways,* Burney *Road, West Humble, Dorking.*
1922 White, Augustus, 14 Florida *Road,* Thornton Heath.
1943 White, J. F,. *c/o Macdonald & Co. Ltd.,* 19 *Ludgate Hill, E.C.*4.
1947 Whitgift School, *Haling Park, South Croydon.*
1945 Whitmore, R. F., 439 *London Road, West* Croydon.
1945 Whitmore, Mrs. W. I., 439 *London Road, West* Croydon.
1945 Whitton, K. R., *The Old Hall School, Wellington, Shropshire.*
1948 Whitton, Mrs. N., *Nanhoran,* Claremont *Lane, Esher.*
1944 Wigan, Mrs. C. M., Bradstone Brook, *Guildford.*
1944 Wigan, E. C., Bradstone *Brook, Guildford.*
1949 Williams, Miss A. M., *The* Mount, *Coulsdon Rise,* Coulsdon.
1930 Williams, H. B., LL.D., Croft Point, *Bramley, Guildford.*
1947 Williamson, Mrs. E. L., 5 *Camden* House, Guy *Road,* Beddington.
1923 Willis, Cloudesley S., F.S.A., 9 *High* Street, Ewell.
1926 Willis, Mrs. R. L., 9 *High* Street, Ewell.
1944 Willy, Stephen, *Ashbourne, Orchard Avenue,* Thames Ditton.
1944 Wilson, Mrs. A., B.A., 16 *The Woodlands, Esher.*
1933 Wilson, Miss C. B. Hutton, *Wideways, Blechingley.*
1946 Wilson, M. A., 16 *The Woodlands, Esher.*
1944 Wilson, P. G., 65 *Headcorn Road,* Thornton *Heath.*
1930 Wilson-Haffenden, J., *Home Wood, Eyhurst* Close, *Kingswood.*
1930 Wiltshire, R. G., *Longhouse Lodge, Ermyn Way, Leatherhead.*
1903 Wimbledon Free Library, *Wimbledon, S.W.*19.
1947 Windebank, Miss M., Turrets, 98 Grove *Road,* Sutton, *Surrey.*
1944 Winton-Lewis, B. A. P., A.R.I.B.A., 12 *City Road,* London, *E.C.*1
1944 Wisconsin, U.S.A., The General Library, *University of Wisconsin,* **816** State *Street, Madison* 6, *Wis., U.S.A., per Hy. Sotheran Ltd.,* **23-25** *Sackville Street, London, W.*1.
1946 Wiseman, Mrs. P. B., *Northview, The* Mount, Fetcham.
1933 Wiseman, R. A., B.A., C.M.G., *Northview, The* Mount, Fetcham.
1947 Woking Public Library, *Woking.*
1947 Wood, Miss A. E., Greenways, Sutton *Abinger, Dorking.*
1943 Wood, Miss D., 1 *Mickleham Hall, Dorking.*
1948 Wood, E. S., B.A., 21 *Ganghill, Guildford.*
1945 Wood, Miss E., Greenways, Sutton *Abinger, Dorking.*
1948 Wood, Mrs. M. C., 21 *Ganghill, Guildford.*

1947 Wood, Miss M. E., M.A., F.S.A., *Little* Fir *Knob, Churt Road, Hindhead.*
1936 Woodcock, H. C., M.B.E., M.R.C.S., L.R.C.P., *Cope Hill, Peaslake.*
1949 Woodley, G. M., A.R.I.C.S., 11 Kingsway, *Ewell.*
1934 Woods, Miss E. M. C., M.A., *Glebe Lodge, Shalford Road, Guildford.*
1937 Woods, F., 56 *Temple Road, Epsom.*
1944 Woodward, Mrs. A. M., *Southcote, Castle Hill, Guildford.*
1922 Worsley, C. F., 36 *St. Stephen's Gardens, Twickenham, Middlesex.*
1944 Wright, F. R., M.A., *Midway, Oxted.*
1944 Wright, H. G., M.A., *St. Glave's Grammar School,* Tower Bri*dge,* S.E.1.
1949 Wylie, A. A., A.C.A., 46 *London Road, Guildford.*

1911 YALE University Library, U.S.A., *per E. G. Allen & Son, Ltd.,* 14 Grape Street, *W.C.2.*
1948 Yates, Miss D., *Squirrel Cottage, Rectory Close, Byfleet.*
1945 Yates, E., F.S.A., *Elm* Court, *Hampton, Middlesex.*
1946 Yates, H. R., M.A., *East Hill Hotel, Oxted.*
1945 Yeatman, D. G., *High* Street, *Walton-on-the-Hill.*
1926 York, The Most Rev. The Archbishop of, Bis*hopthorpe, York.*
1946 Young, D. H. W., M.B.E., 10 *Queensbury Place, S.W.7.*
1944 Young, M., *Greenwood, Longdown, Guildford.*
1944 Young, Mrs. V. M. G., 43 *Pewley Way, Guildford.*

SOCIETIES, &c., IN UNION

WHICH EXCHANGE PUBLICATIONS.

BERKSHIRE ARCHÆOLOGICAL SOCIETY, c/o P. S. Spokes, F.S.A., 26 Charlbury Road, Oxford.
BRISTOL AND GLOUCESTERSHIRE ARCHÆOLOGICAL SOCIETY. c/o Roland Austin, 24 Parkend Road, Gloucester.
BRITISH ARCHÆOLOGICAL ASSOCIATION. 11 Chandos Street, Cavendish Square, London, W.1.
BUCKINGHAMSHIRE ARCHITECTURAL AND ARCHÆOLOGICAL SOCIETY. c/o The Curator and Librarian, Bucks County Museum, Aylesbury.
CAMBRIDGE ANTIQUARIAN SOCIETY. Museum of Archæology and Ethnography, Cambridge.
CAMBRIDGESHIRE AND HUNTINGDONSHIRE ARCHÆOLOGICAL SOCIETY. c/o J. R. Garood, M.D., Alconbury Hill, Huntingdon.
CHESTER ARCHITECTURAL AND ARCHÆOLOGICAL SOCIETY. c/o H. C. Wickham, 13 St. John Street, Chester.
DERBYSHIRE ARCHÆOLOGICAL SOCIETY. St. Mary's Bridge Chapel House, Derby.
DORSET NATURAL HISTORY AND ARCHÆOLOGICAL SOCIETY. County Museum, Dorchester.
DUMFRIESSHIRE AND GALLOWAY NATURAL HISTORY SOCIETY. R. C. Reid, Editor, Cleughbraes, Dumfries.
EAST HERTFORDSHIRE ARCHÆOLOGICAL SOCIETY. 27 West Street, Hertford.

EAST RIDING ANTIQUARIAN SOCIETY. The Museum, Hull.

ESSEX ARCHÆOLOGICAL SOCIETY. Holly Trees, Colchester.

HAMPSHIRE FIELD CLUB. c/o Frank Warren, Staple Gardens, Winchester.

HEREFORD, THE WOOLHOPE NATURALISTS' FIELD CLUB. 267 Upper Ledbury Road, Hereford.

IRELAND, THE ROYAL SOCIETY OF ANTIQUARIES OF. 63 Merrion Square, Dublin.

KENT ARCHÆOLOGICAL SOCIETY. The Museum, Maidstone.

KUNG VITTERHETS-HISTORIE-OCH ANTIKVITETSAKADEMIEN, Storgatan 71, Stockholm, Sweden.

LANCASHIRE AND CHESHIRE ANTIQUARIAN SOCIETY. Hon. Sec., Mrs. Richardson, 43 Newcombe Road, Holcombe Brook, Bury, Lancs.

LEICESTERSHIRE ARCHÆOLOGICAL SOCIETY. The Hon. Librarian, The Guildhall, Leicester.

LINCOLNSHIRE ARCHITECTURAL AND ARCHÆOLOGICAL SOCIETY, Jews Court, Steep Hill, Lincoln. The Editor, G. N. Tupling, Ph.D., M.A., B.Sc., 16 Alexandra Terrace, Haslington, Lancs.

LONDON, THE SOCIETY OF ANTIQUARIES OF. Burlington House, Piccadilly, W.1.

LONDON AND MIDDLESEX ARCHÆOLOGICAL SOCIETY. Bishopsgate Institute, London, E.C.2.

MONTGOMERY ARCHÆOLOGICAL COLLECTIONS. Welshpool, Wales.

NEWCASTLE-UPON-TYNE, THE SOCIETY OF ANTIQUARIES OF. The Library, The Castle, Newcastle-upon-Tyne.

OXFORD ARCHITECTURAL AND HISTORICAL SOCIETY. Ashmolean Museum, Oxford.

ROME, THE BRITISH SCHOOL AT. Librarian, R. Goodchild, Valle Giulia, Rome, 51.

ROYAL ARCHÆOLOGICAL INSTITUTE. Lancaster House, St. James's, London, S.W.1.

ROYAL HISTORIC SOCIETY. 96 Cheyne Walk, London, S.W.10.

ROYAL INSTITUTE OF BRITISH ARCHITECTS. 66 Portland Place, London, W.1.

SCOTLAND, THE SOCIETY OF ANTIQUARIES OF. National Museum of Antiquities, Queen Street, Edinburgh.

SHROPSHIRE ARCHÆOLOGICAL AND NATURAL HISTORY SOCIETY. Public Library and Museum, Shrewsbury.

SOCIÉTÉ JERSIAISE. The Museum, 9 Pier Road, Jersey, C.I.

SOMERSET ARCHÆOLOGICAL AND NATURAL HISTORY SOCIETY. W. A. Seaby, F.S.A., The Museum, Taunton.

SUFFOLK INSTITUTE OF ARCHÆOLOGY. Newbourne, Woodbridge, Suffolk.

SUSSEX ARCHÆOLOGICAL SOCIETY. Barbican House, Lewes.

THORESBY SOCIETY. c/o The Librarian, Brotherton Library, The University, Leeds, 2.

WILTSHIRE ARCHÆOLOGICAL AND NATURAL HISTORY SOCIETY. The Museum, Devizes.

WORCESTERSHIRE ARCHÆOLOGICAL SOCIETY. c/o E. A. F. Keen, F.L.A., Victoria Institute, Worcester.

YORKSHIRE ARCHÆOLOGICAL SOCIETY. The Library, 10 Park Place, Leeds.

LIBRARIES

RULES OF THE
SURREY ARCHÆOLOGICAL SOCIETY

The Rules of the Society were altered and amended by a Special General Meeting presided over by Mr. I. D. Margary, F.S.A., Vice-President of the Society, at Epsom on Saturday, 12th November, 1949. The new Rules as agreed at that meeting are printed herewith.

I.—The Society shall be called THE SURREY ARCHÆOLOGICAL SOCIETY.

II.—The objects of the Society shall be :

1. To promote the study of archæology and antiquities within the County by the collection and publication of material and information of archæological or antiquarian interest concerning the Geographical County of Surrey. This material to include : Antiquities (of all periods) ; Earthworks ; Roman Roads ; Buildings of Architectural or Historical interest ; Records and Manuscripts ; Heraldry and Genealogy ; Costume ; Numismatics ; Ceramics ; Ecclesiastical History and Endowments ; Charitable Foundations ; Records and anything concerning the history or pre-history of the County.

2. To watch for the discovery of Antiquities in the progress of public and private undertakings (making of Highways ; Sewers ; Building Works ; Quarrying, etc.) ; to procure their preservation and to ensure a careful record of the same and of all the circumstances attending their discovery.

3. To encourage those qualified to carry out such work, to undertake excavations on behalf of the Society, especially in the case of sites of archæological interest or potential interest, which are threatened with destruction.

4. To collect funds whereby financial assistance can be granted to assist the carrying out of specific excavations within the County, and the compilation of histories or materials for the histories of places or Parishes in the County.

5. To oppose and, if possible, prevent the destruction of or damage to any site, building, monument or record of archæological or antiquarian interest in the County, and to co-operate with Public or Private bodies or Persons desirous of safeguarding all such sites, monuments or records.

6. To encourage by means of lectures and visits an interest in and knowledge of local archæology and especially of the various archæological sites, monuments and antiquities situated in the County.

III.—The Society shall consist of Members, including Societies or Institutions, and Honorary Members.

IV.—The affairs of the Society shall be conducted by a Council of Management to consist of the President, Vice-Presidents, Treasurer, Secretary or Secretaries and Editor, who shall be elected annually ; and of twenty-four members, six of whom shall be elected each year for a period of four years and shall then retire and be ineligible for re-election till after a lapse of one year. In addition to these the Council may co-opt annually for a period of one year not more than six additional members. The Council may, upon the death or resignation of an elected member, co-opt another member in his place for the unexpired portion of his period of membership. Three members of the Council, exclusive of the Secretary or Secretaries, shall form a quorum. Every person whom it is intended to nominate as a candidate for election to the Council (other than candidates nominated by the Council) shall be nominated in writing by not less than two members of the Society, and the nominations shall be sent to reach the General Secretary not later than the 1st day of March preceding the next Annual General Meeting, and shall be accompanied by the written consent of the person so nominated to serve if elected. If the number of candidates for election to the Council at the Annual General Meeting exceeds the number of vacancies, the election shall be by ballot by members of the Society present at the meeting, and the ballot shall be held in such a manner as the Council may determine. No person shall be eligible for membership of the Council who is not a member of the Society. Any member of the Council elected for a period of four years or co-opted in place of one so elected who after notification and without reasonable excuse shall be absent from four consecutive meetings of the Council shall be deemed to have resigned his membership of the Council immediately after the fourth such meeting.

V.—The names of candidates for membership shall on a written nomination of two members of the Society on the prescribed form be submitted to the Council for election ; the Council shall have power to appoint a committee of not less than two to receive and deal with such nominations.

VI.—Each member elected on or after the 1st day of January, 1950, shall pay an entrance fee of TEN SHILLINGS and an annual subscription of ONE POUND to be due on 1st January in each year in advance, or £20 in lieu thereof, as a composition for life. Those persons who were members prior to that date shall pay an annual subscription of ten shillings as hitherto, or £15 in lieu thereof, as a composition for life. Societies and Institutions shall not be entitled to pay a composition. Wives of members may be elected, without entrance fee, on payment of an annual subscription of ten shillings and be entitled to all privileges of membership, except that they shall not receive the Society's publications.

The Council may remit the entrance fee of any member who is under the age of 21 years at the date of his nomination and may reduce his annual subscription to ten shillings while under that age. Any member intending to resign must signify this intention in writing before 1st January, otherwise he will be liable to pay his subscription for the ensuing year.

VII.—Subject as provided in Rule VI, the subscriptions of members shall entitle them to one copy of every volume of the Surrey Archæological Collections as issued ; and no publication shall be issued to members whose subscriptions are in arrear. Members whose subscriptions are upwards of one year in arrear may, after due notice, be removed from the List of Members. The Council may remove any member whose conduct shall in the opinion of the Council render him unfit for membership of the Society. Before any such member is removed, seven days' written notice shall be given to him to attend a meeting of the Council, which notice shall contain particulars of the complaints against him, and no member shall be removed without first having an opportunity of appearing before the Council to answer the complaints against him, nor unless at least two-thirds of the Council vote in favour of his removal.

VIII.—All payments shall be made to the Treasurer, to the account of the Society, at such Banking House as the Society may direct ; and every cheque shall be signed by the Treasurer on behalf of the Society.

IX.—The Lord-Lieutenant of the County, Members of the House of Peers residing in or who are Landed Proprietors in the County, also Members of the House of Commons representing the County or its Boroughs ; the High Sheriff of the County for the time being ; the Chairman of the Surrey County Council, and such other persons as the Council may determine, may be invited by the Council to become Vice-Presidents, if members of the Society.

X.—Persons eminent for their services to archæology or antiquarian research shall be eligible to be associated to the Society as Honorary Members, and be elected at a General Meeting ; but no person shall be nominated to this class without the sanction of the Council. Honorary Members shall have all the rights of members, except that of voting.

XI.—An Annual General Meeting, of which at least seven days' notice shall be given, shall be held at such date, time and place as the Council shall appoint, to receive and consider the Report and Accounts of the Council on the state of the Society, and to elect the officers for the ensuing twelve months.

XII.—There shall be meetings for the reading of papers and other business, to be held at such times and places as the Council may direct.

XIII.—The Council may at any time call a Special General Meeting, and they shall at all times be bound to do so on the written requisition of ten members, specifying the nature of the business to be transacted. Notice of the time and place of such a meeting shall be sent to the members at least fourteen days previously, mentioning the subject to be brought forward ; and no other subject shall be discussed at such meeting.

XIV.—The Council shall meet for the transaction of business connected with the management of the Society on such days as the Council shall from time to time direct.

XV.—Save as provided in Rule VII, at every meeting of the Society, or of the Council, the resolutions of the majority present shall be binding, and at such meetings the Chairman shall have a casting vote, independently of his vote as a member of the Society or of the Council, as the case may be.

XVI.—The Council shall be empowered to appoint members as Local Secretaries in such places in the County as may appear desirable.

XVII.—The whole effects and property of the Society shall be under the control and management of the Council, who shall be at liberty to purchase books, drawings, engravings, plans, maps or other articles, or to exchange them or dispose thereof.

XVIII.—The Council shall have the power of publishing such extra volumes, local histories, special articles, papers, drawings, engravings and maps as may be deemed worthy of being printed, and shall issue a Report of the Proceedings of the Society in the form of an annual volume or otherwise.

XIX.—Two members shall be appointed annually to audit the accounts of the Society, and to report thereon at the Annual General Meeting.

XX.—No religious or political discussions shall be permitted at meetings of the Society, nor topics of a similar nature admitted in the Society's publications.

XXI.—The Trustees of the Society for all purposes shall be the President and the Treasurer for the time being.

XXII.—No change shall be made in the Rules of the Society, except at a Special General Meeting.

ROMANO-BRITISH CEMETERIES AT HASLE-MERE AND CHARTERHOUSE

BY

JOHN M. HOLMES

THE Romano-British cemeteries at Haslemere and Charter-house were both discovered in 1903, and are already known to archæologists. Some account of the Haslemere cemetery, illustrated with plans of the site and photographs of the pottery, was published at the time of excavation, though nothing has been published concerning the Charterhouse cemetery ; fortunately the finds have been preserved in the Haslemere Educational Museum and the Charterhouse School Museum, respectively. Some of the pots in Haslemere Museum have been quoted by archæological writers, more often by reference to the published photographs than from personal inspection ; but both museums are rather too far from the usual haunts of archæologists for their contents to be generally well known.

At the time when these two cemeteries were excavated, the study of Roman coarse-ware pottery had not been carried very far, especially that of the less romanized types of the more back-ward, native areas ; moreover, the interpretation of the Hasle-mere cemetery was coloured by the then comparatively recent work of Sir Arthur Evans on the Aylesford cemetery ; it is not surprising, therefore, that the Haslemere cemetery should at first have been called "Late Celtic," though its post-conquest date was quickly recognized when an account of the excavations was read before the Society of Antiquaries. As for the Charterhouse cemetery, the Roman date of the bead-rim urns has long been recognized, but the other vessels in the collection have never been studied.

The present account of the two cemeteries is, therefore, an attempt to give a detailed account of the pottery, with a measured drawing of every piece large enough to be of interest, and to date as much of it as possible in the light of knowledge accumulated during the past twenty years. It has, in fact, proved possible to put on record, not only a number of pots datable by comparison with the pottery from other sites, but also a range of native, coarse-ware types in quite closely dated burial groups, some of the types having only a regional distribution. Without taking into account these two cemetery sites, any general discussion of the Romano-British pottery of Surrey in the 1st century would disregard much of the available evidence.

A description of each cemetery will first be given, with a list of all the pottery found, group by group. Roman pottery in quantity is notoriously rather a dull subject, and any attempt to discuss dating evidence in this section would have made it too indigestible ; a plain statement of its probable date has therefore been placed after the description of each pot, and a discussion of the evidence on which this has been based has been reserved for the next section. Here, all the pottery has been classified into two terra sigillata forms and 34 coarse-ware types, each denoted by a number ; type numbers and burial-group numbers have been cross-referenced, using an obvious notation. This section is largely of technical interest and necessarily involves many comparisons and references ; where many examples of a type are known, it has not always seemed necessary to give a full list of references, but general statements about distribution are, nevertheless, based on the evidence of recorded examples, carefully collected. In the final section an attempt has been made to discuss the cultural and historical background of the two cemeteries, based partly on the evidence of the pottery and partly on a general knowledge of the romanization of lowland Britain after the conquest.

THE HASLEMERE CEMETERY

The site of the burials at Haslemere is now occupied by Beech Road and the houses alongside it, and is shown on the map published in *Proc. Soc. Antiq.*, Vol. XXI, p. 219, Fig. 2. The burials were first discovered in 1903, when some ground was being dug for the planting of fruit trees ; further discoveries were made in 1905, when the land was sold for building purposes and the road was made through it. After each discovery, excavations were carried out under the direction of Mr. Swanton, Curator of Haslemere Educational Museum ; all the finds (with the exception of one or two vessels which were given away by the owner and cannot now be traced) were eventually presented to the museum, where the whole vessels are now exhibited and the fragments are carefully stored, in their groups as found. A short account of the excavations in 1903 was published in *Surrey Archæological Collections*,[1] together with a photograph of some of the vessels found in 1905, and a paper on both excavations was read before the Society of Antiquaries and published in their proceedings,[2] together with photographs of the three best-preserved burial groups.

Of the seven burials excavated in 1903, four groups can be identified and dated, while the other three are represented only by the bases of single urns ; another six urns, at least, were represented by fragments dug out by the gardeners in trenching the soil, and thus not found *in situ*; this makes a total of at least thirteen burials in this part of the cemetery, which was in use from the Roman conquest until about A.D. 80. Another thirteen

---

[1] *S.A.C.*, Vol. XIX, pp. 33-38 ; Plates I, II, III, and a sketch plan of the site, facing p. 37.

[2] *Proc. Soc. Antiq.*, Vol. XXI (New Series), pp. 221-228; Fig. 2 (map of the Haslemere urnfield) and Figs. 3-5 (photographs of burial groups).

burials were excavated in 1905, of which three groups can be identified and dated ; the remainder are represented by portions of vessels and fragments, only some of which can be grouped or dated. This part of the cemetery came into use about A.D. 80 and was used until about A.D. 120 ; nothing has been found on the site which can be dated later than about A.D. 120.

The following burials were discovered and excavated in 1903 :

GROUP I. A.D. 60–80. (Fig. 1, top.)

The vessels of this group were discovered by the gardener and were subsequently brought to the museum, cracked by the frost. The first ten are shown in the photograph in *S.A.C.*, Vol. XIX, p. 38, Plate III. Their relative positions are not recorded, but the gardener asserted they were arranged round some of the larger fragments. By analogy with other groups, the bowl No. 2 was probably used as a cover for the cinerary urn ; if so, the diameter of the mouth of the urn would have been slightly smaller than is shown in the figure, or else the dish would have rested directly on the contents.

1. Jug, restored from fragments, handle missing. Dark grey ware, with a reddish core. (Type 15. Claudian or a little later.)

2. Shallow bowl of hard, dark grey ware, unbroken. The bowl is shouldered half-way up the side and the shoulder is marked off from the lower part by a narrow and slightly irregular ridge of clay. (Type 22. Flavian.)

3. Bowl of hard, dark grey ware, much broken on one side. It has a sloping rim, a shoulder half-way up the side, a shallow girth-groove below the shoulder and a slightly pedestal-shaped base. (Type 8. Claudian or a little later.)

4. Shallow saucer of coarse, red ware, not quite perfect, with circular grooves on both the upper and the underside of the base. (Type 13. A.D. 60-80.)

5. Piece of a jar rim of dark grey, sandy ware ; a bead-rim with a narrow, incised groove on the shoulder. It had been used as the cinerary urn of the group and was found with many fragments of calcined human bones. (Type 18. A.D. 50-80.)

6. Small cup of coarse, light red ware, almost unbroken. (Type 7. Claudian.)

7 Part of the base of a small jar or jug of dark brown ware. The form of the missing upper part is uncertain. The pedestal-shaped base, grooved on the underside, is typical 1st-century work.

8. Small cup, rather similar to No. 6 and of the same light red ware. (Type 1. A.D. 50-100.)

9. Another of the same pattern, not quite intact. (Not figured.)

10. Base only of a small bowl of dark grey ware, grooved on the underside of the base. Possibly the upper part was similar in form to No. 3.

11-14. Fragments of red ware, representing at least four vessels, one of them similar to No. 8. (Not figured.)

15. Fragments of another saucer similar to No. 4. (Not figured.)

The earliest dating for the group is suggested by the bowl (No. 2), which is of a type not normally found in Surrey before the Flavian period and can hardly be earlier than about A.D. 60. On the other hand, the flagon (No. 1) is of early type and is not likely to be much later than Claudian. The smaller vessels of the group

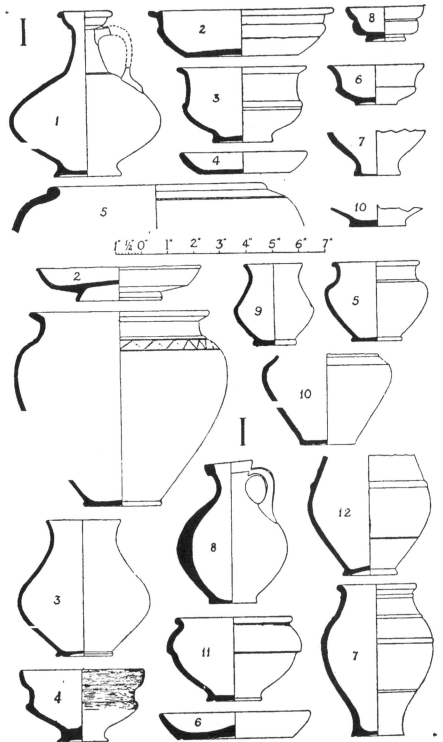

FIG. 1.—POTTERY FROM THE HASLEMERE CEMETERY, EXCAVATED IN 1903 (*top*)
AND IN 1905 (*bottom*).

are all copies of imported types of the Claudian period. The group also includes a large bead-rim jar ; such jars were superseded by other types after the Claudian period, though there is no reason why this example should not be early Flavian. A date not later than about A.D. 80 is therefore suggested for the burial of this group.

GROUP II. A.D. 50–80. (Not figured.)

1. Part of a bead-rim urn, 8 in. in diameter at the mouth, of thick, coarse, dark grey ware. It was found with a quantity of calcined bone. (Type 18. Claudian or early Flavian.)

2. Two small fragments of a vessel ornamented with groups of incised lines. These fragments are figured in *S.A.C.*, Vol. XIX, p. 34. They are most likely of Claudian date, representing a native tradition of decoration.

GROUP III. A.D. 50–80. (Not figured.)

1. Fragments of a bead-rim urn of grey ware, 7 in. in diameter at the mouth. (Type 18. A.D. 50-80.)

GROUP IV. Mid 1st Century. (Fig. 2.)

1. The lower part of an urn of dark grey ware, restored from fragments. At least one fragment of out-turned rim was found with it, but could not be fitted to the pot. This urn is shown in the photograph in *S.A.C.*, Vol. XIX, p. 35, Plate II (*a*). (Type 29. Mid 1st century.)

GROUP V. 1st century. (Not figured.)

1. The lower part of an urn of coarse, grey ware.

GROUP VI. 1st century. (Not figured.)

1. The fragmentary base of an urn of grey ware.

GROUP VII. 1st century. (Not figured.)

1. Fragments of an urn of thick dark grey ware.

The form of the upper parts of the last three jars is uncertain, but they were most probably bead-rim jars (Type 18).

GROUPS VIII–XIII. Undatable. (Fig. 3, bottom, and not figured.)

Many fragments of pottery were collected from a heap of stones formed when the garden soil was being trenched. "Altogether we obtained evidence of 13 cineraries and 16 accessory vessels, including two or three of Samian ware." Seven cineraries and fifteen accessory vessels are accounted for in groups I to VII, so that at least seven vessels must have been represented by the fragments from the stone heap. Of these, the only recognizable fragment is part of the bead-rim of a large, high-shouldered storage jar in coarse, light-brown, sandy ware. This rim is decorated with thumb-marks on the bead and there are deep finger impressions on the inside. (Type 32. 1st century.)

The relative positions of the first seven of these burials are shown on the plan in *S.A.C.*, Vol. XIX, opposite p. 37 ; the others must have come from the piece of ground marked as trenched. The dating of the individual groups suggests that this part of the cemetery was in use from about A.D. **50 to** A.D. **80,** group I probably being the latest.

The following burials were discovered and excavated in **1905** :

GROUP I. A.D. **70–80.** (Fig. 1, bottom.)

This burial group was first discovered by a man digging a hole for a fencing post ; the group was then carefully excavated. The cinerary urn with its lid was found surrounded by thirteen other vessels, in the positions shown in the photograph in *Proc. Soc. Antiq.,* Vol. XXI, p. 220, Fig. 3.

1. Cinerary urn containing calcined human bone, charcoal, sand, two rudely-chipped flints and two fragments of a bronze fibula. The urn is of hard, brittle and rather sandy ware, with a grey surface but brown and less well fired in the centre. It is a round-shouldered pot, decorated with a cordon at the base of the neck, below which is burnished a band of zig-zag ornament. It has a sloping rim and there is a narrow groove round the underside of the base. (Type 19. Flavian.)

The bronze fibula (Fig. 2): both fragments of this fibula are thoroughly burnt, but sufficient remains to show that it was of the "Swarling" type, with pierced catchplate, such as is found throughout the Belgic area of Britain. Its date should be about A.D. 50, but, like some of the accessory vessels in this group, it may well have been a number of years old when the burial took place.

2. Dish of terra sigillata of brick-red paste, used as a cover for the urn. Much of the glaze is worn off. (Form 18. Claudian.)

3. Beaker of coarse, reddish-brown ware, with a rough surface. It has a plain rim, which has been very roughly finished by flattening, and the sides bulge widely ; the base is slightly raised and is grooved on the underside. (Type 23. A.D. 50-100.)

4. Cup of hard, grey ware. The upper part has been burnished a darker grey. (Type 6. Claudian.)

5. Small jar of hard, brittle, grey ware. It has a high, rounded shoulder and a cordon at the base of the neck. (Type 21. Flavian.)

6. Dish, light brown to dirty grey in colour, of a hard, flaky paste with a rough surface. The centre of the base is raised into an abrupt cone and the underside is grooved. (Type 14. A.D. 50-100.)

7. Cordoned beaker of fine, brick-red paste. (Type 25. Flavian.)

8. Small jug of thick, heavy, reddish-brown ware, with a rough surface. (Type 16. A.D. 45-65.)

9. Beaker with a wide, almost carinated, bulge, similar to No. 3 but smaller. It is of hard, dark grey ware with a reddish core. (Type 23. A.D. 50-100.)

10. Small jar of hard, grey ware, with a high, slightly angular shoulder; it has a cordon at the base of the neck, which is missing. (Type 21. Flavian.)

11. Wide bowl of hard, brittle and flaky, grey ware. The deep girth groove has caused the upper part to overhang the lower part. The underside of the base is slightly raised and is grooved. (Type 9. A.D. 50-100.)

12. Cordoned, butt-shaped jar of light red ware. The rim is missing and the base is raised. (Type 25. Flavian.)

13-15. These three vessels are not shown in the photograph and have not been identified.

Although a Claudian date would suit most of the vessels in the group, the absence of bead-rim jars and the presence of the high-shouldered jars Nos. **1, 5** and **10** suggest that the group was buried not earlier than about A.D. 70 ; the terra sigillata dish, the small cup and the jug, to which an earlier date has been given above, could well have been many years old when buried.

GROUP II. A.D. 80–90. (Fig. 3, top.)

This burial group was found a yard away from group I. The positions of the vessels are shown in the photograph in *Proc. Soc. Antiq.*, Vol. XXI, p. 221, Fig. 4 ; their arrangement was similar to that of group I.

1. Cinerary urn of hard, grey ware with traces of a black coating; it contained bones, sand and three flint chips, and part of the lower jaw of a woman was said to be amongst the bones. The urn is a round-shouldered pot with a cordon at the base of the neck, below which is a burnished pattern of wavy lines; it has a sloping rim and a narrow groove round the underside of the base. (Type 19. Flavian.)

2. Shallow bowl of hard, light grey ware, used as a cover for the urn. The side of the bowl is shouldered, with a narrow, incised groove below the shoulder; the upper edge of the rim and the underside of the base are grooved. (Type 22. Flavian.)

3. Dish, similar to I.6, of a hard paste with a rough surface, light brown to dirty grey in colour. The base is marked with circular grooves both inside and underneath. (Type 14. A.D. 50-100.)

4. Dish of coarse, sandy, red ware. (Type 3. A.D. 80-160.)

5. Small, deep bowl of hard, grey ware. The lower part is almost conical, the mouth flared, and there is a slight shoulder at the junction. The base is flat and grooved on the underside. (Type 8. Claudian or a little later.)

6. A similar but slightly larger bowl of the same ware, with a more pronounced shoulder. (Type 8. Claudian or a little later.)

7. Carinated beaker of coarse, reddish-brown ware, with a rough surface, similar to I.3. The rim is missing. (Type 23. A.D. 50-100.)

8. Jar of hard, coarse, reddish-brown ware, decorated with a pattern of large, raised dots arranged in sloping rows. Most of the rim has been broken off, but enough remains to show its recurved form. The base is slightly raised in the centre and grooved on the underside. (Type 28. A.D. 70-80.)

9. Small dish of terra sigillata of a good brick-red ware; most of the glaze has worn off. There are traces of a potter's stamp on the centre of the base, inside, but it is so worn as to be illegible. (Form 27. A.D. 55-80.)

10. Beaker of fine, light red ware decorated with a "roulette" pattern of burnished lines, separated into zones by lightly incised grooves. Similar in type to I.7. (Type 25. Flavian.)

11. Globular jar of fine, buff-coloured ware, thin, and well made. Most of the rim and one side have been broken away. (Type 12. Flavian.)

12. Small jar of hard, grey ware, with a high, carinated shoulder, similar in form to I.10, but slightly larger. The neck and rim are missing. (Type 21. Flavian.)

13-14. These two vessels are not shown in the photograph and have not been identified.

The earliest date for this group is determined by No. 4, imitating a terra sigillata form, and is thus about A.D. 80 ; this dating is supported by the decorated jar No. 8 and the Flavian types. But the group also includes the terra sigillata cup No. 9, which cannot have been made much later than A.D. 80, though it may have been buried some years later. The two cups Nos. 5 and 6, imitating Claudian forms, must actually be dated rather later.

GROUP III. A.D. 70–100. (Fig. 4, top.)

This group was found close to the fence ; the vessels are shown in the photograph in *Proc. Soc. Antiq.*, Vol. XXI, p. 226, Fig. 5.

1. Cinerary urn containing calcined human bones. The jar is of similar type to the urns of groups I and II but rather larger. It has a rounded shoulder and a cordon at the base of the neck, below which is a burnished, zig-zag pattern. The body of the jar is decorated with a burnished pattern of wavy lines, separated by narrow, incised grooves. The shoulder and lower part of the jar have traces of a black coating. (Type 19. Flavian.)

2. Small jar of hard, grey ware, ridged at the shoulder and with a cordon at the base of the neck. (Type 21. Flavian.)

3. A similar but slightly wider jar of the same ware The shoulder is carinated and there is a narrow, incised groove encircling the lower part the jar. The centre of the base is raised and the underside lacks the usual groove. (Type 21. Flavian.)

4. Small shallow bowl of hard, dark grey ware. The side is shouldered and both the upper edge of the rim and the underside of the base are grooved. (Type 22. Flavian.)

All the vessels in this group are of Flavian date.

GROUPS IV–XIII. A.D. 80–120. (Fig. 4, bottom.)

Other cinerary urns and accessory vessels were found near to group II in the positions indicated on the plan (*Proc. Soc. Antiq.*, Vol. XXI, p. 219, Fig. 2). These vessels were all incomplete, mostly fragments ; they cannot be placed in separate burial groups and only the larger pieces are figured.

1. Rim of a large jar of coarse, brown ware with a grey surface; probably used as a cinerary urn. (Type 34. A.D. 80-120.)

2. Rim and lower part of a large jar of dark ware. The shoulder is missing, but the rim form is similar to No. 1 ; the underside of the base is grooved. Probably used as a cinerary urn. (Type 34. A.D. 80-120.)

3. Base of an urn of hard, coarse, grey ware, repaired with a lead plug where the thin base has broken through.

4. Small jar of coarse, sandy ware, reddish in colour, with traces of a grey slip. The high shoulder is rounded and decorated with a cordon. The base is raised and grooved on the underside. The missing rim was possibly similar to that of the large urn III.1. (Type 19. Flavian.)

5. Small jar of hard, grey ware, with a high, slightly carinated shoulder. The rim is missing, but there is the trace of a cordon at the broken edge. The jar is almost identical with I.10. (Type 21. Flavian.)

6. Bowl of brick-red ware. It is decorated with burnished grooves above and below the cordon and just above the carination ; it has a raised, hollow base. The exact shape of the upper part of this bowl is a little uncertain owing to its fragmentary condition and the absence of the rim. (Type 2. Flavian.)

7. Base of a cinerary urn of hard, grey ware. It contained calcined human bones, including pieces of skull. Many fragments of the sides were found with it, but not enough to restore the form.

8. Small bulbous beaker of hard, grey ware. The rim is missing and it has a raised base. (Type 24. A.D. 80-120.)

9. Small beaker of hard, grey ware with a reddish core. It is decorated with a lattice pattern of burnished lines on a rough body ; the band below the rim is coated a darker grey and burnished. The rim is missing. (Type 33. A.D. 80-120.)

The above vessels belong principally to the period A.D. 80–100 and some may be as late as A.D. 120.

Two cinerary urns and some accessory vessels had been disturbed and broken up by the road-makers, who had cut through a circle of interments.

  10. Rim of a jar, probably used as a cinerary urn. (Type 19. Flavian.)
  11. Rim of a bead-rim jar, probably used as a cinerary urn. (Type 18. A.D. 50-80.)
  12. Fragments of a bowl with shouldered sides. (Type 22. Flavian.)
  13. Fragments of another similar bowl. (Type 22. Flavian.)
  14. Fragments of a small jar. (Probably type 21. Flavian.)
  15. Fragments of a cordoned jar. (Probably type 25. Flavian.)

These vessels form a group, possibly two groups, of Flavian date.

Fragments of a cinerary urn, with two flints and a piece of burnt bronze, were found on the other side of the fence.

  16. Fragments of a jar in hard, coarse, grey ware. (Type 19. Flavian.)

A total of 13 interments (cinerary urns) and 46 accessory vessels was discovered during the excavations.

  17. Fragments of a bead-rim urn (Type 18. A.D. 50-80.)
  18. Fragments of a jar of rough, brown ware with a grey surface and traces of black, burnished lines decorating it. (Probably type 19. Flavian.)
  19. Base of an urn of brown ware with a grey surface.
  20-26. Fragments not identified.

The part of the cemetery excavated in 1905 was thus in use up to A.D. 100 and probably as late as A.D. 120. It is not likely that any of the groups were buried before about A.D. 80, and it seems, therefore, that this part of the cemetery was the successor of the older part excavated in 1903.

THE CHARTERHOUSE CEMETERY

The site of the burials at Charterhouse is on a promontory south of Charterhouse School and is marked on the 6 inch Ordnance

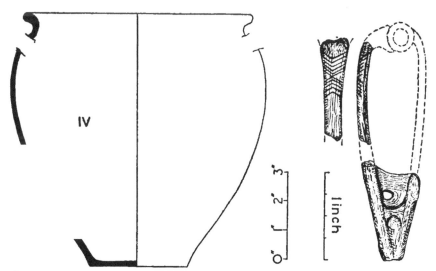

FIG. 2.—BURIAL URN FROM THE HASLEMERE CEMETERY, 1903. FRAGMENTS OF BRONZE BROOCH FOUND INSIDE THE URN OF GROUP 1 OF THE HASLEMERE CEMETERY, 1905 (*see p.*5).

Survey map of Surrey, Sheet XXXI S.E. Four urns were discovered when planting an oak tree in 1903 ; as a result of this
discovery excavations were carried out early in 1904, and the
remainder of the pottery was found. There is no published
account of the excavations and no plan was kept; the pottery,
however, is in the Charterhouse School Museum, where a few
details about the excavations are recorded on the museum labels.
The oak tree which led to the discovery of this cemetery is now
growing at the south-east corner of the Green, and the site of the
other burials is partly overlaid by hard tennis-courts ; the digging
of air-raid shelters during the recent war did not lead to any further
discoveries, but there is still plenty of open ground where further
burials might be found.

The pottery consists of the urns from five burials, each accompanied by accessory vessels, and ranges in date from the Roman
conquest up to not later than A.D. 100 ; it is thus about contemporary with the earlier part of the Haslemere cemetery.

The following burials were excavated from the Charterhouse
cemetery :

GROUP I. A.D. 70–80.   (Fig. 5, top.)

This group was discovered near the newly planted oak tree.

1. Small bead-rim urn of grey ware with a light brown, sandy core.
The urn contained burnt bones. (Type 18. A.D. 50-80.)
2. Small jar of thick, rough, dark grey ware with a light brown, sandy
core. It has a cordon at the base of the neck, a sharply carinated shoulder,
and the underside of the base is grooved. (Type 20. Flavian.)
3. Small jar of dark grey ware, very similar to No. 2 . (Type 20. Flavian.)

The bead-rim jar could be of Claudian date, but the two small
jars make an early Flavian date more probable for the group.

GROUP II. A.D. 50–70.   (Fig. 5, centre.)

The vessels of this group were found at the base of the newly
planted oak tree and a foot or two to the south-west.

1. Bead-rim urn of hard, light brown, sandy ware. (Type 18. A.D. 50-80.)
2. Jar of hard, light grey, sandy ware. The rim has been broken off,
leaving the remains of a cordon. (Type 30. 1st century.)
3. Carinated and cordoned jar of hard, grey ware with a light brown,
sandy core ; it has a high, hollow, pedestal base. (Type 27. A.D. 40-70.)

GROUP III. A.D. 43–55.   (Fig. 6, bottom.)

This is the largest group found and the ashes were contained in
two vessels. The group was about 8 ft. north-east of group II.

1. Jar of hard, grey ware with a light brown, sandy core ; it contained
burnt bones. The shoulder is decorated with a pattern of burnished
diagonal lines   There is a narrow cordon at the base of the neck, but the
rim is missing. (Type 31. 1st century.)
2. Base of another urn, of the same grey ware, containing more burnt
bones. It was most probably a bead-rim urn, but none of the rim is
preserved. (Probably type 18. A.D. 50-80.)
3. Tall barrel-shaped jar of the same grey ware. (Type 11. Claudian.)
4. Small bowl of hard, black, sandy ware. (Type 26. c. A.D. 50.)

5. Dish of hard, black, sandy ware, with several grooves on the underside of the base and one round the lower part of the side. (Type 10. Claudian.)

6. Another exactly similar dish. (Not figured.)

7. Dish of dark grey, sandy ware. (Type 5. Claudian.)

All the vessels of this group are of very early types and the group cannot be much later than mid 1st century.

GROUP IV. A.D. 43–60. (Fig. 6, top.)

These three vessels were found about 12 ft. north-east of group III.

1. Bead-rim urn of dark grey ware, containing burnt bones. (Type 18. A.D. 50-80.)

2. Bulbous beaker of hard, grey ware with a light brown, sandy core. The rim is missing. (Type 23. A.D. 50-100.)

3. High-shouldered jug of hard, grey ware. (Type 17. Claudian.)

The jug cannot be much later than mid 1st century in date, though the other two vessels might be a little later.

GROUP V. A.D. 70–100. (Fig. 5, bottom.)

These two vessels were found about 6 ft. east of group IV.

1. Urn of hard, grey ware with a light brown, sandy core. It is similar in form to I.3, but is rather larger. (Type 20. Flavian.)

2. Globular urn of thin, hard, red ware decorated with a wide, shallow groove just above the widest part of the body. (Type 4. Flavian.)

Both the vessels of this group are of Flavian date.

Of the five groups recovered during the excavation of this cemetery, group III is probably the earliest and may date from very soon after the Roman conquest. Group V may be the latest burial, but the cemetery (or this part of it, if it extends farther than these discoveries) cannot have been in use later than about A.D. 100.

THE POTTERY

The pottery includes two vessels of terra sigillata, which have been dated on their own merits ; all the rest is of coarse ware. Nevertheless, the coarse wares can be grouped into those types which are direct imitations of contemporary imported pottery of various kinds, terra sigillata, Belgic wares, flagons, and those types which, although obviously influenced by Belgic work, are really developments of native pottery traditions ; the imitations can be dated by reference to the dating evidence available for the originals.

Thus, ultimately, the dating of both cemeteries is made to depend on terra sigillata and on dated Belgic sites. The native types ought then to be datable by the groups in which they occur, but it does not happen that every group contains closely datable pots ; it has, of course, been necessary to take into account the dating of comparable native vessels from other sites. The local character of the pottery must here be emphasized ; for these native vessels represent a process of romanization of

E

several different tribal traditions. The Charterhouse pottery will be seen to contrast strongly in its details with the contemporary Haslemere pottery ; yet it has a certain family resemblance, due to the common Belgic origin of both and the same romanization process influencing both. The Charterhouse pots are hard and angular in outline, wholly undecorated, but with carefully moulded cordons, typical of Belgic fashions ; the Haslemere vessels have a rounder outline, still obviously Belgic, but mixed with the Celtic traditions of the Wessex of earlier times, and they are sometimes decorated with linear patterns, in the old Celtic manner. Hence, close parallels for these pottery types will be found only over a certain region. This regional character of the pottery has an important bearing on the cultural and historical background of the Haslemere and Charterhouse people, which will be discussed below.

TERRA SIGILLATA.

Form 18. (*Haslemere*, 1905 ; *I*.2.)

This dish may be compared with one from Silchester (May, *Silchester Pottery*, p. 91 and Plate XXXII, 30 ; Oswald and Pryce, *Terra Sigillata*, Plate XLV, 10). Its features are a rudimentary lip, a continuous, low base, shallow depth, and a footstand of early shape ; it is thus not a late example of its type. The Silchester dish was stamped OF LICIN, a well-attested pre-Flavian potter. A Claudian date has therefore been given to the Haslemere example.

Form 27. (*Haslemere*, 1905 ; *II*.9.)

A cup of this form, of almost exactly the same size, though slightly taller, was found at Silchester (May, *Silchester Pottery*, p. 88 and Plate XXXI, 18 ; Oswald and Pryce, *Terra Sigillata*, Plate XLIX, 14). It has a groove encircling the foot-stand (a pre-Flavian feature), and a narrow groove on the internal surface just below the lip—again characteristic of early work. It is of large size for this type of cup, though the larger sizes occur both early and late. The Silchester cup is stamped MEMORIS M and dated Nero-Vespasian ; this dating has been given to the Haslemere example.

IMITATIONS OF TERRA SIGILLATA FORMS.

Several of the coarse ware vessels in both cemeteries were made in imitation of terra sigillata forms, often in red ware to imitate the colour, but sometimes in grey ware. In date, these copies cannot be earlier than the forms they imitate, and may be later, especially when copied at second hand from foreign imitations in terra rubra or terra nigra ; these Belgic wares were quite common at Silchester and were often copied in coarse-ware by local potters.

Type 1. *Imitation of form* 27. (*Haslemere*, 1903; *I*.8, *I*.9, *I*.11, all in red ware.)

These cups are quoted by May (*Silchester Pottery*, p. 174, under type 176) as "cup 27 Drag. rudely imitated in Late Celtic technique." It is not possible from so rude an imitation to recognize any

13

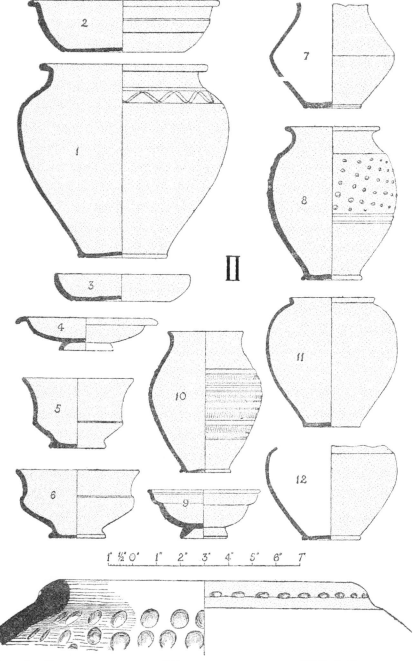

Fig. 3.—Pottery from the Haslemere cemetery, 1905 (*top*); rim of large store-jar from the Haslemere cemetery, 1903 (*bottom*).

features which might determine its date precisely, but the form was in use abundantly in the Claudian period and survived up to about A.D. 140. The example I.8 looks like a copy of the more markedly constricted early form.

Type 2. *Imitation of ʹform* 29. (*Haslemere*, 1905; *IV-XIII*.6, *in red ware.*)

This form, in terra sigillata, becomes more definitely carinated, and the rim decidedly everted, as it develops ; the present imitation might therefore be expected to belong to the Flavian period. May (*Silchester Pottery*, p. 115 and Plate XLVIII, 56) shows a rather similar bowl of soft, brown clay, finished in "bronzed" technique. Pieces of bowls of rather similar form were found at Ashtead villa (*S.A.C.*, Vol. XXXVIII (ii), p. 145, Fig. 7, 2, in coarse, reddish ware with black surfacing ; *S.A.C.*, Vol. XXXVII (ii), p. 160, 11, and Fig. 3, in hard, grey ware coated with white slip) ; these were not closely dated, but are likely to be Flavian. The upper part of a more elaborate bowl, in brownish-grey ware, was found with the "Mavins" kiln, near Farnham (*Farnham Survey*, p. 245, R.87) ; this kiln was in use during the first half of the 2nd century. The type may also owe something to the Gallo-Belgic pedestal beakers in terra rubra, such as Camulodunum, form 78.

Type 3. *Imitation of ʹform* 36. (*Haslemere*, 1905; *II*.4, *in red ware.*)

This form, in terra sigillata, was abundant in the Flavian period and in the 2nd century up to about A.D. 160. May (*Silchester Pottery*, p. 115 and Plate XLVIII, 57) illustrates a similar dish in brown ware, with a varnished, "bronzed" finish. The characteristic leaf ornament is absent from these imitations.

Type 4. *Imitation of form* 67. (*Charterhouse; V*.2, *in red ware.*)

This variety of form 67 is illustrated by Oswald and Pryce, *Terra Sigillata*, Plate XXI, 9, from Lezoux (?), or 12, from the first period at Newstead. Girth grooves near the greatest diameter of the vessel are a constant feature of these terra sigillata beakers, imitated on the copy by the wide, shallow groove. The form belongs exclusively to the Flavian period. The proportions of the imitation, 74 : 120 : 54, may be compared with those of an example in terra sigillata from Silchester, 82 : 115 : 51 (May, *Silchester Pottery*, p. 87 and Plate XXX, 2).

Type 5. *Imitation of form* 18. (*Charterhouse; III*.7, *in grey ware.*)

This dish has the low, curved sides and flat internal base characteristic of the Claudian period for form 18 in terra sigillata.

Type 6. *Imitation of ʹform Ritterling* 5. (*Haslemere*, 1905; *I*.4, *in grey ware.*)

Although Ritterling 5 is a comparatively rare form in Britain in terra sigillata, it was common at Colchester in Belgic terra rubra and native copies (*Camulodunum*, 56, 57). It is not surprising to find it copied at Haslemere, for the form was known at Silchester in both terra sigillata and Belgic wares (May, *Silchester Pottery*, p. 11 and Plate IV, 2 ; p. 174 and Plate LXXIII, 174 in terra nigra). The cup-shaped mouth and the high foot-stand are features strikingly copied in the Haslemere cup, while the burnished upper part may represent the rouletting on the original. The form belongs to the Tiberio-Claudian period and the copy has, therefore, been dated Claudian.

Type 7. Imitation of form Ritterling 9. (Haslemere, 1903; I.6, in red ware.)

This cup probably represents a crude copy of the smaller variety of Ritterling 9 in terra sigillata, a form known at both Silchester and London. A similar cup in even more crude technique, from Pitland Farm, Thursley, is in Guildford Museum. Three others were found at Yateley, Hants (photograph in *Berks. Arch. Journ.*, Vol. XXXII (1928), p. 73, group II, 3, 4, and possibly 5).

Type 8. Imitation of form Ritterling 9. (Haslemere, 1903; I.3. Haslemere, 1905; II.5, II.6. All in grey ware.)

These cups may be compared with examples from Silchester (May, *Silchester Pottery*, p. 174 and Plate LXXIII, 176, 177) ; May suggests imitation of the form Drag. 24/25, but he was evidently judging from photographs and actually they more closely resemble Ritterling 9. Four similar cups were found at Tilford (*Farnham Survey*, p. 260). Another, associated with 1st century pottery, is recorded from Richborough (*Richborough I*, p. 100 and Plate XXVI, 74). Ritterling 9 is a Claudian form, though it may have been made as late as the beginning of the Flavian period. The imitations should thus be Claudian or a little later.

IMITATIONS OF GALLO-BELGIC POTTERY.

Type 9. Grey pedestal bowl. (Haslemere, 1905; I.11.)

A degenerate copy of bowls of the type *Hofheim*, 127, dated A.D. 40–51. The Haslemere bowl may be compared with one from the ditch of the Roman enclosure at Ram's Hill, Uffington, Berks., of mid 1st century date (*Antiq. Journ.*, Vol. XX (1940), p. 478 and Fig. 7, 6). Two bowls from Silchester are closer to the Belgic prototype (May, *Silchester Pottery*, p. 171 and Plate LXXI, 166). A fine grey bowl in this series was imported to the coastal site of Angmering, Sussex, and found in the earliest, mid 1st century, ditch (report forthcoming). The Haslemere bowl might be of any 1st century date after about A.D. 50. Other bowls made in the same tradition have been recorded from Swarling, Richborough, Verulamium, Welwyn (Lockleys Estate), but belong to the eastern Belgic area of Britain and differ somewhat from the present examples.

Type 10. *Plate with moulded side.* (*Charterhouse; III.5 and III.*6.)

A copy in coarse ware of a common form of Belgic plate. The prototype is represented by Loescheke's type 72, from Haltern, and is derived ultimately from an Arretine plate form. The Charterhouse plates have two concentric grooves on the underside, which are all that remain of the footring on the original Belgic plates. Varieties of the type occur sparingly in the western Belgic area, for example, at Arundel, Sussex, at the "Shepherd's Garden" site (*Sussex Arch. Collns.*, Vol. LXXVII, p. 230, 3, 4, 5, 6), and at Silchester (May, *Silchester Pottery*, p. 176 and Plate LXXIV, 186), where a crude variety was also made at the kilns (May, *Silchester Pottery*, p. 194 and Plate LXXIX, 9) ; it was even found at Hengistbury Head with La Tène style decoration on the inside (*Hengistbury Head*, Plate XXVII, Class L, 39).

The type is, however, much more abundant in the eastern Belgic area and is common at Colchester (*Camulodunum*, Plate L) ; it occurs at Richborough (*Richborough I*, p. 93 and Plate XX, 9, 10) and at Verulamium (*Verulamium*, p. 175 and Fig. 23, 9) ; at all these sites it is of Claudian date. It occurs also in London, for example from London Wall (Wheeler, *London in Roman Times*, p. 143 and Fig. 53), and is likely to have reached Charterhouse by contacts from this direction up the River Wey. A similar, but smaller, example, from a site at Bourne, near Farnham, is also in the Charterhouse School Museum. A larger example was found at Leigh Hill, Cobham (above the River Mole) (*S.A.C.*, Vol. XXII, Fig. 35, figured upside down as a lid). A fragment was found with bead-rim pottery in a post hole at the Farnham Gravel Company's pit, Green Lane, near Farnham (*Farnham Survey*, p. 230, R.68 on Fig. 103). The Charterhouse plates are thus Claudian in date and the type is more common in the eastern Belgic area.

Type 11. *Tall jar with ovoid body.* (*Charterhouse; III.*3.)

This tall jar may be compared with *Hofheim*, 125B, which is of almost exactly the same size and proportions (Charterhouse 47 : 86 : 34, Hofheim 54 : 86 : 35). The type has been found also at Colchester, where it is common both before and after the conquest (*Camulodunum*, 232Aa), and at Richborough, in pit 14, dated Claudian (*Richborough I*, p. 92 and Plate XX, 4). The Charterhouse vessel must, therefore, be of Claudian date. A smaller example was found at Silchester (May, *Silchester Pottery*, p. 165 and Plate LXVIII, 143), but the type seems more common in the eastern Belgic area of Britain.

Type 12. *Globular beaker.* (*Haslemere, 1905; II.*11.)

This beaker, of a fine, buff-coloured ware, is clearly not of local manufacture. The form is of Belgic origin, and it forms a pre-Flavian local type at Colchester (*Hofheim*, 118 ; *Camulodunum*, p. 237 and Plate LVI, 108) ; it was found in Belgic terra nigra at Silchester (May, *Silchester Pottery*, p. 169 and Plate LXX, 156). In a thoroughly romanized form it is common on military sites,

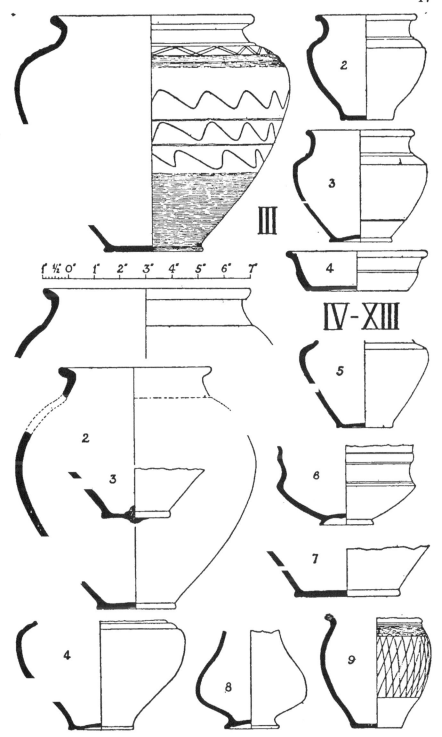

FIG. 4.—POTTERY FROM THE HASLEMERE CEMETERY, 1905.

such as Richborough and Newstead, in the Flavian period and later. But the only close parallel to the Haslemere beaker comes from London, from the Midland Bank site in Princes Street, which was dated by terra sigillata to the Flavian period ; this beaker, also, was in fine, light brown ware (*Antiq. Journ.*, Vol. IX, p. 227, 2). Another similar vessel was found at Woodmansterne, Surrey (*S.A.C.*, Vol. XLVIII, p. 153, Fig. 2).[1] The proportions of these vessels are of interest :

Haslemere	A.D. 80–90	67 : 104 : 45
London	Flavian	69 : 103 : 46
Silchester	1st century	61 : 100 : 37
Hofheim	A.D. 40–83	79 : 110 : 38
Camulodunum	Pre-Flavian	77 : 106 : 36
Woodmansterne	1st century	79 : 109 : 42

These proportions suggest that a Flavian date for the Haslemere beaker is correct, while the Woodmansterne example may be pre-Flavian.

Type 13. *Red plate with flat base and curved wall.* (*Haslemere, 1903 ; I.4, I.15.*)

The Belgic type is seen in *Camulodunum*, 17, where the cruder examples are post-Claudian. An example from Richborough, in red ware, was dated "second half of the 1st century" (*Richborough I* p. 100 and Plate XXVII, 87). Plates of this type have been found with burials at Shackleford (Guildford Museum) and at Yateley Hants (*Berks. Arch. Journ.*, Vol. XXXII, p. 72, Photo. II.6). The associations of the type are thus consistent with a date about A.D. 60.

Type 14. *Plate with curved side and raised base.* (*Haslemere, 1905 ; I.6, II.3, in greyish-brown ware.*)

A native rendering of a series of Belgic plates with moulded side and foot-ring (*Hofheim*, 98, 99), in which grooves represent the foot-ring and moulding of the original. Similar plates have been found in the Farnham district, one in a burial group at Farnham Fair Field, and a group of eight at Tilford (*Farnham Survey*, p. 228, R.52, and p. 260) ; both these finds were associated with pottery of Flavian date. An example was found at Silchester (May, *Silchester Pottery*, p. 177 and Plate LXXIV, 191).

FLAGONS.

Type 15. *Small flagon with cup-shaped mouth.* (*Haslemere, 1903; I.1.*)

The features of this flagon are the cup-shaped mouth with three rings externally ; the tapering neck, wider at the bottom ; the foot-ring ; the handle, shown by the stumps to have been of the high, early shape. It is of native coarse ware. Except for the widely bulged body (which may be due to inexperience in

---

[1] There are some sherds of hard, pink ware, from vessels of this type, decorated with "circles" similarly to the London and Woodmansterne beakers, in Richborough Museum (from pit 125, Flavian).

turning fiagon bodies) the form is similar to *Camulodunum*, 155A (A.D. 48–65). A burial group from Folkestone included a closely similar fiagon, associated with a terra sigillata cup of form 27, dated mid or late 1st century (*Swarling*, Plate V, Fig. 1). An example dated mid or late 1st century was found at Richborough.

Type 16. *Small square-lipped flagon.* (*Haslemere*, 1905; *I*.8.)

In this flagon the handle is fixed to the lower edge of the squarish lip. The external form is closely similar to *Camulodunum* 141B, a flagon of about the same size in brittle, brown-buff ware, and dated A.D. 43–65. The thick rim and unusual thickness of the body may be due to an attempt to copy the externals of a form unfamiliar to the potter.

Type 17. *Flagon with cordoned neck.* (*Charterhouse; IV*.3.)

The form of this flagon is very similar to that of the two-handled Gallo-Belgic jugs, such as *Camulodunum*, 161-163, which were imported to Britain during the early 1st century ; it is, however, in native, dark grey ware, and has only one handle. The Gallo-Belgic jugs did not long survive the Roman conquest, and this copy in native ware is not likely to be later than about A.D. 60.

Native Wares.

Type 18. *Bead-rim jar.* (*Haslemere*, 1903; *I*.5, *II*.1, *III*.1, *and possibly V*.1, *VI*.1, *VII*.1. *Haslemere*, 1905; *IV-XIII*.11, *IV-XIII*.17. *Charterhouse; I*.1, *II*.1, *IV*.1, *and possibly III*.2.)

The development of the bead-rim pot has been discussed by Hawkes ("Belgae of Gaul and Britain," in *Arch. Journ.*, Vol. LXXXVII). In Surrey it scarcely occurs before the Roman period, by which time it has developed into a distinctive, high-shouldered jar, common in London, recorded from more than a score of sites in Surrey, and distributed sporadically in the neighbouring counties. It has generally been given a date A.D. 50–100, most examples being found without more closely datable associations. It is certainly more abundant in the Claudian period than later ; at the Ashtead villa it was found mainly below the floors of the first building, erected about A.D. 70–80, and it has not been recorded in any deposit closely dated to the Flavian period. It has, however, been found in association with other coarse wares to which a Flavian date has been given, and it is likely that it survived, although being superseded, up to about A.D. 80.

At Haslemere, of the seven identified burial urns in the early cemetery, three were bead-rim jars and three probably were ; only two fragments of bead-rim jars came from the later cemetery. At Charterhouse, out of five urns, three were bead-rim jars and one was possibly of this type. All the six undoubted bead-rim jars were found in groups which have been dated within the period A.D. 50–80.

Type 19. *Jar with high, rounded shoulder.* (*Haslemere,* 1905; *I.*1, *II.*1, *III.*1, *IV-XIII.*4, *IV-XIII.*10, *IV-XIII.*16, *and probably IV-XIII.*18.)

This type supersedes the bead-rim jar as the standard, native jar-type of the Flavian period in Surrey. At Haslemere it is not found in the early cemetery, and the three whole examples occur in groups dated A.D. 70–100. It has been found on a number of sites in Surrey and occurs in graves in London, but seems to be rare elsewhere. The following examples have been found in Surrey :

Byfleet	... *S.A.C.,* Vol. XLVI, p. **134,** 4, **19.**
Cobham, Leigh Hill ...	... *S.A.C.,* Vol. XXII, Fig. **16.**
Cobham	... *S.A.C.,* Vol. XLII, p. **112,** 1.
Farnham Fair Field ...	... *S.A.C.,* "Farnham Survey," p. **228,** R.51.
Wotton	... *S.A.C.,* Vol. XXXVII, p. **222,** photo.
Frimley, Yorktown ...	... Guildford Museum.
St. Martha's, Tyting Farm	... Guildford Museum.

Type 20. *Jar with high, carinated shoulder.* (*Charterhouse;* *I.*2, *I.*3, *V.*1.)

This is similar to the preceding type, though usually rather smaller ; the shoulder is angular, instead of rounded, and lacks the distinctive decoration. It does not occur in the three Charterhouse groups that have been dated early, but must certainly be dated early Flavian in group V ; this makes it probable that, in group I, where it is associated only with a bead-rim urn, it is also of this date. The following examples have been found in Surrey :

Byfleet	... *S.A.C.,* Vol. XLVI, p. **134,** 11, **12.**
Cobham	... *S.A.C.,* Vol. XLII, p. **112,** 2.
Thorpe	... Unpublished.

These may be compared with examples from Silchester (May, *Silchester Pottery,* Plate LXXIX, 13) and Worthy Down (*Hants Field Club,* Vol. X (ii), Plate V, 75) ; they evidently represent earlier stages of the type, which is of Belgic origin.

Type 21. *Small jar with high, carinated shoulder.* (*Haslemere,* 1905; *I.*5, *I.*10, *II.*12, *III.*2, *III.*3, *IV-XIII.*5, *and possibly IV-XIII.*14.)

This may be regarded as a smaller size of the preceding type, 3-4 inches high. It is clearly a Flavian type at Haslemere. It appears to belong exclusively to the western part of Surrey ; an example from Wrecclesham was found with a cremation burial (*Farnham Survey,* p. **230** and Fig. 96, R.62), while others were found at Puttenham and in making the by-pass road at Compton (Guildford Museum).

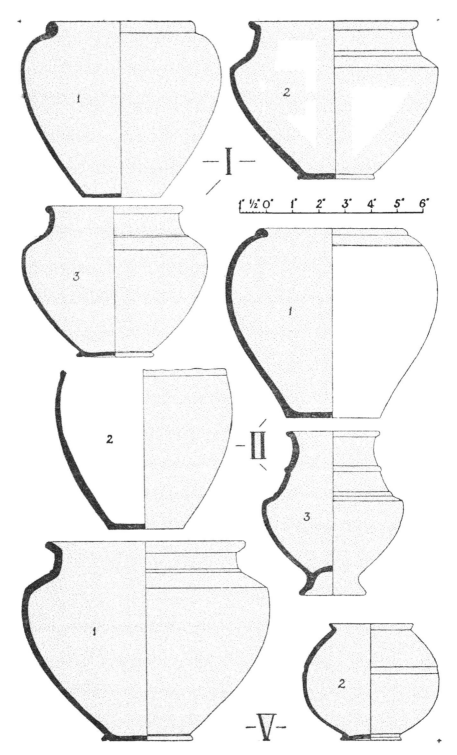

FIG. 5.—POTTERY FROM THE CHARTERHOUSE CEMETERY.

Type 22. *Bowl with shouldered side.* (*Haslemere*, 1903; *I*.2. *Haslemere*, 1905; *II*.2, *III*.4, *IV-XIII*.12, *IV-XIII*.13.)

This bowl, with its distinctive shouldered side and grooved rim, is common on 1st century sites in Surrey, and several examples have been found in London. At Ashtead villa it was dated Flavian or later, but at Haslemere is found in one group dated possibly as early as A.D. 60 ; it does not occur, however, at Charterhouse. A crude example was found at Silchester and a more normal example was excavated there in 1939 (May, *Silchester Pottery*, p. 184 and Plate LXXV, 12 ; *Arch*., Vol. XCII, p. 153, Fig. 11, 22.) Several of these bowls have been found in neighbouring counties, but usually in a cruder technique than the Surrey bowls ; one at Alfoldean, on Stane Street, just over the Surrey border, is of the Surrey type and was dated A.D. 70–120 (*Sussex Arch. Collns*., Vol. LV, p. 151, Fig. 20).

These bowls appear to be a local type, developed during the Claudian period in the western Belgic area, and in common use all over Surrey during the Flavian period. The footnote in *Arch*., Vol. XCII, p. 154, refers to them as a "typical Surrey type," and states that they were "much commoner during Period II" at Silchester (A.D. 65–120).

Type 23. *Developed carinated beaker.* (*Haslemere*, 1905; *I*.3, *II*.7 *and the very small example I*.9. *Charterhouse* ; *IV*.2.)

Although the carinated beaker is found throughout the Belgic areas, it did not long survive the Roman conquest ; in this developed form, however, with the rounded carination, it is a common 1st century type in west Surrey and the parts of Hampshire and Berkshire adjoining ; the form has also been found in London and at Ashtead villa. At Charterhouse it was associated with Claudian pottery, while at Haslemere it occurred in Flavian groups. The more angular examples such as the one from Ashtead villa, dated pre-Flavian, are likely to be earlier (*S.A.C.*, Vol. XXXVII (ii), p. 160, Fig. 3, 15 ; May, *Silchester Pottery*, p. 173 and Plate LXXII, 173) ; while the more rounded examples such as that from Hogwood Shaw, Finchampstead, and from a burial group at Yateley, Darby Green, Hants (*Berks. Arch. Journ*., Vol. XLI (1937), photo, p. 36 ; Vol. XXXII (1928), photo, p. 71) also others, unpublished, from "Over Compton," near Farnham, and Alice Holt, Hants, are likely to be of Flavian dates. Degenerate examples occur even later.

Type 24. *Degenerate carinated beaker.* (*Haslemere*, 1905 ; *IV-XIII*.8.)

The rounded carination of the previous type has degenerated, in this beaker, into a low, sagging bulge, while the neck is weakly formed ; the foot-ring characteristic of 1st century vessels is retained, but the beaker should probably be placed late in the series, perhaps as late as A.D. 120.

Type 25. *Devolved butt-beaker.* (*Haslemere*, 1905; *I*.7, *I*.12, *II*.10, *IV-XIII*.15.)

These beakers, all in brick-red ware, are late and highly devolved variations of the Belgic butt-beaker. On all these examples the bulge of the body bears two cordons on the upper part, and a groove on the lower part, while in *II*.10 the two zones into which the body is thus divided are decorated with a "roulette" pattern. The type is discussed under *Camulodunum*, 119. The Haslemere beakers are not earlier than A.D. 50 and are not out of place in these groups, dated A.D. 70–90. An example was found at Richborough in pit 34, dated A.D. 80–120 (*Richborough III*, p. 175 and Plate XXXVII, 271). A similar beaker in red ware was found at West Wickham (*Antiq. Journ.*, Vol. XIII, p. 306, Fig. 3).

Type 26. *Squat bowl.* (*Charterhouse; III*.4.)

An unusually squat variation of a common Belgic bowl. A rather similar vessel of about the same size, from Tong, Kent, was found in the same clay pit as pottery of about A.D. 50 and is probably about this date (*Antiq. Journ.*, Vol. VI, p. 310, Fig. 8.) The more normal form is shown by *Camulodunum*, 221.

Type 27. *Jar with tall, cordoned neck.* (*Charterhouse; II*.3.)

The high pedestal, carinated shoulder, and cordons are typical of Belgic pots of about A.D. 50, but no closely dated parallels are available for this form. Fragments of the necks of two similar jars have recently been found among the first century pottery from "Over Compton," near Farnham. Two unusual rim and base fragments from Colchester may be from a vessel of this form (*Camulodunum*, Plate LXXIV, sub 204). The pedestal type of base did not long survive the Roman conquest.

Type 28. *Globular beaker with studded body.* (*Haslemere*, 1905; *II*.8.)

This vessel is referred to by May, *Silchester Pottery*, p. 293, Table IV, among "fumed ollae, with Late Celtic concave profile, ribbed and ridged *en barbotine*." He there dates it "Late Celtic," or pre-Roman, and regards it as the prototype of his series. It may be compared with a Belgic example from Urmitz, but is much less globular in its proportions (63 : 86 : 41), besides being in coarse, native ware (*Camulodunum*, p.235, form 95, and Plate LVI, 95A). This weakening of the form, together with the rim, which is turned over to a much flatter angle than on similar Belgic vessels, suggests that it is, in fact, much later in the series. The form is commoner under Nero (*Camulodunum*, p. 235), so that the Haslemere pot need not be earlier than A.D. 70–80, which is about the date of the group in which it occurs.

Type 29. *High-shouldered jar.* (*Haslemere*, 1903; *IV*.1.)

The upper part of this jar is uncertain, but the complete jar was probably similar to one from the bottom of well I at Richborough,

24

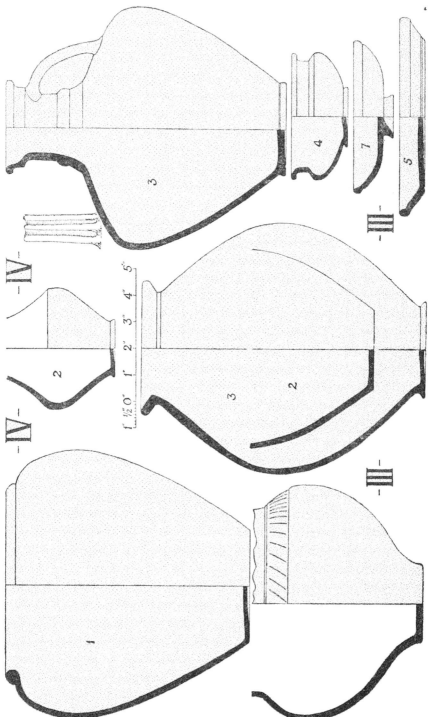

FIG. 6.—POTTERY FROM THE CHARTERHOUSE CEMETERY.

dated mid 1st century (*Richborough I*, p. 95 and Plate XXII, 26). Whether the rim belongs to the jar or not, the form of the body indicates a date about A.D. 50.

Type 30. *Jar with beaded rim.* (*Charterhouse; II.2.*)

This jar is comparable to one from Richborough dated A.D. 80–120 (*Richborough III*, p. 172 and Plate XXXV, 245).

Type 31. *Jar with wide, bulged body.* (*Charterhouse; III.1.*)

This jar may be compared with a smaller jar found in a 1st century deposit at Richborough (*Richborough III*, p. 172 and Plate XXXV, 249) ; such jars are stated to have been common in Flavian deposits at Richborough, but the present example is earlier, as it was found with other pottery of Claudian date.

Type 32. *Large jar with thumb-marked rim and internal finger-marks.* (*Haslemere*, 1903; *VIII.1.*)

Large jars of a rather similar appearance have been discussed in connection with the Roman ditches excavated at Ewell Council School (*S.A.C.*, Vol. XLVIII, pp. 51-3, and Fig. 6, 12) ; the Haslemere rim, however, is not quite of the same form as these 3rd century jars. The rim is that of a large store-jar of bead-rim form, while the thumb-mark decoration and internal finger-marks are a fairly natural result of finishing by hand the heavy rim of such a large jar. No other pottery has been found on, or anywhere near, the site which can be demonstrated to be later than A.D. 120 ; hence this rim is best regarded as that of a large, bead-rim store-jar of mid-1st-century date.

Type 33. *Jar with lattice decoration.* (*Haslemere*, 1905; *IV-XIII. 9.*)

This form is intermediate between the ovoid beakers of the Flavian period and the normal cooking pot of the first half of the 2nd century. It has not lost the incurving of the sides just above the base, but it has the trellis pattern normal on 2nd century pots. It may be compared with a slightly larger jar from Richborough, found in pit 34, dated A.D. 80–120 (*Richborough III*, p. 181 and Plate XL, 319).

Type 34. *Round-shouldered jar with tapering neck and everted rim.* (*Haslemere*, 1905; *IV-XIII.1, IV-XIII.2.*)

These jars may be compared with one found at Blackheath, Surrey, and now in Guildford Museum. The tapering neck and sloping rim are similar to those of the high-shouldered jars discussed under type 19 ; the body form, also, is rather similar, but the shoulder is lower and more rounded ; they are more roughly made and of thicker ware. No parallels can be traced outside West Surrey, and they may represent a late, local development of the type. In date, therefore, they are probably late 1st or early 2nd century.

THE BACKGROUND

The existence of a cemetery necessarily implies the existence of a community, and it remains to be shown to what extent the furnishings of their graves will throw light on the nature of these communities who inhabited West Surrey in the 1st century A.D. No community had inhabited either site before ; it is true that flints from the hunting and food-gathering ages have been found in the neighbourhood, but no earlier food-producing community had settled in this area. Moreover, none of the pottery in either cemetery can be shown to date earlier than A.D. 43. The sudden appearance of village communities here, at the time of the Roman conquest, must be part of the process, begun under the Belgic rulers but quickened under Roman influence, of penetrating the hitherto impenetrable forest and cultivating more and more land hitherto considered unfit for cultivation. The pottery from the cemeteries, together with an inspection of the map, shows that in the case of Haslemere the penetration was from the territory of the Atrebates of Hampshire, while in the case of Charterhouse it came by the River Wey from the Thames valley and the eastern Belgic area. Although the general direction of this expansion seems thus established, the detailed steps of the process have not yet been traced in the archæological record of either area.

The process is bound up with the growth of London, for Prof. C. F. C. Hawkes has shown, on the evidence of bead-rim and pedestal jars, that artisans were brought to the growing town from both Wessex and Kent[1] ; the evidence of other coarse-ware pottery types is in agreement with this. South of the Thames, Surrey had long been settled by Early Iron Age communities who had penetrated up the river valleys, chiefly those of the Mole and Wey ; this penetration was intensified by the growth of London and aided by the building of Stane Street, so that both the eastern (Charterhouse) and the western (Haslemere) pottery types fused together in the Flavian period to form several distinctive Surrey coarse-ware types, such as are found in the later part of the Haslemere cemetery.

No trace of any building has been found at either Charterhouse or Haslemere ; at Charterhouse, the most likely ground has never been searched and may well be now occupied by playing-fields and school buildings, while at Haslemere, the ground has been so thoroughly ploughed and afterwards built upon that nothing is likely to remain. In any case, the traces would be slight, consisting only of a few post-holes, some pits and perhaps some shallow ditches, for the buildings would have been of timber, and the sandy surface soil would be easily washed away, leaving little trace of any occupation. In Whimster's book, *The Archæology of Surrey*, there is a suggestion that a "villa" once existed at Haslemere, but this is an error resting on a misunderstanding. During the 1903

---

[1] "Belgae of Gaul and Britain," *Arch. Journ.*, Vol. LXXXVIII, p. 253 and p. 287.

excavations, a "pavement of flat stones" was found "three feet or more below the surface, arranged to resemble a huge shallow saucer about six feet across." This was interpreted at the time as the remains of a kiln, as it was "filled with a great quantity of fine sand and charcoal and small fragments of pottery," and it is so recorded in the Archæological Gazetteer of Whimster's book. The author has, however, misinterpreted the word "pavement" to mean "tesselated pavement" and concluded that a building formerly existed here ; in fact, no tesseræ were found. The excavators' interpretation of this "pavement" as a kiln is equally unacceptable when the description quoted above is compared with that of a typical Romano-British pottery kiln, such as those found in the Farnham district, or at Silchester. These kilns were commonly about three feet in diameter, and substantially constructed of clay, baked hard and blackened by the heat of firing. The flat stones could, however, have been the bottom of one of the storage pits common on Romano-British sites of the period, and into which rubbish and ashes had been thrown when it ceased to be used. If so, it represents the only clue as to the direction in which the farmstead or village lay, but the excavations were not carried far enough to the south to prove or disprove the existence of other such pits.

Close to the last burial group excavated in 1903 there was discovered a "large mass of burnt bones, charcoal and sand, resting on a layer of rough stones." This was interpreted by the excavators as probably the site of a funeral pyre.

An examination of the plan of the Haslemere cemetery shows that the burials are arranged in two groups, each of a long and narrow shape, with a third group indicated in another place. It is likely that cemeteries of the Romano-British period would occupy strips and patches of waste land, between the cultivated fields, and that the grouping of the Haslemere burials was determined by the existence of such patches. When the original burial patch was full, about A.D. 70, a new patch would be found for the next burials. All the area not occupied by burials, therefore, must represent the space taken up by the squarish Celtic fields belonging to these first inhabitants of Haslemere. The site is one of the few fairly level pieces of ground in the neighbourhood, besides being situated well above the damp and wooded valleys, and would have been well suited to Celtic agriculture. The promontory on which the Charterhouse burials were found is similarly a piece of fairly level ground well above the river, and might also have been the site of Celtic fields, though the pattern is not so convincing.

Thus the picture of these early Romano-British settlements is completed in outline, and if some of it is speculation, at least it is no more than the evidence will bear. It is part of the larger picture of the romanization of the countryside, together with the growth of London and an increase in the population of Surrey. By the first quarter of the 2nd century the picture has changed and

F

the old sites have ceased to be occupied ; from what causes this change proceeded can only be decided by building up a complementary picture of Surrey in the 2nd century A.D., but they are probably not unrelated to the growth of the villa system and the great increase in the size and prosperity of London soon after its recovery from the Boudiccan disaster. The common pots of the Haslemere and Charterhouse people can tell us no more.

ACKNOWLEDGMENTS

The pottery from both sites was drawn at the museums in 1943 and 1944. Permission to draw the Haslemere vessels was readily given by Mr. E. W. Swanton, curator of the Haslemere Educational Museum ; he gave much valuable assistance in identifying the pots and arranging them in their burial groups, and he put the resources of the museum freely at my disposal. For permission to draw the Charterhouse vessels, I am indebted to the President of the Charterhouse School Museum and to Mr. P. J. Mountney, the curator, who also freely gave his services in bringing out the pots and explaining the site where they had been found. In addition, much information about the Haslemere excavations has been taken from the published accounts, but this is sufficiently apparent to need no further acknowledgment.

ABBREVIATIONS used in the foregoing article :

Oswald and Pryce, Terra Sigillata	*An Introduction to the Study of* Terra Sigillata, by F. Oswald and T. D. Pryce ; Longmans, Green & Co., 1920.
Hofheim	*Das fruhromische* Lager *bei Hofheim im Taunus.* Annalen des Vereins f. nassauische Altertumskunde xl. Wiesbaden, 1913.
May, *Silchester Pottery*	The Pottery *found at Silchester*, by T. May ; Reading, 1916.
Camulodunum ...	Camulodunum, by C. F. C. Hawkes and M. R Hull ; Society of Antiquaries, 1947.
Richborough I (II) (III)	*Excavations of the Roman* Fort *at Richborough*, Kent, First (Second) (Third) Report, by J. P. Bushe-Fox ; Society of Antiquaries, 1926-32.
Verulamium	Verulamium, a Belgic and two Roman Cities, by R. E. M. and T. V. Wheeler; Society of Antiquaries, 1936.
Swarling	*Excavation of the Late Celtic Urnfield at Swarling*, Kent, by J. P. Bushe-Fox; Society of Antiquaries, 1925.
Hengistbury Head ...	*Excavations at Hengistbury Head, Hampshire*, in 1911-12, by J. P. Bushe-Fox ; Society of Antiquaries, 1915.
Farnham Survey ...	A Survey of the Prehistory of the Farnham District; Surrey Archæological Society, 1939.
Wheeler, London in Roman Times	London in Roman Times, by R. E. M. Wheeler ; London Museum Catalogue, No. 3, 1930.
Arch.	Archæologia.
Proc. Soc. Antiq. ...	Proceedings of the Society of Antiquaries of London. (New Series.)
Antiq. Journ.... ...	Antiquaries Journal.
Arch. Journ. ...	Archæological Journal.
S.A.C.	Surrey Archæological Collections.
Sussex Arch. Collns....	Sussex Archæological Collections.
Berks. Arch. Journ. ...	Berkshire Archæological Journal.
Hants Field Club ...	Hampshire Field Club and Archæological Society, Papers and Proceedings.

THE FOURTH-CENTURY ROMANO-BRITISH POTTERY KILNS AT OVERWEY, TILFORD

BY

ANTHONY J. CLARK

IN the Society's *Survey of the Prehistory of the Farnham District*, p. 224, appears a short note on a Romano-British pottery kiln found in a trial trench made in 1937 at Overwey, Tilford, and on pp. 247-9 there is a description of some of the pottery found in the trench. The site lay forgotten throughout the war, but it has since come into the hands of Major C. W. De Roemer, a member of the Society, who was anxious to revive interest in it. A trench was dug at the beginning of 1947 by Major A. G. Wade, producing a large quantity of pottery sherds and the remains of an oven, and as a result of these finds Major De Roemer invited the writer to organize a full-scale excavation of the whole site.

Work was begun by members of the Society in May, 1947, and continued during week-ends until May, 1948. About half-way through this period, the excavators were reinforced by parties of children from Sheephatch School, Tilford, who, under the able leadership of Mr. H. J. Grant, not only did the bulk of the heavy work on site B, but continued after the termination of the main excavation with the digging of trial trenches and the filling of trenches no longer required.

The writer is indebted to many people for kindness and generosity since the excavation began. Firstly we must thank Major and Mrs. De Roemer, who not only allowed us every facility for the work, but provided the diggers with refreshments on a great number of occasions. Special thanks are due to the volunteers, both members of the Society and others, who gave so freely of their spare time to work on the site and who are too numerous to mention individually. The writer gratefully acknowledges the help of Mr. Donovan Box, Mr. F. Clark and Mr. P. R. Stuart, who photographed the site ; of Mr. Lowther, Major Wade and Mr. Sheppard Frere, all of whom visited the site and gave much helpful advice ; and of the members of the staff of the Natural History Department of the British Museum who examined the charcoal and animal remains. Without the interest of Mr. R. V. Gould, Headmaster of Sheephatch School, and the unfailing energy of Mr. Grant and his boys and girls, the complete excavation of the site would have been impossible. Repairs to some of the pottery were very finely executed by Mr. David Baker.

The site of the kilns is in a rough field sloping down to the River Wey on the southern edge of the level plateau of Folkestone

sands, extending northward from the river to the range of greensand hills of which Crooksbury Hill forms the highest point
hereabouts. The plateau is sparsely populated and thickly wooded
to the present day, and must have been extremely remote in
Roman times. The site is situated in the grounds of the house
"Overwey," in Tilford parish, half a mile N.E. of the village, and
is to be found on O.S. 6-inch Sheet, Surrey XXX S.E., the National
Grid Reference being **880440**.

The three kilns excavated were found to occupy two distinct
sites, immediately at the top of the slope on either side of a broad
gully or hollow running down the side of the plateau in the direction of the river, 1,100 feet away. This hollow disappears half-way
across the field below, but an old inhabitant of the village stated
that sixty years ago, when this lower field was cultivated for hops,
the workers obtained water from a spring issuing from the bank
between the two fields at a point in the centre of the hollow[1]. This

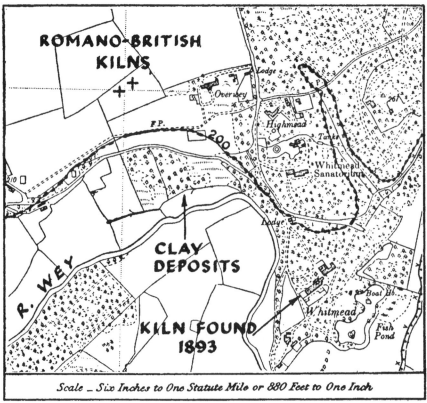

Scale — Six Inches to One Statute Mile or 880 Feet to One Inch

[*This map is reproduced from the Ordnance Survey Map, with the sanction of the Controller
of H.M. Stationery Office.*]

Fig. 1.—The Site of the Kilns.

---

[1] Information kindly supplied by Miss Maud, who lives in a house adjoining
the site, and was told about the former existence of the stream by her gardener,
a former labourer.

spring has now disappeared, but it is probable that the hollow
was formed by it and that in Roman times the water flowed from
higher up the slope, providing a reason for the grouping of the
kilns round the hollow. Trial trenches were cut across this hollow
in an attempt to discover whether there were remains of clay-
puddling floors beside the former course of this stream, but the
hollow was found to be filled with top soil for a depth of as much
as 2 feet 6 inches, below which the yellow sand subsoil was badly
discoloured, and no remains, apart from a few worn pottery sherds,
were to be found.

It thus seems that the site had the advantage of a convenient
water supply, and timber for firing the kilns would have been
abundant in the area ; but suitable deposits of clay, the essential
raw material of pottery making, appear at first sight to be absent.
The geological map shows that the nearest recognized deposits of
the local gault clay lie two and a half miles to the north, under the
southern slope of the Hog's Back. The gault also occurs at a
roughly equal distance to the west in the Frensham district,
but it seems most unlikely that clay would have been brought so
far, connection with the Frensham deposits being further hindered
by the intervening River Wey. It was therefore decided that
during the excavations search should be made for hitherto unsuspected deposits in the vicinity of the kilns, and the investigation

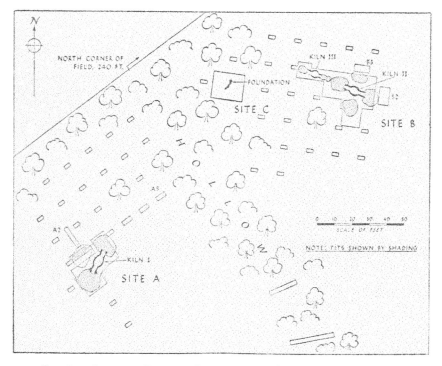

FIG. 2.—GENERAL PLAN OF SITE SHOWING LAYOUT OF TRENCHES.

was rewarded by the discovery, 300 yards away, of pockets of grey clay in the alluvium close to the river. It appears that these small deposits were found and used by the potters, possibly explaining the predominance among their products of grey wares, which modern potters find impossible to reproduce with the normal gault.

Site A.

This site was chosen as the field of operations for the first trenches for two main reasons : it appeared to be the point where the 1937 trench had encountered remains of a kiln, and the amount of burnt sand and wasters showing on the surface indicated that better results would be obtained here than elsewhere.

To begin with, a narrow trench was cut roughly along the contour of the hill, which by good fortune intercepted both pit I*a* and pit I*c*. It was assumed that a kiln would be attached to one or both of these pits, and accordingly trenches were put off at right angles from the approximate centre of pit I*c*. Trench A2 revealed nothing except the tip of the pit, but a trench opposite this encountered the masonry of the western furnace of kiln I, and the further excavation of the site was a fairly straightforward matter of clearing the kiln, pit I*b*, and as much as was practicable in the time of the remainder of pits I*a* and I*c*.

Kiln I.

When clearing was begun, it was expected that this kiln would assume the usual form of Romano-British pottery kilns—a circular firing chamber covered by the remains of a perforated clay floor on which the pottery was placed, and connected by a narrow furnace-tunnel with a single stoking-pit. The kiln seemed at first to be following this arrangement, for after the furnace found in the trial trench had been partly cleared, stoke-pit I*b* was found to be connected with it, and in the opposite direction the walls of the furnace broadened into what was apparently a firing chamber. Further excavation, however, revealed that at its N.E. end the chamber narrowed to form a projection connected with pit I*a* in an exactly similar manner to that in which the furnace was joined to pit I*b*. Both the openings were on the same level, rendering it unlikely that one of them acted as a chimney, and the only reasonable conclusion that could be drawn was that the kiln had two furnaces, connected with separate stoke-pits. Apart from this, the kiln was found to be completely lacking in any remains or indications of the normal perforated floor covering the firing chamber, and it was obvious that this kiln was the first recognized example of a type unique to the Farnham area of Britain. A discussion of the distribution, and probable method of working of these kilns, will be found on p. 42. The broad part of the kiln was later found to be almost certainly the oven, and will be called by that term throughout this report.

PLATE I

[*Photo : Donovan Box*

PLATE IA.—KILN I FROM THE S.W.

Pit I*b* in foreground ; pit I*c* on left showing section of black filling. The ranging pole stands in Pit I*a* and on the further side of this the stones blocking the small oven (3) can be seen.

[*Photo : Donovan Box*

PLATE IB.—KILN I FROM THE N.E.

Pit I*a* in foreground ; pit I*b* behind kiln ; the ranging pole stands in pit I*c*. Note the course of stones capping the S.E. kiln wall.

[*Facing p.* 32

PLATE II

[*Photo : Donovan Box*

PLATE IIA.—SITE B FROM THE W.
Kiln III in foreground ; kiln II at rear. Note the double stoke-pit (IIIa) on
the further side of kiln III.

[*Photo : Donovan Box*

PLATE IIB.—SITE B FROM THE E.
Kiln II in foreground ; kiln III at rear. The ranging pole stands in pit IIc, the
dense black filling of which is shown in section.

[*Facing p.* 33

The walls of both furnaces of the kiln consisted of large sandstone and ironstone blocks mortared with clay, and originally covered with a baked clay facing ; but where the walls opened out into the oven, they were formed of almost pure red puddled clay, baked to a blue or sometimes yellow colour on the surface. The use of masonry was probably confined to the furnaces because of the extra wear they suffered through the stoking of the fires. The floor, of strongly baked clay throughout, was laterally almost level, forming a sharp angle with the steeply sloping walls of the oven, but longitudinally was slightly hollow in the centre of the chamber and in the furnaces (see section A-A^1).

The walls and floor of the kiln had clearly been built against the sides and bottom of a carefully shaped trench in the natural sand subsoil, the top of the oven wall, with a mean height of 18 inches, being level with the subsoil surface. The kiln had been built in a slight dip in the ground, with the fortunate result that charcoal-impregnated sand, similar to that filling the pits, had accumulated over it to a minimum depth of 1 foot, and protected it from damage by subsequent ploughing. Thus it seems probable that the height of the walls had not been appreciably reduced since the kilns were in use, for the kiln showed no sign of having been violently destroyed at the end of its life.

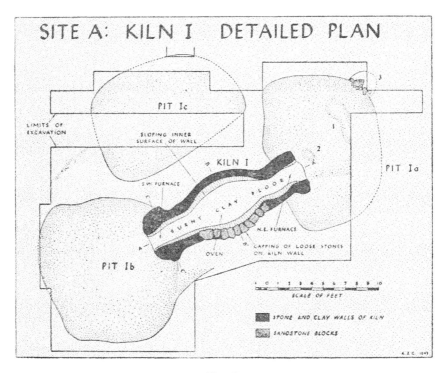

FIG. 3.

The kiln was filled with a mass of unbaked and partly baked red clay, especially solid in the S.W. furnace, mixed with small quantities of sand and many sherds of pottery, some of the vessels being almost complete. At the sides the filling was level with the top of the clay walls, but sagged an average of 8 inches toward the centre, and was separated from the burnt sand layer covering it by a layer of burnt sandstone and clay blocks fallen from the sides of the kiln. The division between the kiln filling and the burnt sand was found to be very clean and the red clay was packed solidly into the kiln up to the mouths of the furnaces, where it ended abruptly on a line with the ends of the walls—a feature not so marked in the N.E. furnace, which had apparently been disturbed and damaged by the excavators in 1937—and gave way immediately to the black pit fillings. The freedom of this kiln from disturbance was well demonstrated by a single course of large sandstone blocks capping the eastern wall of the oven. These were laid without any clay binding, but were neatly arranged and all declined *c.* 10° from the horizontal toward the centre of the kiln ; they projected well above the red kiln filling into the overlying burnt sand, and the stones found lying on the top of the filling probably represented a similar course along the western kiln wall. This feature will be noticed later in connection with the method of working the kilns.

The lack of a perforated clay floor covering the central oven has already been mentioned, and indeed the layout of the oven rendered it almost impossible for one to have been used : the maximum width between the two walls was 4 feet 4 inches ; there was no indication of a central support in the middle of the floor, and it therefore appears that such a floor if used in this kiln would have had an unsupported span of over four feet, and, unless exceptionally massive, would have collapsed under a normal load of pottery. The furnace walls were roughly vertical, and generally showed no sign of converging toward the top, or of being arched, although they remained to a height of as much as 2 feet 6 inches.

The kiln had obviously been in use for several years, as was evidenced by a number of repairs which had been carried out. Sections cut through the floor revealed hard blue layers, similar to the floor and wall surfaces, alternating with softer yellow and red clay layers, each blue layer representing the surface of a former floor. Three reconstructions were counted in the S.W. furnace, two in the N.W. furnace, and one in the oven, where wear had been apparently less than in the furnaces. The walls showed no sign of having been resurfaced in this manner, but very thick sherds, probably pieces of broken storage jars, were embedded in them in places, especially near the tops and at corners more than usually exposed to damage. Relative to the walls, the floor was thin, and the heat of the fire had caused the sand beneath it to be burnt to a dark red colour ; the oven walls, on the

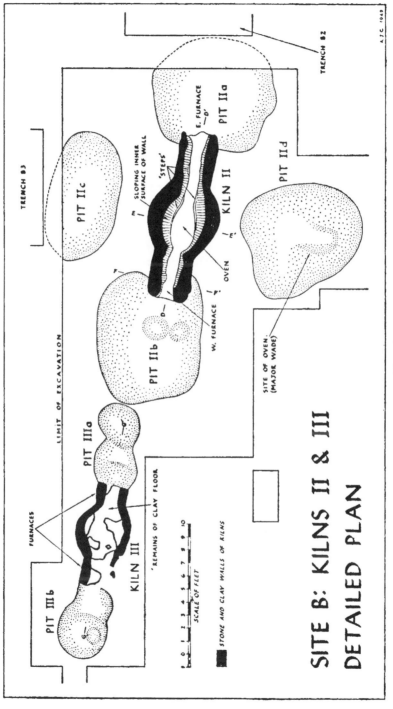

FIG. 4.

SITE B: KILNS II & III
DETAILED PLAN

other hand, being so much thicker, consisted, for the greater part of their thickness, of raw pink clay in a plastic condition, and were fired blue for a thickness of little more than 1 inch.

Particularly noticeable in the S.W. furnace was a spreading out of the top of the wall over the sloping sides of pit I*b* adjacent to the furnace, a device which must have been intended to prevent the loose sand from blocking the furnace mouth and interfering with stoking (see section C-C^1).

The Pits.

Three large pits, I*a*, I*b*, and I*c*, were found and excavated on this site, pits I*a* and I*b* being stoke-pits connected with the two furnaces of the kiln. All of the pits were filled with a remarkably homogeneous filling of sand burnt black and mixed with charcoal, most of which was in minute fragments, and pottery sherds from cast-away wasters. The outline of the pits was extremely easy to establish, as their black contents contrasted sharply with the yellow sand of the subsoil. Although careful search was made, no sign of any revetments of wood or other materials to retain the sides of the pits could be found, in spite of the fact that the sides were very steep, in pit I*c* sometimes vertical, and the sand into which they were cut was extremely fluid. Indeed, after excavation, the sides collapsed almost immediately, which strongly suggests that very little time could have elapsed between the kilns becoming disused and the filling of the pits with the blackened sand.

Pit I*a*, the N.E. stoke-pit, provided the most interest. The trial trench of 1937 had cut through its filling to encounter the furnace, as mentioned before, but this trench missed three almost complete vessels, two of them in a small depression (No. 2) dug into the pit floor. A bowl (No. 24 in pottery description), perfect except for a crack in the side, was found lying at the bottom of this depression in a large piece of the side of a jar (No. 55) which must have acted as a kind of saucer to retain liquid leaking from the bowl. A mass of sandstone blocks at the top of the northern side of the pit was found on removal to be blocking the loose filling of what appeared to be a small oven (3 in Plan) cut into the sand and containing two sherds of a rough type of pottery and a small amount of charcoal. These two small details probably represent domestic activities of the potters, and the bowl in the depression would almost certainly have been placed in position after the kiln had ceased to operate, for if a stoker had been working in the pit after it had been deposited it would not have escaped being crushed. Depression I, a small sharply cut hole, contained no objects of interest and was probably the work of the 1937 excavators. On the nothern side of this pit, where the ground is already beginning to slope down to the hollow, there had been little disturbance, and the Roman soil level was found 2 feet below the surface, beneath a scatter of 9 inches of the black **pit-**

37

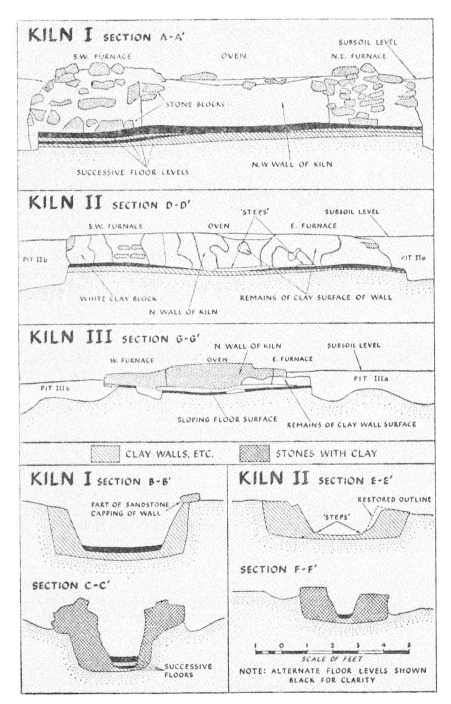

FIG. 5.—SECTIONS.

filling. The greatest depth of pit I*a* below the Roman level was 3 feet 3 inches ; below the present level, 5 feet 3 inches, a considerable depth which made the complete clearance of the pit impracticable in the time available, as was also the case with pit I*c*. A small barbed and tanged flint arrowhead, of Bronze Age type, was found on the subsoil surface close to the S.E. edge of the pit.

Pit I*b*, the S.W. stoke-pit, was entirely cleared, and presented no remarkable features. The sides sloped at about 45°, and access to the pit was apparently gained by a rather more gentle slope close to the S. side of the furnace. The filling was evenly black, except that a very slightly lighter layer, 1 foot thick, covered the pit bottom, and had a scatter of small sand-stones on its surface around the furnace mouth : this seems to have constituted the level of accumulated filling when the kiln was abandoned, and before the pit was filled up with the normal black sand. A section of this pit close to its S.W. side revealed furrow-marks in the form of regularly spaced V-shaped pockets of yellow sand dragged into the black filling from outside the pit by the ploughshare. The tips of two of these furrows were at the abnormal depth of 1 foot 3 inches, and it is obvious that a considerable accumulation of top soil must have taken place since they were made : it is just possible that these are the marks of the plough used by the Romano-British inhabitants after pottery production had ceased and the site had been levelled, a hypothesis which will be considered below.

Pit I*c*, although two-thirds cleared, was found to have no connection with kiln I, although it approached as close as 2 feet 6 inches to the oven, nor did it appear to act as a stoke-pit for any other kiln. The filling was of the normal burnt sand with the usual proportion of sherds, the only notable feature being a considerable quantity of baked clay lumps close to the floor in the western corner. The sides of this pit were unusually steep and actually overhung on the S.W. side, the greatest depth being 5 feet 3 inches from the present surface. The only reasonable explanation of this isolated pit, and another in an exactly similar situation on site B, is that it would probably have been used to supply sand for covering the pottery after it had been loaded into the oven of the kiln.

SITE B.

This site was 140 feet from site A, in an exactly similar position at the top of the slope, but on the opposite side of the hollow. A considerable amount of burnt sand and wasters was noticeable in rabbit-burrows, especially in the neighbourhood of a slight hump in the ground close to where a trial hole dug by Major Wade in January, 1947, had unearthed the remains of a small oven.

Trenches soon encountered the pits associated with kiln II, and the actual kiln was found to lie beneath the slight hump already mentioned. It became obvious as the work proceeded that the scale of this site was altogether smaller than Site A, and that since the kiln had not been built in a slight hollow, the height of its walls had been badly reduced by ploughing.

Kiln II.

This kiln, although closely similar in design, was smaller than kiln I, the total length being 13 feet, as opposed to 15 feet 2 inches and the length and maximum breadth of the oven 4 feet × 3 feet, as opposed to 6 feet 9 inches × 4 feet 4 inches in kiln I ; the walls of the oven were, however, more massive, and had a thickness of as much as 18 inches in places (see section E-E^1).

When the top soil, about 9 inches in depth, had been removed from the kiln, the whole of the filling and the tops of the walls were found to have been flattened and scored with parallel grooves by ploughing, and it was clear that only the lower part of this kiln would be preserved intact. Clearing was easy, the filling consisting mainly of a soft, grey-black burnt sand, similar to that contained in the pits, but not so dark. Pink, unbaked clay was present in this filling, but in isolated lumps only. As in kiln I, the furnace walls had been reinforced with stone, while the oven walls were largely of clay. The floor, which dipped markedly in the centre of the oven, was in good condition, but the burnt blue clay surface of the walls had weathered badly, exposing the soft, unfired interior in large patches. The W. furnace was well preserved, and the clay roughly plastered over the stones at the ends of the walls was deeply marked all over with finger-prints, which unfortunately crumbled away as the kiln dried out. The N. wall was terminated with a large smooth, soft block, apparently formed of some kind of clay, a curious substance also used sparingly in the furnaces of kiln I. The E. furnace had suffered in the same way as the N.E. furnace of kiln I, and the ends of the walls, especially on the N. side, were badly battered and reduced in height.

An interesting detail was the appearance of slight "steps" at the junction of the walls with the floor at the E. end of the oven (see plan and section E-E^1). These may have had some use in supporting the pottery load, although that on the N. side was seen to reappear in the E. furnace, where such an explanation could hardly apply. It was also noticed that at the point of junction of the oven with the W. furnace, both walls projected sharply inward to form a narrow opening that did not appear to be repeated at the opposite end of the oven, although it is doubtful whether this had any significance.

In common with kiln I, the oven walls sloped steeply, while the furnace walls seemed to have originally been more or less vertical, and once again showed no sign of having been arched over. The floor, 2 inches thick, had not been remade in the oven but had been resurfaced once in each of the furnaces, which explains the relatively low level of the floor in the oven itself. Large sherds of pottery had been used to strengthen the walls in places, and their fabric contained several neatly squared baked clay slabs, 1½ inches thick, and resembling bricks. These, before being incorporated in the walls, would probably have been intended as supports for the pottery load, for no other signs of a brick industry were found on the site.

The Pits.

These were smaller in size and shallower than the pits on site **A**. They were, however, equally featureless, showing no signs of any attempt at lining or revetment of the sides, and contained an exactly similar black filling of burnt sand and sherds, presenting a perfectly even appearance from top to bottom of the pits, with no signs of stratification. On this site, as mentioned before, the plough had shorn away the upper levels, and the fillings of the pits were not joined by an overall black layer as in site A.

Pit II*a* constituted the E. stoke-pit of kiln II, and was completely cleared except at its eastern end. It had a maximum depth below the surface of 2 feet 6 inches with sides sloping at about 45°, and a broad, flat floor. No continuation of the pit was found in trench B2.

Pit II*b* was the counterpart of pit II*a* for the W. furnace; the whole filling was removed, and the pit found to have a depth of 2 feet 6 inches. Two shallow depressions cut in its floor in front of the furnace were probably connected with some stoking operation. The clearing of this pit led to the discovery of pit III*a*, the E. stoke-pit of kiln III.

Pit II*c*, 3 feet deep, had no connection with any kiln, and with its relatively steep sides and its position close alongside kiln II corresponded exactly with pit I*c* on site A. It will be remembered that pit I*c* was thought to be a quarry to provide material to cover the pottery loads, and there is nothing to suggest any other role for pit II*c*. Trench B3, cut with the object of finding something to explain the presence of this pit, drew a complete blank.

Pit II*d*, although it occupied a position corresponding to that of pit II*c* on the other side of the kiln, filled a more definite function, for in it Major Wade found an oven when cutting his trial hole prior to the main excavation, and he has very kindly supplied the writer with notes on its structure. It consisted of large ironstone slabs, each about 1 foot square and 2 inches thick, packed together upright and at right angles to the sides of the excavated hole in which they stood; a length of about 2 feet of this walling remained, and no clay whatever had been used in its construction. The depression in which this oven had obviously stood was in the bottom of pit II*d* and is shown in the site plan, and its position, together with its wide divergence from the usual kiln plan, tempts one to suggest that it was used as a domestic oven. Major Wade, however, states that this could hardly have been so, owing to the fact that the surrounding sand had been baked hard for a thickness of as much as 1 foot from the outside of the oven wall, which indicates that a very fierce heat must have been used, fiercer, indeed, than seems to have been used in the normal kilns. It would appear, therefore, that we have here some special kind of small kiln for the firing or drying of pottery. The maximum depth of pit II*d* was 2 feet 9 inches.

Kiln III.

This was the smallest of the three normal kilns and certainly the most fragmentary, and the pottery found associated with it suggests that it was used exclusively for the production of the finer types of wares made at Overwey. Although similar to kilns I and II in general layout, this kiln differed from them in several respects, and it is advisable to consider the kiln and its stoke-pits as a whole.

The walls, which nowhere remained to a height greater than 1 foot, consisted throughout of small sandstone slabs laid horizontally and bound together with only a minimum of clay. The slabs had originally been faced with a thin layer of burnt blue clay internally, as was evidenced by a few remaining patches. The floor was nowhere more than 1 inch thick and was broken away in large patches, revealing the underlying sand subsoil, which had been burnt red to a depth of 2 inches below the floor. The W. end of the S. wall had been completely destroyed, but as this kiln was standing entirely above the subsoil level it was very fortunate that so much of it survived. The floor sagged slightly between the two furnaces in common with the floors of the other kilns, and it was also observed to dip as much as 3 inches between the sides of the oven, which was exceptionally large in proportion to the size of the furnaces.

The stoke-pits were also unusual. Instead of the normal large, round excavations, they consisted of two holes, 2 feet 6 inches deep, with diameters nowhere greater than 4 feet, joined to the furnace mouths by similar but considerably shallower extensions. That this arrangement was intentional is proved by the remarkable similarity of the two stoke-pits, although the meaning of it is a debatable point. All that can be definitely said is that while the stoker must have worked in the stoke-pits themselves when firing the other two kilns, he must have stood outside the pits to operate this kiln.

The slight construction and lack of restorations to the floor indicate that this kiln was abandoned early. Its approximate alignment with kiln II and the remarkably close gap between pits II*b* and III*a* strongly suggests that both kilns were in operation at the same time. Careful probing of the surrounding ground revealed no signs of pits similar to II*c* adjacent to kiln III.

TRIAL TRENCHES.

Two groups of trial trenches, each 2 ft. ×4 ft., laid out on a grid of 15 feet squares, were based on sites A and B, with the object of picking up any further remains of kilns or of dwellings, working floors, etc. Special attention was paid to the hollow in whose protection it was considered that the potters would have built their huts, but, apart from a considerable accumulation of burnt sand from the kilns, nothing was found except at site C. Here a trench cut across what appeared to be a foundation consisting of large sandstone slabs associated with several pieces of pottery, including a fragment of Samian ware. Sheephatch School removed a large area of the top soil here, but the results were disappointing. The stones were laid directly upon the subsoil, and no other remains accompanied them. The presence of the Samian ware, however, suggests that they represented vestiges of a small-scale earlier settlement of the site, probably between A.D. 50 and 138, which has been attested by certain pieces of pottery found with the kilns (see pottery report). A coin of Gratian, in good condition, was found in the soil taken from trench A5, and appeared to have been lying on, or slightly below, the Roman surface level at a depth of c. 18 inches. The two trenches put across the lower part of the hollow have already been described.

DESTRUCTION OF THE SITE.

Several pieces of evidence seem to permit us to think that the kilns, after a long period of use, were peacefully dismantled and the pits levelled by the potters or other Romano-British people who had succeeded them, presumably in order that the site could be turned over to agriculture. The absence of stratification in the pit fillings and the steepness of the pit sides renders it almost certain that they were filled quickly and immediately they had ceased to be used, for a certain amount of silting would have taken place if the process had lasted even so short a time as a week. Furthermore, we have the neatness with which kiln I was dismantled and its clay filling packed inside it ; and the deep plough-marks across the top of the filling of pit I*b*. The blackened sand would have been lying in great heaps in the vicinity of the kilns, and apart from providing the obvious material for levelling the site, would have produced one of the richest soils imaginable. A possible reason for such a change in use of the site is discussed in the conclusion.

OPERATION AND DISTRIBUTION OF THE KILNS.

The method of operating the kilns is the most important question which has arisen out of the excavation, but the clues available do not allow us to come to anything but provisional conclusions which may well have to be revised when other kilns of this type have been scientifically excavated.

In none of the kilns was there found the slightest remnant of the usual perforated clay floor which, in normal kilns, was placed over the firing chamber, providing a base for the oven containing the pottery, the heat being introduced through the perforations or vents in the floor. This oven usually consisted of a dome of alternate layers of clay and straw, probably supported on a framework of boughs, and covered on the outside with earth or sods to retain the heat ; the whole thing would have been built up round the pottery load and destroyed after each firing. The Overwey kilns, although they lacked this floor, were provided with an unusually level clay floor to what is normally the bottom of the firing chamber, and it seems that the pottery was actually placed on this floor or perhaps raised a few inches on bricks such as were found in kiln II, in order to allow the heat to circulate beneath them. This suggestion is supported by the finding in kiln I of a complete jar standing upright on the floor, while many others were scattered about over the floor surface. Such an arrangement would also explain the need for furnaces at opposite ends of the oven, for if only one were used, as in the normal type of kiln, the heat would have by-passed pottery close to the floor at the rear of the oven, causing very uneven firing of the load. With two furnaces, however, such "blind" spots would have been effectively overcome and the potters would have stood some chance of achieving the beautifully even firing which is typical of Overwey wares. The oven would, of course, still have to be domed over and irregular slabs of burnt clay, covered with straw-impressions, were found here as at more normal sites, indicating that this was actually done.

Sand seems to have been used exclusively for covering the dome, as is suggested by the masses of burnt sand filling all the pits. The sand excavated from the stoke-pits would have been used at first, and when this was exhausted, special quarries like pits Ic and IIc would have been excavated. The furnaces showed no sign of permanent roofs, and it is probable that these too would have been specially built for each firing, so that they could be removed to allow easy access to the load when firing was completed. With two furnaces, a wind blowing consistently in one direction would have caused trouble and the kilns, or at least kiln I, were sunk deeply in the ground to avoid this, the necessary draught probably being provided by a chimney in the top of the dome. The course of loosely laid stones capping the S.E. wall of kiln I appeared to represent the remains of a footing for the sides of the dome.

Four large iron nails, apparently of a square-headed type, were found in the pit-fillings on both sites A and B, showing that the workers made use of reasonably well-constructed wooden articles, possibly small carts or frameworks for potters' wheels.

The distribution of this type of kiln is almost certainly limited to the Farnham area. A good many kilns have been found in this

G

district, but it is unfortunate that few of them have been excavated sufficiently thoroughly for an accurate idea of their form to be gained. A kiln excavated at Snailslynch by Major Wade, and described and illustrated by him in *Ant. Journ.*, VIII, January, 1928, was closely similar to the Overwey type, with the remains of its last load standing on the floor exactly as has been surmised for the Overwey kilns, but in Major Wade's opinion the opening opposite the first furnace constituted a flue leading to a chimney. In the light of the Overwey evidence, however, I am inclined to the belief that this flue was more likely a second furnace and that in the Snailslynch kiln we have a counterpart of those at Overwey. It is noteworthy that the pottery produced at Snailslynch is more closely similar to Overwey wares than that of any other Farnham kiln.

Mr. W. F. Grimes, in his extremely valuable classification of Romano-British pottery kilns,[1] bases his Type VII, the horizontal-draught kiln, entirely upon the evidence of the Snailslynch kiln, but it now seems that the characteristics of this type should be modified to accord with the Overwey findings.

Less than half a mile from the Overwey site, a Roman kiln was found at "Whitmead" in 1893, and was described as being "floored with Roman tiles."[2] It was destroyed, and in the absence of any detailed description of the kiln or of the pottery, it is impossible to say whether it represents an expansion of the Overwey industry, although its proximity renders this very likely.

THE POTTERY.

In describing the pottery, care has been taken to include a representative selection of both the normal products of the kilns, and the rare forms, of which in many cases only one or two examples were found.

The most common Overwey product was the hard, light grey ware *cooking jar* with horizontally striated outer surface, a typical 4th-century type whose prevalence allows us to date the kilns with confidence to that century. It was found in greatest numbers in kiln I, which seems to have been almost entirely devoted to it, especially towards the end of its existence. It was found in quantity in association with kiln II, although the last load contained mainly "fine" wares ; kiln III, however, contained only a few sherds, for this small kiln seems to have been used almost exclusively for the manufacture of "fine" pottery.

Other forms include all the remaining types except the large storage jars, and consisted mainly of jars and bowls in "fine" ware —smooth grey paste with a coating of slip on the rim and shoulder. Many of the most carefully made vessels, especially from kiln II, were "fumed," giving the surface of the pot a black colour, and the slip coating a very shiny black finish. Apart from these, and

---

[1] Grimes, *Y Cymmrodor*, XLI (1929).
[2] *S.A.C.*, XIII (1895), p. 151 ; and *Preh. Farnh.* (1939), p. 224.

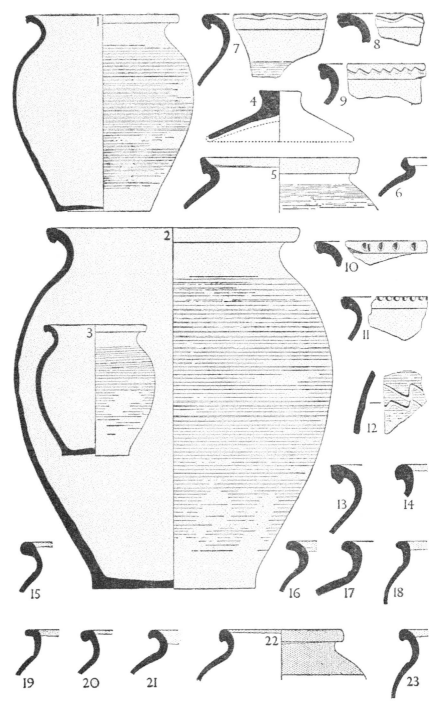

Fig. 6.—Coarse Striated Cooking Jars and Miscellaneous Jars.

underfired examples which ranged in colour from pink to buff, the ware was invariably grey and the slip used of a white or creamy colour.

The majority of the big *storage jars* were made of a buff paste, a colour which seems to have been intentional, and is probably due to the use of a different mixture of clay in their production. An analysis of the relative frequency over the whole site of striated cooking jars, miscellaneous wares, and storage jars, gave the approximate result 6 : 3 : 1 respectively.

Good 4th-century *red colour coated ware* was rare at the site, hardly more than half a dozen pieces being found, and was probably imported from elsewhere. A single sherd of real Samian found in trench C was probably a relic of the scant early occupation of the area.

Jars and Bowls.

1-3. Three examples of the hard, sandy, light grey ware cooking jars. The rim is always undercut, and the body covered with horizontal striations executed with a comb, apparently to enable the vessels to be picked up easily with wet hands. The type is common throughout the south in the 4th century, especially its latter half. *Cf. Lockleys,*[1] Welwyn, Fig. 12, 1, dated *c.* A.D. 340 ; *Park Street,*[2] near St. Albans, Fig. 20, 8, in a group containing other vessels strikingly similar to Overwey types, dated second half of 4th century. The three vessels figured were found in the lower part of the filling of the oven of Kiln I.

5-13. Variants of the same type, including most of the decorated pieces present among the great amount of this ware which was absolutely plain. Except in the case of 12, the decoration was confined to the rim, and consisted of a roughly executed wavy line or row of notches. Slip was never used on this class of ware.

1. An example of the normal size ; almost complete.
2. Largest example found ; reconstructed diagrammatically from fragments.
3. One of the smallest of this type.
4. Lid, from which the underside and outer edge have flaked away ; underfired. Only two lid fragments were found.
5, 6. Two of the few examples with lid groove. Diam. of 6, 4·8 in.
7. Large jar with shallow wavy line on edge of rim ; diam. 9·6 in.
8. Another large example, with wavy groove on outside of widely splayed rim; diam. *c.* 11 in.
9. Similar to 8, but with a zig-zag groove ; diam. 7·8 in.
10. Widely splayed rim similar to 8, but decorated with impressions possibly made with the flat end of a stick ; diam. 8·4 in.
11. Decorated in a similar manner to 10. The impressions are shallower, and made along the top edge of the rim; diam. 7·6 in.
12. The only example of this type found with decoration on the body : two very shallow wavy lines superimposed upon the normal horizontal combing.
13. Variant of the normal undecorated type, with lower edge of rim bevelled ; diam. 9·7 in.

14-26 are miscellaneous jars and bowls which do not appear to fall into the category of main products of the kilns. None was found in abundance, and some are represented by only one example. The rims and shoulders of all examples, except 17, which is not contemporary with the kilns, were coated or intended to be coated with slip.

[1] The Roman Villa at Lockleys, Welwyn, *Ant. Journ*, XVIII (Oct. 1938).
[2] The Roman Villa at Park Street, near St. Alban's, Hertfordshire, *Arch. Journ.*, CII (1945).

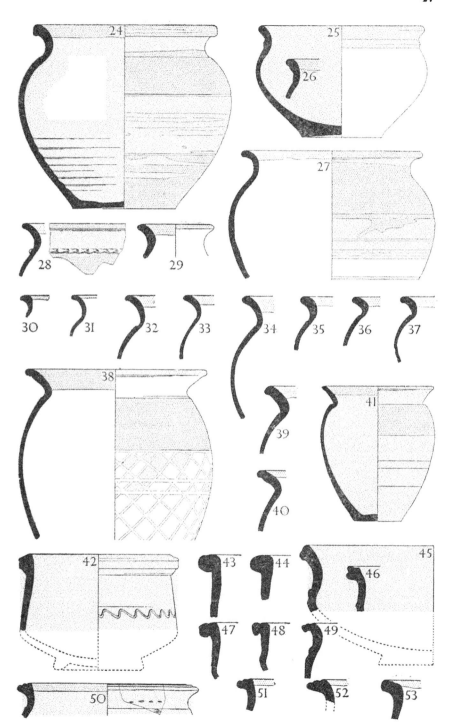

FIG. 7.—JARS AND BOWLS.

14. Light grey ware with white slip ; diam. 6·4 in.

15. Rather soft light grey ware with white slip ; slight cordon at base of neck ; diam. 7·6 in. *Cf. Lockleys*, Fig. 15, 5, dated mid 4th century.

16. Very hard dark brown ware with grey core. An overfired example on which the slip has been burnt to a green-grey colour. Diam. 7·2 in.

17. Large, globular jar in coarse light grey ware, diam. 5·4 in. Exactly similar to a jar from Ewell Council School (Frere, *S.A.C.*, XLVIII, Fig. 5, 9) dated to the Hadrianic period. An early intrusion in this case.

18. Smooth, light grey-buff ware with fumed surface and slip. The lower edge of the slip band on the shoulder is marked by a groove, a very common feature at Overwey ; diam. 6·4 in.

19. Similar to 18, and possibly made at the same time, both being from kiln II ; diam. 6·2 in.

20. Rather soft, gritty buff ware with grey core ; white slip fumed black in places ; diam. 6·6 in. Variants of this type—*e.g.*, 23 and 24—are fairly common, especially in pit 1*a*.

21. Smooth light grey ware with white slip ; diam. 4 in.

22. Smooth dark grey ware with white slip ; a fairly common type.

23. Dark grey ware with light grey slip ; diam. 7·2 in.

24 Bowl in smooth, soft dark brown ware, with fumed surface, and bands of shiny black slip on rim and shoulder, and extending upward from the base The rough band round the middle of the body, separated from the upper slip band by a groove, and from the lower by a deeply burnished line, has three irregular burnished lines round its centre. The slip bands also appear to have been burnished after firing. This vessel, a slightly cracked waster, was found almost complete, lying in a piece of the side of a large jar (No. 55), inside a small depression at the bottom of pit 1*a*. (see p. 33).

25. A most exceptional bowl in rather coarse and very flaky orange-pink ware, badly overfired, also from the bottom of pit 1*a*. Probably intended to be decorated with slip, but thrown out after the first firing.

26. Soft orange-buff ware with cream slip ; diam. 7 in. The only sherd found of a type similar to 25.

27-41. Recurved and sharply everted rims, together with intermediate forms which are difficult to assign definitely to either type. Although the arrangement here suggests an evolutionary sequence, it seems certain that all these forms were in production at the same time. These rims were found always to be coated with slip on the rim and shoulder, the lower edge of the band on the shoulder generally being marked by a shallow horizontal groove. The paste was smooth and grey in most cases, although a buff ware was sometimes used for the recurved-rim type. It is interesting to note that in no case did the everted rims have a diameter greater than that of the body of the pot, as is the usual tendency of this type in the 4th century.

27. Recurved-rim jar, of which large numbers were found ; white slip roughly applied to rim and shoulder, and narrow burnished lines on lower part of body.

28. The same type, but with cordon at base of neck, decorated with rouletted notches ; diam. 6·6 in. The only example found with this form of decoration.

35. One of a few examples with surface and slip fumed black, the slip being very shiny, and perhaps burnished after firing; diam. 6·2 in.

37. An example with the exceptional feature of two girth grooves below the shoulder, the upper one being very deep ; diam. 5·6 in.

38. Large jar in hard, light grey ware, with white slip on rim and shoulder , right-angled burnished trellis design on lower part of body, with two horizontal lines running through it. Only two jars bearing this decoration were found, both in kiln II *Cf. Lockleys*, Fig. 10, 23, dated A.D. 300-340. The wide angle of the trellis is characteristic of the 4th century.

40. An example lacking the usual offset between the shoulder and rim ; diam. 6·2 in.

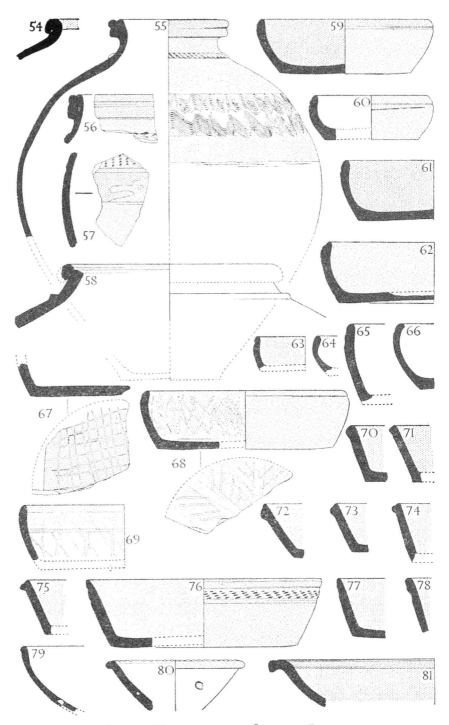

FIG. 8.—NARROW-NECKED JARS AND DISHES.

41. A small and almost complete everted-rim jar in light grey ware, with disintegrated white slip on rim and shoulder. This vessel was over-fired on one side, with the result that it has become distorted, and the slip burnt black on that side.

42-53. Vertical-sided bowls with knobbed, undercut and reeded rims. All these types were rare at Overwey, and one at least (46) was probably made elsewhere. Excepting the distinctive types 43, 44 and 50-53, the ware was generally grey-buff and coarse and sandy in texture.

42. Crudely moulded rim, and inscribed zig-zag on side. Probably a rude imitation of Samian form Ludowici Sh.

43. Rather smooth and soft buff-grey ware with signs of burnishing on rim ; diam. c. 11 in.

44. Smooth, soft orange-pink ware ; diam. c. 11 in.

45. Sandy, buff-grey ware, probably based on a vessel similar to 46.

46. Soft white paste with red slip; diam. 8·8 in. An importation, possibly from the New Forest, which would have been used as a pattern for vessels such as 45. A bowl almost identical in ware and form is figured in *Richborough* 2,[1] Fig. XXXI, 162. A common 4th-century type also found at Silchester and Chatley Farm.

47. Coarse buff-grey ware with two slight offsets on side ; diam. 11·4 in.

48. Sandy bright pink ware ; diam. 9·6 in.

49. Coarse cream-grey ware with reeded rim ; diam. 7·4 in. *Cf. Richborough* 1, Pl. XXIX, 130, for a similar vessel, but without reeded rim, dated mid 4th century.

50. Small sherd of reeded-rim bowl in smooth, dark grey ware with white slip on rim. Decorated with a rough line of small incisions on neck, and similar incisions in groups of three on cordon at base of neck.

51. Similar to 50, but without incisions ; diam. 8 in.

52. Smooth, light grey ware, white slip ; diam. c. 12 in.

53. Smooth paste, cream slip on rim and shoulder ; diam. c. 9 in. *Cf.* Chatley Farm, Cobham, *S.A.C.* L, Fig. 7, 28, found in a 4th-century context.

Large, narrow-necked Jars.

54. Plain, rolled-over rim with white slip ; diam. 5 in.

55. Light grey ware with cordon at base of neck decorated with rouletted notches, and a double band of combed waves on shoulder ; white slip on rim and on body above and below the decoration. Reconstructed from pieces of two examples : rim and neck from kiln III, body found with 24 at bottom of pit Ia. An attractive and very distinctive Farnham type made in small numbers at Overwey, and also found at Alice Holt Forest, "Six Bells" pit, and Kingsley, Hants (*Preh. Farnh.*,[2] R115, R130). Sherds of this kind were found in the 4th-century bath-house at Chatley Farm, Cobham, which ceased to be used c. A.D. 360 (*S.A.C.*, L, Fig. 7, 31).

56. Similar to 55, but with V-shaped impressions on cordon ; diam. 6 in.

57. Piece of body of the same type, but with decoration on shoulder consisting of vertical lines of impressed dots.

58. Light grey ware ; lid groove and upstanding cordon on shoulder. An exceptional type to which the writer can find no parallel, and perhaps dating back to the earlier settlement of the site. From kiln III.

Dishes and Flanged Bowls.

59-66. Dishes with curved sides, generally with a single groove dividing the rim from the body. These were very common in kilns I and II, and are of a late type, frequently found with 4th-century pottery. At Overwey they are either made of a coarse, sandy ware without slip, or of smooth, usually light grey ware, carefully burnished all over and coated with polished slip over the

---

[1] Society of Antiquaries : *Excavation of the Roman Fort at Richborough*, Kent (1926-1932).

[2] S.A.S. : *Survey of the Prehistory of the Farnham District* (1939).

51

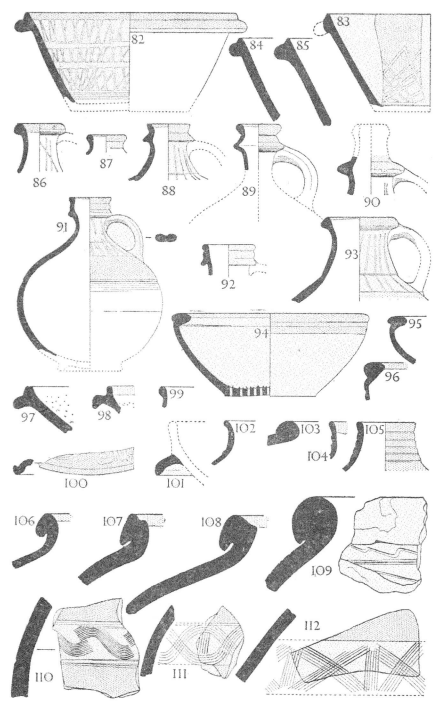

FIG. 9.—FLANGED BOWLS, FLASKS AND STORAGE JARS.

whole of the inside. This latter type was often fumed black, and sometimes decorated with burnished patterns internally.

59. Smooth ware fumed black. A curious feature, found on many other examples, is a single irregular zig-zag line burnished on the underside of the base. An alternative to this was a rough cross, and these marks may have been used to differentiate the products of two workers.

60. Coarse buff ware.

61. Smooth, orange-pink ware with white slip.

62. Large example in very coarse grey ware ; three grooves below rim.

63. Light grey ware, fumed.

64. Coarse, orange-pink ware, no groove below rim ; diam. 6 in.

65. Sandy cream-coloured ware, two grooves below rim ; diam. 9 in.

66. Underfired, grey-pink ware ; diam. c. 7 in.

67-69. Examples with internal burnished lines, probably in imitation of basket-work (cf. flanged bowls, 82-3). 68-9 are closely paralleled by *Park Street*, Fig. 20, 4, dated second half of 4th century, and less particularly by *Lockleys*, Fig. 9, 5, dated A.D. 325-330.

67. Light grey ware base with trellis pattern.

68. Light grey ware with surface and internal slip fumed black ; two irregular superimposed zig-zag lines on side, giving a "trellis" effect, and the base decorated with a herring-bone pattern radiating from the centre.

69. Similar to 68, but horizontal burnished line divides trellis pattern from band of dark grey slip extending upward to rim.

70-75. Shallow versions of the common 4th-century straight-sided flanged bowl (cf. 82-5). All the examples figured are in rather soft buff or grey ware, burnished over the whole of the outside, and coated with smooth slip internally, and with the exception of 72 were fumed to a shiny black finish. Diams. ranged from 7·8 in. to 9·2 in.

76-81. Miscellaneous dishes.

76. Grey ware with fumed outer surface and internal slip ; zone of comb-impressed decoration between grooves below rim.

77. Similar to 76 but undecorated ; diam. 7·8 in.

78. Buff ware with fumed black surface and slip ; diam. 7 in.

79. Soft orange-pink ware ; diam. 7·8 in. Imitation of Samian form 31.

80. Sandy buff-grey ware ; cordon on inside of rim decorated with rouletted notches. Possibly a pedestalled cup.

81. Soft grey-buff ware with fumed black surface and internal slip. Possibly a lid, but disposition of slip renders this unlikely, and more probably an imitation of Samian form 35.

82-85. Straight-sided flanged bowls typical of the 4th century, especially its earlier half. These vessels were either in a coarse, undecorated ware, or in smooth ware burnished all over, with a band of slip covering the rim only. Those with internal trellis decoration were found only in kiln II.

82. Grey-black ware with fumed surface and slip on rim. Irregular internal trellis of burnished lines, crossed by two horizontal bands, apparently imitating basket-work in the same manner as the dishes 67-69. A very similar vessel is figured in *Park Street*, Fig. 20, 1, where it is assigned to the second half of the 4th century.

83. Light grey ware with white slip on rim ; similar to 82, but without horizontal bands, and trellis largely confined to lower part of side.

84. Buff ware with white slip on rim ; internal trellis similar to 82, but more open, and crossed by only one horizontal band ; diam. 8·6 in.

85. Rather coarse, dark grey ware, undecorated.

86-93. Flasks and jugs. The necks of these vessels appear always to have been ornamented with roughly applied vertical burnished lines, similarly to examples in an early 4th-century context from No. 1 Kiln, Sloden Inclosure (*New* Forest,[1] Pl. XVIII).

86. Soft light grey ware, white slip on rim ; handle missing.

87. Light grey ware, coated with white slip ; probably upper part of flask similar to 90.

---

[1] Heywood Sumner: *Excavations in New Forest Roman Pottery Sites* (1927).

88. Orange-buff ware, white slip on rim ; handle missing.

89. Grey ware, cream slip on rim.

90. Light grey ware with white slip ; possible reconstruction shown. A late 3rd- and 4th-century type.

91. Dark grey ware with white slip on rim and shoulder, the lower edge of the latter band being marked by a heavily tooled groove ; burnished zone extending upward from the base. The most complete flask found.

92. A similar vessel, but larger, in orange-pink ware that has not undergone the second, or ' slip,'" firing.

93. Jug reconstructed from fragments of two vessels ; white slip on rim and shoulder. The joining of the handle to the rim is a practice typical of the 4th century.

Miscellaneous Types.

94-5. Strainers in grey ware with fumed black surface and slip on rim, the whole of the outside and base being burnished ; the holes are clean and round, at an average interval of ¼ inch, and punctured from the outside ; incurved rim to prevent the spilling of liquid. An unusual type, of which several examples were found here. Two closely similar bowls in *Richborough* 3, Pl. XLI, 341-2, were probably of this type, although their bases were missing. One is dated mid 4th century, the other was found in a pit filled in *c.* A.D. 400.

96. A variant of the type in underfired orange-pink ware with white slip ; diam. 7·6 in.

97, 98. Two of the only three mortaria rims found at Overwey. The rarity of this type suggests that it is an importation to the site, and its remarkable similarity to 4th-century examples from Richborough renders it almost certain that both sites were supplied with mortaria by the same kilns. 97 is in grey-white ware, with a lid groove, and bears signs of a white slip coating ; diam. *c.* 10 in. *Cf. Richborough* 3, Pl. XLI, 360. 98 is one of two very similar sherds in red-grey clay with light buff slip, identical in treatment with *Richborough* 1, Pl. XXVIII, 102, dated mid 4th century.

99-101. Examples of the few pieces found of the common 4th-century red colour coated ware. These, too, have remarkably close parallels at Richborough, and were probably not made at Overwey. (See also 46.)

99. Small bowl in soft orange-pink paste with grey core and smooth, dark red slip on surface ; diam. 6·4 in. *Cf. Richborough* 1, Pl. XXVIII, 113.

100. Similar ware to above ; diam. 12·6 in. Small rim sherd with a pattern of alternating scrolls and lines of white paint, in imitation of the barbotine decoration on Samian form 36. *Cf. Richborough* 2, Pl. XXXII, 175.

101. Dark blue clay coated with bright red slip ; flange from bowl derivative from Samian form 38, of which two examples were found. Exactly similar in paste and form to *Richborough* 1, Pl. XXVIII, 112, but without pattern in white paint. Dated mid 4th century.

102-3. Rims of a cordoned pot and a bead-rim jar, both in a distinctive coarse, gritty ware, belonging to types common in the period A.D. 50-100. From the lowest part of the filling of pit I*a*. Together with 17 and 58 these sherds must represent intrusions from the scattered debris of an earlier settlement.

104-5. Orange-pink ware with cream slip. 104 is a jar, diam. 4 in., with two offsets on the neck, to which the writer can find no parallel. 105 seems to be a variant of the common 4th-century tall, narrow-necked jar, with the unique feature of regularly spaced grooves covering the neck. *Cf. Lockleys*, Fig. 12, 6, for an example with a strongly wheel-marked surface, dated early 4th century. The groove treatment on the Overwey sherd may be a development from the wheel-marking, and is probably rather later. A similarly decorated but much larger vessel was found at "Mavins" kiln (*Preh. Farnh.*, Fig. 104, R82.)

Large Storage Jars.

106-112. Sherds of massive jars, probably intended for storage purposes, and found in association with kilns I and II. They are all 4th-century types.

106-8. Smooth buff ware coated on rim and shoulder with cream slip ; diams. respectively 7·6, 12, 13 in. 106 is unusually small, 107 and 108, with lid groove, being the more normal size. This type seems always to have been decorated on the lower part of the shoulder with a band of simple, incised comb pattern. The interior is often "clawed-out," a treatment which is obviously intended to produce a rough surface. This feature has a wide distribution in Surrey and Sussex, but more usually in vessels with rough rims like 109, and is discussed by Frere in *S.A.C.*, XLVIII, pp. 52-3. No. 107 is closely paralleled by a sherd from the Kingsley kiln (*Preh. Farnh.*, Fig. 108, R129), and rather similar jars, but with more upstanding rims, were found in the Snailslynch kiln (*ibid.*, Fig. 102, R53a and R53).

109. A large, coarse example, with a crudely executed incised decoration below the rim. This, and a similar rim with "cable" decoration, was found in pit I*b*, and is typical of degenerate late 4th-century technique. *Cf. New Forest*, Pl. XVII, 10, from the 4th-century No. 1 kiln, Sloden Inclosure ; Frere, *S.A.C.*, L, Fig. 8, 41, dated before A.D. 360 ; and *Preh. Farnh.*, Fig. 108, R127, from Kingsley kiln.

110-112. The more common forms of comb-decoration used on jars of types 106-8. *Cf. New Forest*, Pl. XXII, 22, from Black Heath Meadow, for a pattern similar to 111. The frequent use of flowing curves in these simple designs is typical of a resurgence of native Belgic feeling in decoration, which was general in the southern pottery industry during the 4th century, and has been noted particularly among the late New Forest kilns.

APPENDIX I

The coin found in trench A5 was kindly examined by Mr. A. W. G. Lowther· F S.A., who reported on it as follows :—

3Æ of Gratian (A.D. 367-383).

Obv.   Bust, diademed and draped, to r.
      Ins.   D N GRAT(IANUS) AUGG AUG
Rev.   GLOR(IA ROMANORUM)

Emperor advancing or standing r., placing r. hand on head of kneeling captive, and holding labrum in left.

Lyons mint mark   O | FII   Type, Cohen 24.

                     | ʊ

                   ‾‾‾‾‾
                   LVGS

APPENDIX II

ORGANIC REMAINS

These were kindly examined by members of the staff of the Natural History Department, British Museum, whose reports are embodied in the following notes.

Charcoal (examined by Mrs. F. L. Balfour-Browne).

All charcoal samples which were sufficiently large to be identified were found to be of either ash, birch, hazel or oak, all of which are to be found in the vicinity of the kilns at the present day. It is instructive to note the absence of the Scottish pine, which is now so abundant in the area, especially around Crooksbury Hill, and would almost certainly have been used by the potters if it had been available. Of the 25 identifiable charcoal samples examined, five were hazel, six ash, six oak, and eight birch, a result which seems to show that no special preference was shown toward any one of the four types, all of which were used in both kiln I and kiln II. No pieces large enough to be worth preserving could be found in association with kiln III.

Animal Remains (examined by Mr. J. E. King).

These consisted of two ox teeth, found at different levels on Site A, and an ox horn core fragment from the upper part of the filling of kiln II. The ox would presumably have been kept not only to provide food, but also for the haulage of timber and for conveying the wares to the potters' scattered customers. The question of what animal was used by potters to transport their goods has always been a matter for conjecture, and Mr. Heywood Sumner suggested that the New Forest people employed donkeys for this work.

CONCLUSION.

Apart from a small amount of occupation c. A.D. 50–138, during which pottery may not have been made on the site, the period of activity of the Romano-British pottery kilns at Overwey was during the latter part of the 4th century A.D.

The only definitely dated object found was the coin of Gratian (A.D. 367–383) which, although of little significance alone, fits in well with the general picture obtained from the pottery. The kilns were apparently peacefully dismantled and filled in with the accumulation of burnt sand and wasters that lay around them, in order that the site could be used for agriculture. This change may have taken place after the fierce barbarian raids of c. A.D. 368, when widespread destruction of rural settlements in the south of Britain must have seriously affected the livelihood of the potters who served them. Little is so far known about the end suffered by 4th-century settlements in Surrey, but the recently excavated bath-house at Chatley Farm, Cobham, where much pottery of Overwey types was found, may have come to a violent end at this time.

If we may accept this mere hypothesis as true, the coin would have to be assigned to the agricultural period, and bearing in mind the fact that the kilns show signs of reconstruction, the west furnace floor of kiln I having been resurfaced three times, it would be reasonable to allow the site a period of activity of about five years, probably c. 363-8. There was no stratigraphical evidence of any period when the kilns may have been temporarily disused, and the identical nature of much of the pottery from kilns I and II renders it almost certain that sites A and B were operating at the same time. The remoteness of the site from the relatively thickly inhabited, but earlier, pottery-producing area at Farnham itself may indicate that the potters were forced to seek the security of a position well away from the main E.W. route, which must have provided a very easy road for invaders. The area certainly has no advantages over the Wrecclesham plateau so far as clay supplies are concerned.

Was there any connection between the pottery industries at Overwey and in the New Forest ? Many of the products of the two places are remarkably similar, but the absence from Overwey of such characteristic New Forest types as the purple-glazed "thumb-beakers," and rosette-stamped ware, seems to preclude any direct contact, and the similarity of other wares is probably due to competition in satisfying popular demand. Pottery was manu-factured on a large scale at Alice Holt Forest, Hants, throughout

the Roman period from shortly after the conquest,[1] and it is
probable that the whole group of Farnham kilns, including Overwey, and kilns producing the same wares at Farley Heath, Albury,
all represent an eastward expansion of the Alice Holt industry.
The organization and development of these southern potteries,
and the method of operation of the curious two-furnace kilns, will
become clearer when more sites have been excavated by modern
methods.

---

[1] See A. G. Wade and A. W. G. Lowther, *Alice Holt* Forest (British Archæology, 1949).

INVESTIGATIONS ON WALTON HEATH AND BANSTEAD COMMON

BY

J. M. PREST AND E. J. PARRISH

THE two areas which were investigated by the writers during 1948 and 1949 are shown on the site map (Fig. 5). Of the two detail maps (Figs. 6 & 7) showing these areas, map No. 2 covers the area comprising the site of the Roman villa which was found on Walton Heath in 1770, and the other, map No. 3, the area of the earthworks on Banstead Common, situated between Walton-on-the-Hill and Mylenfield Windmill. (Both sites appear on O.S. 6-inch map, Surrey, sheet XXVI, N.W.)

The work which was carried out in each of these areas is here described separately.

1. *The area adjoining the site of the Roman Villa on Walton Heath.*

The first discovery to be recorded consists of a series of ditches and banks, situated both north and south of the villa. These were surveyed by the writers and are marked on map No. 2. Their proximity to the villa raised the hope that they might represent the boundaries of fields connected with it, and of similar date, but when a section-trench was dug across one of them (at the point marked *A* on the map) nothing was found to prove either that they actually are former field boundaries, or that they are of any considerable age, though, in the absence of any evidence to the contrary, this suggestion is still the most probable one. The section referred to is illustrated on Fig. 1.

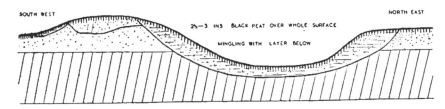

SOUTH WEST NORTH EAST

2½—3 INS BLACK PEAT OVER WHOLE SURFACE

MINGLING WITH LAYER BELOW

SECTION ACROSS DITCH. POINT 'A' ON MAP 2

RED CLAY &
YELLOW CLAYEY
SOIL

SALTED YELLOW
CLAYEY SOIL

SOLID RED
CLAY

YELLOW CLAYEY
SOIL

SCALE IN FEET

0 1 2 3 4

Fig. 1. Section Across Ditch (Point A, Map 2).

The lines of these ditches and banks show up quite clearly on aerial photographs taken in recent years. There are four "spaces" which are more or less enclosed by these ditches and banks, and these are numbered 1-4 on the map. A brief description of these enclosures is as follows :—

No. 1. Bounded on the N.E. and S.E. sides by what appear to be "negative lynchets." (All the other boundaries of the series 1-4 consist of ditches and banks).

No. 2. Separated from No. 1 by a double ditch, and bounded on the S.E. and S.W. sides by the most clearly defined ditch of them all, which is 18 feet in width.

No. 3. Very small, and possibly incomplete ; it is bounded on three sides only and open to the east.

No. 4. Bounded on N. and S. by two ditches that diverge very slightly from east to west. It is an "open-ended" enclosure.

Those ditches marked 5-9 on the map are probably a part of the villa's original boundary ditch. The section marked 7-8 was originally shown on the 25-inch O.S. map of the area, of 1895, but as it has since been obliterated by the golf course, it no longer appears on these maps, and the section marked 8-9 is the only part so indicated.

It must be emphasized that the whole series of these ditches and banks may hold no special interest for archæologists. If, however, an actual date can eventually be assigned to any of them, especially if of the Roman period, they will undoubtedly be of very real interest.

At B on map No. 2 is a bomb-crater, a relic of the recent war, and from the bottom of it was recovered the piece of store-jar

SECTION THROUGH TRENCH DUG ON THE SITE OF THE
ROMAN VILLA ON WALTON HEATH. AUGUST 1948

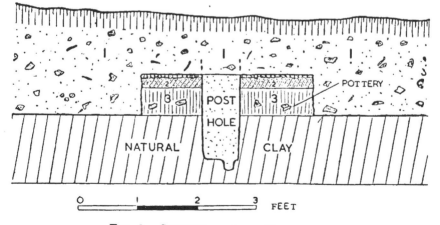

FIG. 2. SECTION THROUGH TRENCH.

rim which is illustrated on Fig. 3 (No. 1) and which is of mid-1st century A.D. (Claudian) date.

The villa itself was discovered in 1770 by one Hoar ("a poor person"—Manning and Bray, ii page 664), and excavations were carried out in the following years :—

1772, by a Mr. Barnes, who found remains of foundations, walls and a flue—also a coin of Vespasian (*S.A.C.*, 1864).

1789, when combed flue-tiles were found (*Arch.*, 1789).

1808, Foundations found, at a depth of two feet ; lumps of clay with burnt wood in them (? wattle and daub) and pieces of bone. (Manning and Bray, ii, p. 664).

1856, by Mr. W. W. Pocock, who found a pavement. (*S.A.C.*, II, pp. 1-13).

1882, by Mr. E. Freshfield, who excavated a room measuring 30 feet by 8½ feet. (*Proc. Soc. Ant.*, Ser. II, IX, p. 110).

1939, by Mr. M. Berry, a member of this Society, who dug a trial trench and made certain finds which, owing to his death (he was killed on active service in Italy), have never been published.

The only other recorded find from the site of this villa is that of the brooch which is described in *S.A.C.*, XLIX., p. 108 (Fig. 4, note by S. S. Frere.)

In the hope that something might be found which would enable the date, or dates, of its occupation to be assigned, the writers dug a single trench at point *C* on the villa site.

Despite the fact that excavating at this much disturbed site is now rather like sorting the rubble of a "blitzed" structure, so thoroughly has it been turned over, the writers were sufficiently lucky to find a small undisturbed portion of a plain tesselated

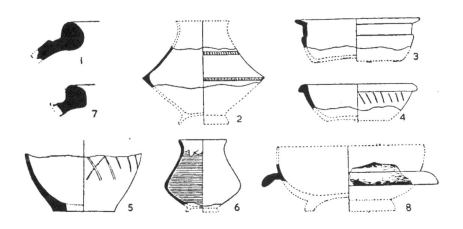

POTTERY FROM AND FROM CLOSE TO THE VILLA ON WALTON HEATH

SCALE ━━━━━━ INCHES

FIG. 3.   POTTERY FROM VILLA.

H

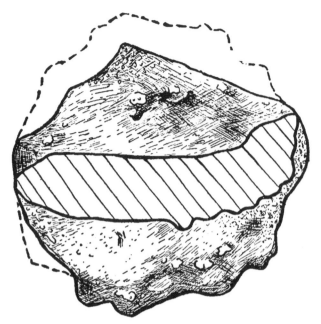

FIG. 4.   IRON CINDER, FOUND AT POINT F ON MAP 2.   Scale ½

pavement (with a hole where a post had penetrated it at a subsequent date), and fragments of a datable pot were recovered from underneath it. Some further pottery was recovered from the loose rubble previously mentioned.

The section-trench, which was dug across both the disturbed and undisturbed layers, is shown on Fig. 2. The pottery found in the disturbed layer (level No. 1) is illustrated on Fig. 3, Nos. 2-5, while the pot from level No. 3, the undisturbed layer beneath the pavement (level 2) is shown by No. 6 on the same figure. All the pottery found is discussed in a note by Mr. Lowther[1], who assigns a 2nd century (Hadrianic) date to the latter vessel. This suggests that the floor itself was laid about the middle of this century. However, the presence at the site of some pottery of Claudian date implies that occupation began early in the Roman period, and at a date considerably earlier than that at which this floor was constructed. Since there is no evidence of the existence at this site of any building before the villa itself was erected, it seems likely that it was either (a) enlarged, or (b) reconstructed at some date in the mid-2nd century A.D., as has been found to have been the case with so many other villas, including the one found at Windmill Bank, a short distance N.W. of this villa. (See report in this volume.)

Other evidence as to date is provided by the pavement which was found by Mr. Pocock in 1856, and which seems to have been, as regards its design, very like one found at Verulamium and to

---

[1] Appendix I, at end of this article.

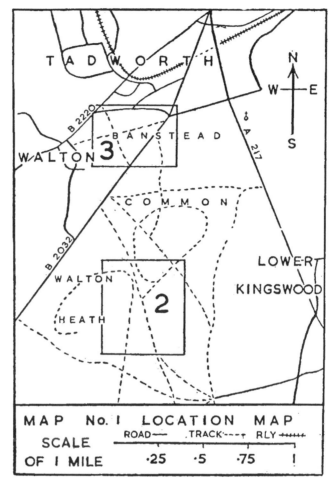

FIG. 5. MAP No. 1, LOCATION MAP.

which a mid- or late-2nd century date has been ascribed (*Verulamium*, Research Report No. 11 of *Soc. Ant.*, pl. 47—mosaic No. 12 from building 4, room 10, *v.* also p. 147). Both pavements depicted a large, two-handled urn ; that from Walton is described in *S.A.C.*, II, pp. 1-13.

A further indication that the villa was reconstructed, or redecorated, and was probably in use for some considerable time, was that of the discovery or a piece of resurfaced wall plaster.

As there is no other known Roman site in the immediate vicinity, a piece of Roman pottery found lying on the surface of the ploughed land between the villa and enclosure *E* (map No. 2) presumably came originally from the villa itself. This sherd (Fig. 3, No. 8) dates from about A.D. 350, the type remaining in use to the end of the 4th century. Thus the villa was probably occupied well into the second half of the 4th century A.D., a conclusion that is supported by some of the material found by the previous excavators.

The finds, other than pottery, from this latest excavation include : a piece of window glass ; iron nails ; a quantity of brick tessera ; coloured wall-plaster, and a number of small bricks (or "brickettes") measuring $2\frac{1}{2} \times 1\frac{1}{2} \times \frac{3}{4}$ in., and of the type used for constructing herringbone paving, but the smallest of their type so far recorded. That they had been employed as stated is shown by the "wear" being restricted to one of the long sides in each case, as well as by the mortar still adhering to each of the brood faces.

As regards other "features" in this area, the small barrow-like mound (D on map No. 2) was sectioned by the writers and proved

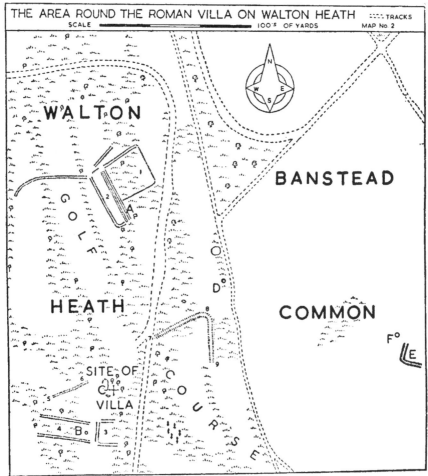

[This map is reproduced from the Ordnance Survey Map, with the sanction of the Controller of H.M. Stationery Office.

FIG. 6. MAP No. 2, ROMAN VILLA, WALTON HEATH.

to be modern, and probably connected with the existing golf course.

The enclosure *E* is plotted from an aerial photograph, and not from a ground survey. From its surface came the store-jar rim No. 7 on Fig. 3. Near by, at *F*, is a small patch of iron cinders, of a type produced by the smelting of iron in early-Roman and pre-Roman times (*v.* "Purberry Shot," Ewell, *S.A.C.*, L, p. 20, Fig. 9). A typical cinder is shown on Fig. 4.

2. *Earthworks in the area between Walton-on-the-Hill and Mylenfield Windmill.* (Map No. 3).

The three earthworks marked *A*, *B*, and *C* on this map are described in *V.C.H.*, *IV*, p. 392, and are shown on the O.S. maps of the district.

To these, a new earthwork, *D*, not previously recorded, must be added. It appears to be of the same type as the others, so that the group consists of four and, as will be seen, arranged in pairs, each pair consisting of a large and a small enclosure, viz., *A* and *B*, and *C* and *D*. The ditches of *D* are not so clearly defined as those of the other three, and its outline on plan is less regular. A trackway crosses its southern corner, the tip of which is spoilt by the presence of a small pit. On the eastern side, its ditches become

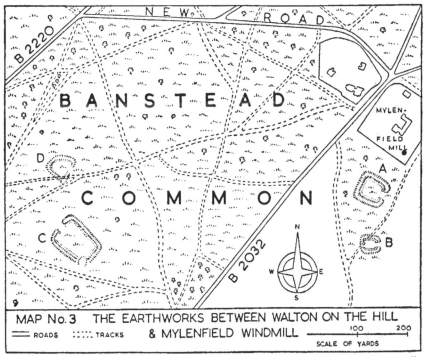

MAP No. 3   THE EARTHWORKS BETWEEN WALTON ON THE HILL
═══ ROADS   ⋯⋯⋯ TRACKS   & MYLENFIELD WINDMILL ────
SCALE OF YARDS

[*This map is reproduced from the Ordnance Survey Map, with the sanction of the Controller of H.M. Stationery Office.*

FIG. 7. MAP No. 3, EARTHWORKS.

quite insignificant, which may explain why it has escaped detection for so long.

Investigations of these earthworks carried out by the late S. E. Winbolt (*S.A.C.*, XXXVIII, 94-96) produced some pottery, incorporated in one of the banks, which was probably (from the brief description published) of late 16th- or early 17th-century date, and it has been suggested (A.W.G.L. in *S.A.C..*, L, p. 170) that these earthworks may belong to the period of the Civil War.

Whether so or not, the "grouping," consequent on the discovery of *D*, implies a relationship between a "large" and a "small" enclosure in the case of each pair, and the writers would suggest this relationship might well be made the subject of some further investigation, which might afford some reasonable explanation as to the purpose of the whole group.

APPENDIX I—A NOTE ON THE ROMAN POTTERY
A. W. G. LOWTHER, F.S.A.

Fig. 3.

1, 7. Bead-rim fragments from large store-jars of "Patch Grove" type. No. 1, of orange-red ware; No. 7, grey internally, with reddish surface. Date—Claudian.

Similar urns have been found at Purberry Shot, Ewell (*S.A.C.*, L, p. 29) Hawke's Hill, Leatherhead, and, beneath the Roman villa, at Windmill Bank, Walton-on-the-Hill. These examples were, however, of a "gritted" ware, whereas 1 and 7 are of typical "Patch Grove" ware, as found by Prof. J. B. Ward-Perkins both at the type site and at Oldbury Camp, Kent (*Arch.*, 90, p. 127 *et seq.*).

2. Part of a small, sharply carinated pot of thin, brownish ware with a fumed and burnished outer surface, and with two surviving bands of rouletted ornament. Date—Claudian. Small pieces from an identical vessel were found at Purberry Shot (*S.A.C.*, L, unfigured).

3. Piece of a shouldered dish of "Ashtead" type, of grey ware (cf. Ashtead Common Villa, *S.A.C.*, XXXVII, p. 160, Figs. 1-8). Date—Flavian. Also found in quantity at Purberry Shot (*op. cit.*, p. 41, Fig. 29).

4. Shallow-sided dish, with bead rim and external lattice ornament. Of brownish-grey ware, with fumed black outer surface. A number of bowls and dishes of this type were found in Hadrianic levels at the Ashtead Common site.

5. Small hard grey-ware pot, with lattice ornament on the outside. Date—Hadrian-Antonine.

6. Small pot of thin, white, slip-coated ware, of a type evolved from carinated vessels such as No. 2. The ware is the same as that formerly known as "Upchurch ware," and of which the commonest type consists of small vessels with applied "dot" ornament, in vertical bands (cf. "Purberry Shot," Fig. 26). Date—Hadrianic.

8. Part of a flanged bowl of red-coated red ware ("New Forest Ware"). Date—4th century, *c.* A.D. 350—400.

ROMAN VILLA AT SANDILANDS ROAD, WALTON-ON-THE-HILL.
EXCAVATIONS OF 1948-49

BY

A. W. G. LOWTHER, F.S.A.

THE presence of a Roman villa at this site (that of the garden of the present bungalow named *Windmill Bank*) was first discovered during 1915, when practice trench-digging was being carried out in what was then an open field (the glebe meadow) by a detachment of the Public Schools Battalion, which was then in training in the area.

An apsidal plunge-bath, and certain other foundations, were then cut through, but no detailed excavations were then possible. Fortunately, the find was reported to Mr. Edward Yates, F.S.A., who visited the site together with the late Mr. Mill Stephenson, F.S.A., and the position of the bath was noted by them and photographs taken (here reproduced—Plate V).

The trenches were filled in and nothing further was done until 1948, when Mr. Frere, with the assistance of boys from Epsom College, commenced excavations which were continued by the writer during the winter and the spring of the following year. Though the meadow had, since 1915, been divided into two separate holdings, and a dwelling erected on the front portion of each plot, practically the whole of the villa (as the excavations showed) lay within the confines of one plot and, despite the fact that it had been laid out as a garden, by careful selection of the points at which the trenches were sited, it was possible to recover the plan of the villa fairly completely and with a minimum of damage to the garden concerned.

Amongst those volunteers who assisted with this work, a special tribute is due to the late Michael Berry of Tadworth, whose death in 1944, while serving in Italy with the R.A.F., has deprived archæology of one of its keenest workers and of one who, had he been spared, was likely to have done much for the archæology of Surrey.

Description of the Site.

The site lies to the north of Walton and close to Tadworth and is on the extreme northern edge of a plateau, or level summit, of the North Downs, at a height of 550 ft. o.d., with Banstead Heath to the south-west and Walton Heath to the south. The subsoil consists of five to six feet of gravel and sand resting on chalk. From the northern end of the villa the ground drops

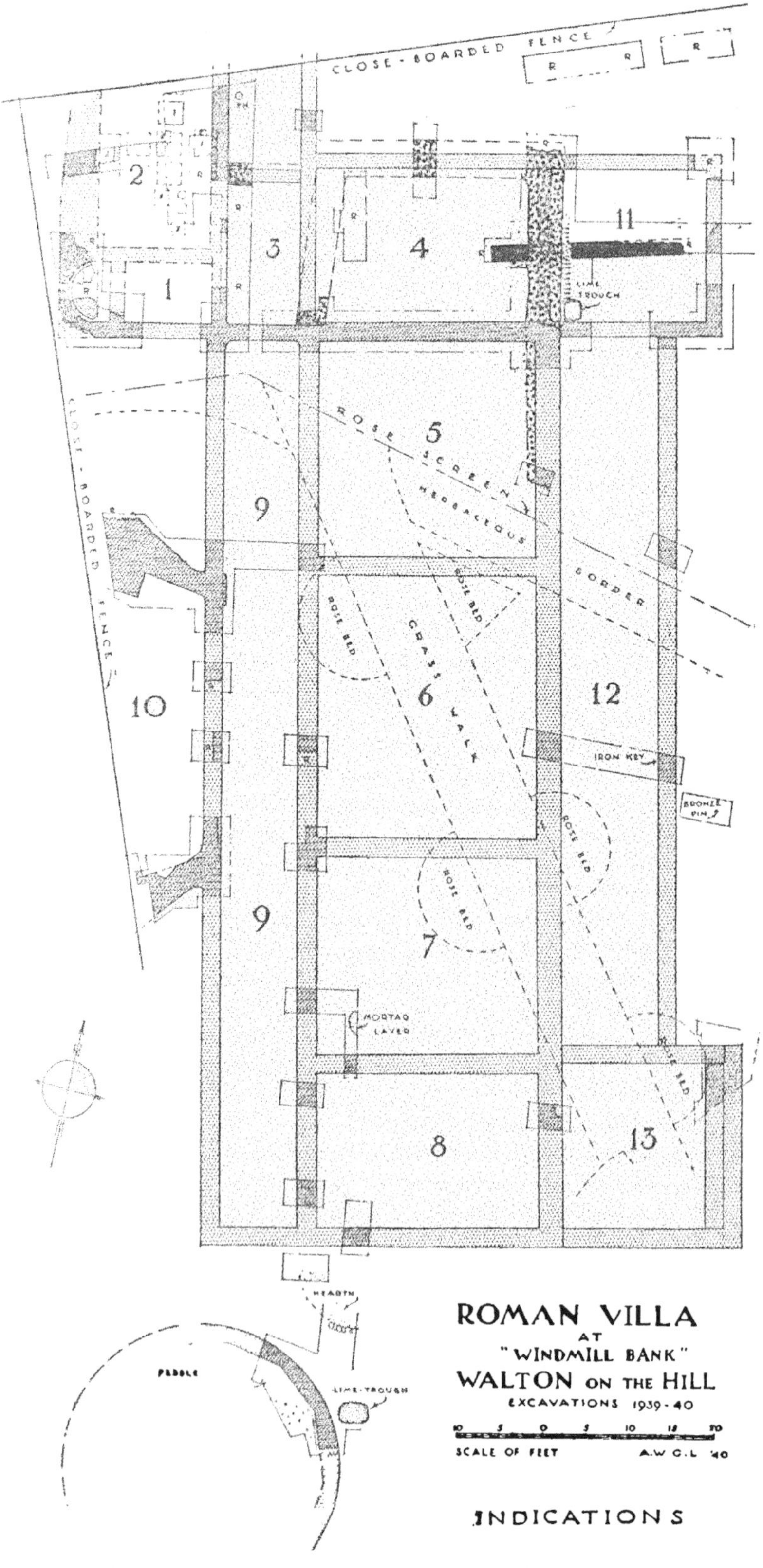

FIG. 1.—PLAN OF SITE.
(Block kindly lent by Society for Promotion of Roman studies.)

ROMAN VILLA
AT
"WINDMILL BANK"
WALTON ON THE HILL
EXCAVATIONS 1939-40

SCALE OF FEET   A.W.G.L. '40

INDICATIONS

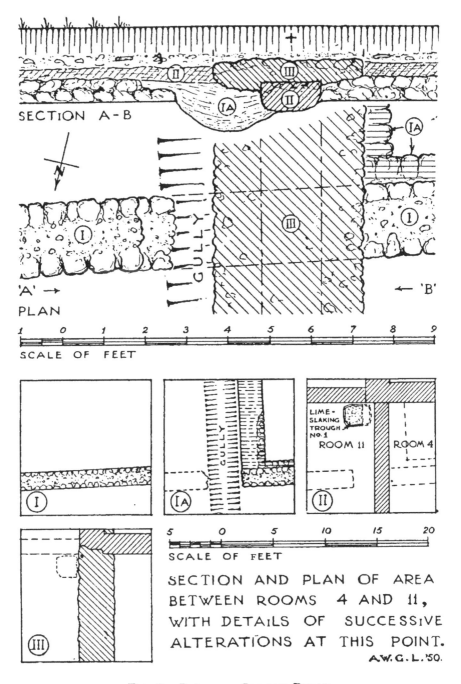

SECTION A-B

PLAN

'A' →   ← 'B'

SCALE OF FEET

LIME-
SLAKING
TROUGH
No. 1
ROOM 11   ROOM 4

SCALE OF FEET

SECTION AND PLAN OF AREA
BETWEEN ROOMS 4 AND 11,
WITH DETAILS OF SUCCESSIVE
ALTERATIONS AT THIS POINT.

A.W.G.L. '50.

FIG. 2.—PLAN AND SECTION DETAIL.

away fairly steeply to the north and there is an uninterrupted view of many miles in this direction, over the Epsom race-course and beyond to the hills of Kingston and Wimbledon. (The site is recorded on the 6-inch and 25-inch o.s. maps, and the grid reference to the site on the one-inch New Popular Edition map, London, S.W., sheet 170, is 223557). It is $1\frac{1}{2}$ miles from the Roman villa on Walton Heath ; the latter, lying in an east-of-south direction, is the subject of a separate report in this volume (p. 57).

The initial work of 1948 exposed once again the apsidal plunge-bath, and a long trial trench dug to the east of it disclosed a complex junction of walls, of three separate periods, (between rooms 4 and 11 on plan) and proved to be the most important find as regards the elucidation of the history of the successive buildings and so is described in some detail later on (p. 72 and Fig. 2).

Summary of Results.

The site proved to have been occupied in pre-Roman times, during the latter part of the Iron Age, and a certain quantity of pottery dating *circa* A.D. 10-43 was found, mostly in an occupation layer (level 3) about two to three inches thick (with charcoal, calcined flints and some roughly worked flints) resting immediately above the gravel subsoil. This pottery includes pieces of a vessel of south-eastern "B" type (Fig. 5, No. 1) with traces of painted ornamentation on the shoulder ; a piece of an (imported) "terra rubra" dish (No. 6), found with the latter, and pieces of several vessels of Patch Grove ware types ; all typical of pottery in use during the decade or two prior to the Claudian invasion of A.D. 43.

It appears that there may then have been a gap in the occupation of this site, until the latter part of the 1st century A.D., though this is not certain as some few of the pieces of pottery found (including one or two of the Samian ware fragments) are of the Claudian-Flavian period. Anyhow, a solitary piece of wall, about 25 feet in length as now surviving, and completely robbed of its material at either end (crossing rooms 11 and 4 on plan) was the only remaining portion of a structure dated (from associated pottery) to *circa* A.D. 100. This wall, which is likely to have been part of a small single room, barn-like structure, was not retained when the subsequent villa was erected (*circa* A.D. 180),[1] and the wall separating rooms 4 and 11 had its foundations trench dug through the remaining lower part of this earlier wall.

There was clearly an interval of some years between the destruction of the period I building and the erection of the villa in period II, as a small ditch or gully (containing a certain amount of Hadrianic pottery, had been cut through the early

---

[1] It was, however, subjected to certain alterations (1*a* on plan) and this alteration appears to have been of the same date as that of the gully.

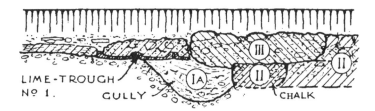

a. E-W SECTION THROUGH LIME -
SLAKING TROUGH №1.

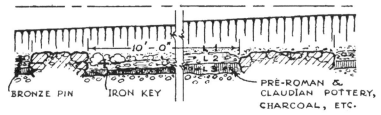

b. E-W SECTION ACROSS CENTRE
OF CORRIDOR 12.

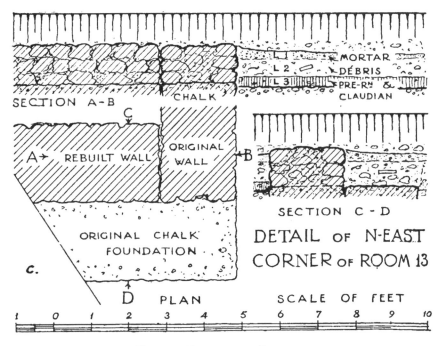

Fig. 3.—Details of Sections.

wall and then filled with soil and debris before the construction of the period II villa took place, since the foundation of the wall between 4 and 11 (made of chalk, like the other wall foundations of this period) rested on the material filling the lower part of the gully. Hence a period of some fifty years, or more, may have elapsed between the destruction of the early building (*circa* A.D. 200) and the date of the erection of the period II villa (*circa* A.D. 250, or later).

The villa (which was entirely of one period, discounting subsequent repairs or the partial rebuilding in period III) had consisted of a single range of rooms running in a north–south direction, with a corridor, or verandah, at the back and another at the front (see plan). The entrance, on the axis of the largest room (6) of the range, was on the eastern side. Two splayed foundations on the west side (extending into the adjoining garden, where it was not possible to excavate) are likely to have formed part of an octagonal room similar to that at the villa at Great Witcombe, Glos. (*Arch.*, XIX, 1821), and at several other Roman villas. If so, it was probably the main room of the villa, and probably had an elaborate mosaic pavement, but (as was the case with much of the villa) only a few inches of the lowermost part of the foundations had survived, and that at a depth much below that of the original floor.

At the north-eastern corner of the villa were the bath quarters, of which only the plunge-bath and the room off which it opened (1) and the hypocaust of the *tepidarium* (2) could be excavated.

The *caldarium*, *sudatorium* and furnace room, with its stokehole, which extended (in this order) to the north of room 2, had been outside the present site, and have clearly all been destroyed both by the present footpath and garden beyond, as well as by reason of the slope of the ground which now drops away fairly sharply to the north from the northern limits of our site.

Room 2, the *tepidarium*, consisted of a hypocaust, of which all the overlying floor had been destroyed, but of which the floor supports (*pilæ*) were for the part excavated, still *in situ*. These consisted of two different types and clearly of different date, so that the bath, if not most of the villa, had become ruinous and had been reconstructed at a later date, but before the date of the final partial rebuilding described later on. A coin of Tetricus II (270-274) found in the débris filling the ruined hypocaust (a coin which was in a very good state of preservation) suggests that the baths were finally destroyed about this date so the reconstruction referred to may have taken place about A.D. 280 or 300.

The purpose of the isolated circular structure (14) with a polygonal-sided internal room, and with some of its *opus signinum* floor and quarter-round angle moulding still in position, is not certain. (More than half of it extended beyond the limits of the site.) It has a fairly close parallel in the polygonal detached room found at the villa at Stroud, near Petersfield, Hants (*Arch.*

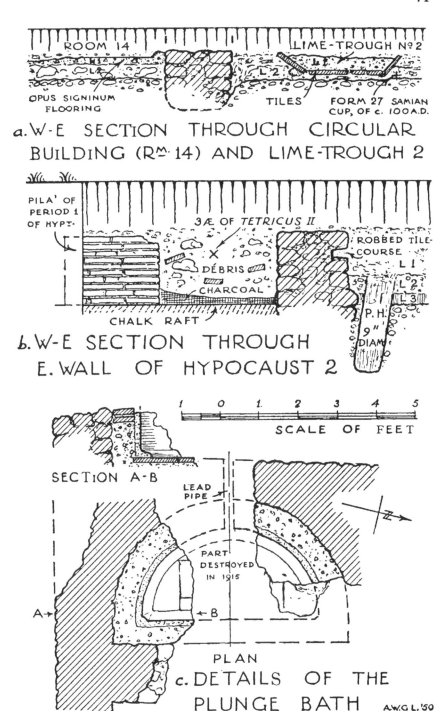

a. W-E SECTION THROUGH CIRCULAR
BUILDING (R^m 14) AND LIME-TROUGH 2

b. W-E SECTION THROUGH
E. WALL OF HYPOCAUST 2

c. DETAILS OF THE
PLUNGE BATH A.W.G.L.'50

Fig. 4.—Hypocaust and Plunge Bath Details.

Journ., LXVI, 38, 1909).[1]   It seems probable, from the care
taken to shape the inner wall-surface, that it was intended for
some domestic, rather than utilitarian, purpose.

The east wall of the small square room (13) at the south end
of the east corridor possessed a feature of particular interest
(Fig. 3c).   It had been built (perhaps only partially) two feet
farther to the east than was evidently intended, or than the
amount of the projection of the corresponding wall at the north
end of the villa (that to room 11).   To correct this, a fresh chalk
foundation was formed inside this wall, and the flint walling
pulled down and rebuilt on the new foundation.   Such a correction,
and of an error which would not have been very apparent if it had
been allowed to remain, implies that the building work was
carried out under the supervision of someone who was the equiva-
lent of a present-day architect, or of a clerk of the works.

Evidence of the latest work—a rebuilding apparently of only a
part of the villa, and at some time late in the 4th Century A.D.—
was found only at the northern end of the site.   It consisted of
the lowest part of some very broad foundations, executed in very
poor materials (flints set in yellow, sandy mortar, with much
chalk and semi-slaked lime), and its nearness to the present
surface of the ground probably accounts for there being no trace
of this rebuilding for the southern half of the villa, where the fall
in the ground level would account for its disappearance.   Three
minimissimæ—minute coins of Lydney type and dating *circa*
A.D. 400—were found in contact with these latest foundations
and immediately above them.

Some of the earlier walls were completely rebuilt in this late
period, and are covered by the broad foundations (*e.g.*, the north
and west walls of 4).   Others were thickened (*e.g.*, the east wall of
5), while the west wall of 4 was rebuilt, overriding the earlier
foundation and on a different alignment.   Some of the earlier
walls must, however, have still been standing, at least as regards
their lowest part (*e.g.*, the south wall of 3 and 4) as the later work
is carried up to and against them.   It is likely that this latest
rebuilding should be dated to the extreme end of the 4th Century
A.D., rather than *circa* A.D. 300 as has been suggested on the plan
(Fig. 1).   In short, the site was occupied from about A.D. 10
to about A.D. 400.

Details of the Excavations.

As regards the recovery of the history of the various buildings,
or rebuilt structures, the most important evidence was obtained
from the part, already mentioned, between rooms 4 and 11.
Here (Fig. 2) walls of three periods,[2] and a ditch or gully of a

---

[1] Or to the octagonal room at the villa at Loose Road, Maidstone, Kent,
published in *Arch. Cant.* X ; 1876.

[2] Also the alterations, previously noted, to the period I wall.

PLATE III

[*Photos by S. S. Frere, F.S.A.*

1. GENERAL VIEW OF NORTH END OF SITE, LOOKING EAST, DURING PROGRESS OF EXCAVATIONS.
2. WALL BETWEEN ROOMS 4 AND 11 ; VIEW LOOKING SOUTH-EAST.
3. INTERSECTION OF WALLS OF PERIODS I-III ; VIEW LOOKING EAST.

[*Facing p. 72*

PLATE IV

[*Photos by S. S. Frere, F.S.A.*

1. PART OF LIME-SLAKING TROUGH, No. 1.
2. NORTH-EAST CORNER OF ROOM 13. (See Fig. 3c.)
3. OUTER WALL AND FLOOR OF CIRCULAR BUILDING (14), LOOKING NORTH-
   WEST.

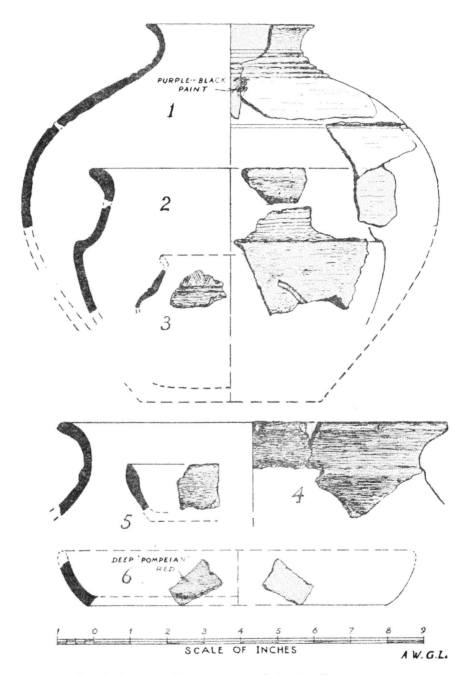

FIG. 5.—NATIVE, AND IMPORTED, PRE-CLAUDIAN POTTERY FROM THE
EARLIEST OCCUPATION LEVEL.

period (I*a*) between that of the two first periods, all either intersect or lie one upon the other. In addition, in the south-west corner of 11 was found the lime-trough (formed of roof-tiles) in which lime used for the plastering of the period II walls was slaked (Fig. 3*a*). In the lime still remaining in this trough were found the pieces of a cooking pot (Fig. 8, No. 29) which are of late 3rd-century, or early 4th-century, date. Also, about half of this trough was cut away when the late broad-wall foundation, between rooms 4 and 11, was constructed.

The pottery from the gully which cuts across the period I wall and underlies, in part, both the period II foundation and the lime-trough, includes some pieces (Fig. 7) which are of Antonine date, but most of it is Hadrianic, while some of it is of still earlier date. From the fact that it consists of stray pieces from a number of vessels, and includes no complete, or even nearly complete, pots, it is likely that this pottery was lying on the surface when the gully was filled in and that it represents pottery used when the period I*a* structure was in use. Also the gully, from an absence of silt, appeared not to have been open for any great length of time and to have been filled deliberately. The fact that it nearly coincides with the wall between rooms 4 and 11, and does not extend beyond the north and south walls of these rooms, implies that it was dug as an external drain for the shortened building of period I*a*.

Some further evidence for dating period II was obtained, in the form of pottery including the Samian ware cup-base (form 33) with the stamp of the Antonine potter Genialis, in corridor 9, and beneath a thin spread of mortar. Another lime-trough and some more stratified pottery was found just outside the isolated, circular room, No. 14, as well as from beneath the remains of *opus signinum* flooring inside this building. As well as some pottery of Hadrianic-Antonine date, it included some earlier pieces, amongst which was the upper part of the native-ware pot, Fig. 6, No. 7.

The small apsidal plunge-bath, originally uncovered in 1915, was located and re-excavated, and calls for no special comment. It had been very well constructed of tiles covered with *opus signinum*, of good hard quality and with a very smooth surface, and with quarter-round angle-mouldings. The narrow trench cut through it in 1915 (when the lead outlet-pipe was discovered) was apparent, and can be seen on the photographs taken at that date by Mr. E. Yates, F.S.A., to whom I am indebted for the copies here reproduced. (Plate V).

Room 2, the *tepidarium* (Fig. 4*b*), originally had square (18 inch by 18 inch, approx.) tile built floor supports. When, as mentioned above, this hypocaust was reconstructed, some additional smaller supports were inserted, and some of these were built against the earlier supports, or *pilæ*. (For the earlier *pilæ*, in addition to tiles of normal dimensions, some of those employed measure 3 inches

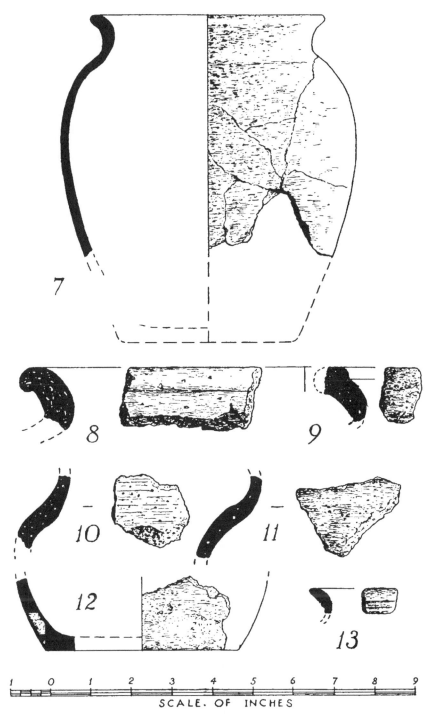

7 8 9 10 11 12 13

1 0 1 2 3 4 5 6 7 8 9
SCALE. OF INCHES

FIG. 6.—NATIVE WARE OF THE EARLIEST OCCUPATION PERIOD.

by 6 inches by 15½ inches. It is a point worth noting that bricks of such unusual size and shape were sometimes employed in the Roman period, since, if found apart from a Roman building, it might be difficult to decide as to their actual date).

The post-hole found immediately outside the east wall of 2, in the northward extension of corridor 9, was probably formed by part of the scaffolding used when the period II building was erected. It had been filled in with soil and débris and had contained a circular post, or pole, of 9-inch diameter, extending to a depth of 2 feet 6 inches below the top of the adjacent wall-foundation (Fig. 4b).

The remains of the buildings were extensively robbed during mediæval times and, at the same period, there was some digging of the site for gravel, extending to a depth of three or four feet, in the area north of rooms 4 and 11, as well as inside room 4. Refuse, including much pottery dating from *circa* 1250-1400, had been deposited in the pits so formed, and it seems likely that this removal of gravel, tiles, etc., took place in connection with building work at Walton Manor, which is at no great distance to the south and which, in addition to the 14th-century work still to be seen there, has a Norman *motte* close to it and on which the foundations of some structures were found (but not properly recorded) during the last century.

Some of the robbing had, however, clearly taken place in Roman times and prior to the erection of the final building. Evidence of this was found in the hypocaust of room 2 of the baths, and in connection with the east wall of this room. The robbing of tiles from the *pilæ* of the reconstructed hypocaust, and from the bonding-course of the east wall (where the removal of tiles had left a slot in the outer face of the wall), had taken place in late Roman times, as shown by the stratification. Hence, as at many other sites, it is clear that the bath annexe was not included in the latest and final reconstruction of the villa.

Building Materials.

In addition to the use of flints for the rubble masonry of the walls, some few pieces of greensand stone were employed, but as roughly broken pieces of stone and not as squared or dressed masonry. One or two large pieces of gravel-iron conglomerate, the so-called pudding stone, were also found built into the walls.

A number of loose, brick *tesseræ* were found, and a few mosaic *tesseræ* (of hard chalk, etc.), but probably as the result of subsequent ploughing and the slope of the site already mentioned, no paving was found *in situ*, apart from the small patch of *opus signinum* in the isolated circular building (14).

The fact that, save for a very few small pieces, no flue-tile fragments were found in the débris filling the ruined hypocaust (2) suggests that these flue-tiles had been carefully removed when the bath annexe was dispensed with, either for re-use at another

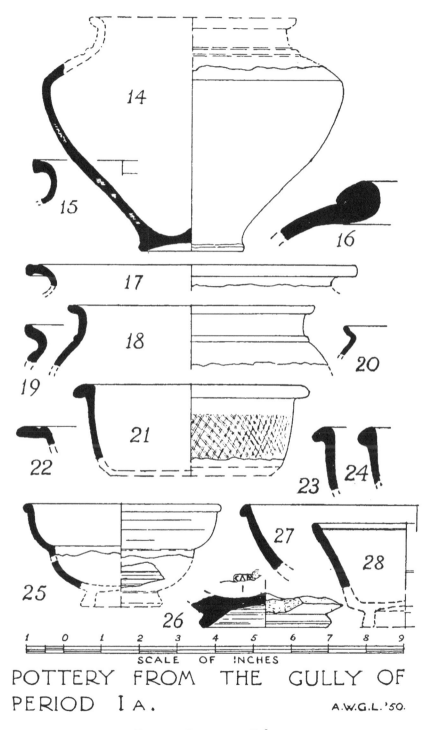

POTTERY FROM THE GULLY OF
PERIOD I A.

A.W.G.L. '50.

FIG. 7.—PERIOD IA POTTERY.

site or (as was sometimes the case, *e.g.*, at the Ashtead Common site) for use as drain pipes.

Finds (*not including the pottery*).

(*a*) *Stone.*

Piece of a quern, of a hard grit-stone, 2 inches thick and of 18 inches diameter, with a central hole, originally about 1¼ inches in diameter. (Not figured).

(*b*) *Iron.*

Key (Fig. 9*a*). Probably a door-key ; of a common Roman type, it was found in level 2, close to the front wall of the east corridor.

Tanged knife-blade (Fig. 9*b*). Found with 4th-century pottery (level 1) beside south wall of room 3.

Two styli (not figured). Both from level 1.

(*c*) *Bronze.*

Pin, 4¼ inches long, with conical head. From level 2, outside wall of east corridor.

(*d*) *Coins.*

The four coins found during the excavations (a 3 Æ of Tetricus II, and three 4th- and 5th-century minimissimæ, of Lydney type) together with three or four coins found (during gardening operations) in the adjoining garden, were, unfortunately, lost in the post when (October, 1940) being sent to an expert for his opinion on them. They were not, however, of much consequence for dating the various periods of the structures, and this can only be arrived at, somewhat approximately, from the pottery from the various stratified levels.

The Pottery.

(*a*) From the earliest occupation level (level 3) on the natural subsoil. (Figs. 5 and 6).

1. Upper part of a large pot, of orange-brown soapy-surfaced ware. Horizontal ribbing at the neck, and with remaining traces of painted ornamentation, in a purple-black paint. This vessel, of "eastern-B" type, has parallels from sites in Sussex. No. 13 may be from a similar vessel.

2, 4, 7, 11 and 12. Pieces of pots of Patch Grove ware, similar to some found at Purberry Shot, Ewell (*S.A.C.*, L.)

3. Shoulder fragment of a small pot of a black, burnished ware and with a band of ornament consisting of alternate sloping lines. Hand-made, Belgic ware.

5. Piece of rim of a dish of brown, soapy, hand-made ware.

6. Dish, of imported terra rubra ware. Buff, micaceous paste, coated internally with a thick coating of deep pompeian red colour.

8, 9 and 10. Pieces of large store-pots of hand-made gritted ware. (Many pieces from the walls of vessels of this type were found in level 3 and later levels).

(*b*) Arretine ware from level 3 (Fig. 9).

41. A single small piece from rim and side of an Arretine platter, apparently of the type S4B as found at Colchester (*Camulodunum*, Hawkes and Hull, pl. XXXIX, and p. 182) was obtained from level 3, outside the east wall of room 2 (Section, Fig. 4*b*). Date :—pre-Claudian, or Claudian.

(*c*) From the gully of Period Ia (Figs. 2 and 7). Samian and coarse ware of typical Hadrianic and Hadrian-Antonine forms, including some pieces (*e.g.*, the store-jar bead-rim, no 16) of earlier ware.

Bowls as 21, 23, and 24, were present in some quantity.

26. Base of Samian bowl, form 18/31, of thick poor quality, Antonine ware. Part of the stamp with letters CAN. . . (Candidus ?).

25 and 28. Samian cups, of forms 27 and 33, of Hadrian-Antonine ware.

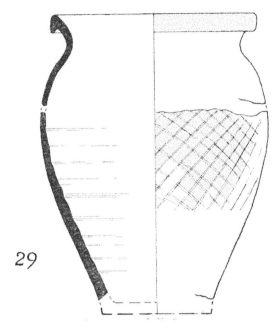

COOKING - POT FROM LIME IN
SLAKING - TROUGH No. I.

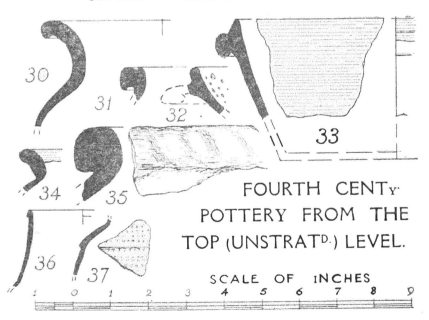

FOURTH CENTy.
POTTERY FROM THE
TOP (UNSTRATD.) LEVEL.

SCALE OF INCHES

FIG. 8.—POTTERY.

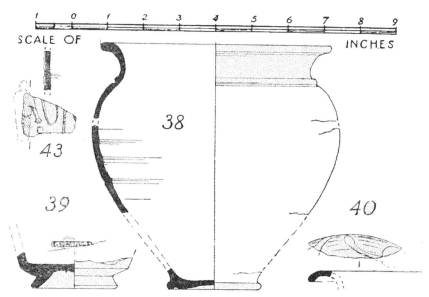

SCALE OF   INCHES

43

38

39   40

POTTERY PRE-DATING PERIOD II
VILLA. (L.2, BELOW E. CORRIDOR)

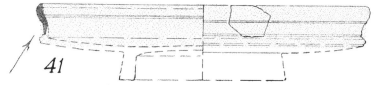

41

PIECE OF 'ARRETINE' PLATTER (L.3, AD NAT)

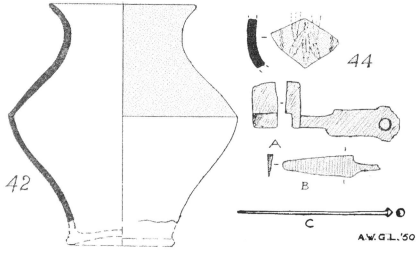

42

44

A

B

C

A.W.G.L.'50

FIG. 9.—POTTERY AND SMALL FINDS (A—C).
A, Iron key ; B, Iron knife-blade ; C, Bronze pin.

PLATE V

[*Photos by E. Yates, F.S.A.*

THE APSIDAL PLUNGE BATH (ROOM 1) AS EXPOSED IN 1915 AFTER
PARTIAL DESTRUCTION BY ARMY TRENCHING.

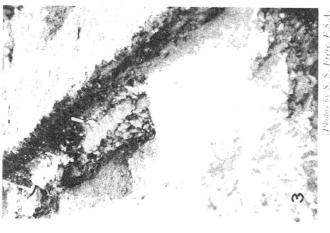

3. VIEW, LOOKING EAST, OF BROAD (PERIOD III) FOUNDATION BE-TWEEN ROOMS 4 AND 11; PERIOD I WALL IN BACKGROUND.

[Photos by S. S. Frere, F.S.A.

Farine

1 AND 2. VIEWS OF HYPOCAUST (ROOM 2).

27. Rim, of form 18/31, of good ware. Early 2nd-century.

(d) From *the lime in the lime-slaking* trough *No.* 1. (Figs. 3a, *and* 8).

29. Pieces, forming about half, but without the base, of a cooking pot of hard, dark blue-grey ware, with band of roughly executed lattice ornament. Probably of early 4th-century date. This pot must have been thrown into the lime in this trough while the lime was still soft, since the pieces were all embedded in it. The trough belongs to the Period II building, but may have been formed to slake lime for re-decorating (replastering) the walls, and need not have been used for the original period II building work. Part of it was destroyed by the broad-wall foundation of period III, the final period.

(e) Late Roman (4th-5th-century) *pottery from the uppermost level* (*level* 1) *and from the top*-soil. (*Fig.* 8, *Nos.* 30-37).

30. Rim of pot, of hard buff ware containing coarse grit particles. 4th-century. Unstratified.

31. Rim of a narrow-necked large jar (probably of globular shape and with band of combed ornament) identical to those made at the Snails-lynch kiln site at Farnham. This much worn fragment has lost all traces of the white slip surfacing which is usual with these vessels. Late 3rd, or early 4th-century.

32. Piece of a mortarium of hard, white ware, with pinkish quartz gritting to inner surface. 3rd-century.

33. Flanged bowl, of grey ware with white slip coating to inside and top of rim. Typical of vessels made at the 4th-century kiln sites at Farnham and in Hants. (Alice Holt, and at the New Forest sites). For similar vessels from the bath-house at Cobham *v. S.A.C.*, L., p. 86, Fig. 6.

34. Rim of grey ware with white slip coating. Typical of vessels produced at the Farnham kiln sites. Late 3rd-century.

35. Cable-patterned rim of a large store-jar of New Forest and Alice Holt type and probably made at the 4th-century potteries in the Farnham district.

36 and 37. Pieces of colour-coated beakers, the latter of a common shouldered and rouletted type. Circa A.D. 300.

(f) Pottery (*from level* 2) *found beneath the east and* west corridors, *and pre-dating the period II villa*. (Figs. 3b and 9).

38. Wide mouthed jar of dark grey ware, flecked with small white and black particles. Antonine—of about A.D. 200·

39. Samian cup base, form 33, with stamp of the Antonine potter Genialis, who worked at the Reinzabern pottery works. West corridor, level 2.

40. Samian bowl rim, with barbotine ornament, form 35. 2nd-century.

43. Piece of a decorated Samian ware bowl, form 30. Draped figure, with extended left arm. Circa A.D. 90-100. East corridor, level 2.

(g) From *beneath lime-slaking* trough *No.* 2, (Section *Fig.* 4a, level 2).

42. Carinated pot of dark brown-grey ware. Date—circa A.D. 100, this type (of which examples were found at the Purberry Shot, Ewell, and Ashtead Common sites) is a late form of the sharply carinated pots of Claudian and Flavian date.

44. (Unstratified).

Piece of a decorated Samian bowl (form 37) with part of a panel of leaf and tendril ornament, between vertical zig-zag lines. Date— circa A.D. 90-100.

SOME SURREY WILLS IN THE PREROGATIVE COURT OF CANTERBURY

BY

HILDA J. HOOPER

PART I

ALL wills in England were proved in the Ecclesiastical Courts up to the year 1858. If a testator owned land in more than one diocese, the will had to be proved in a higher court since a bishop had no jurisdiction over the affairs of another diocese. Such wills had to be proved in the Prerogative Court of Canterbury in London.

All Ecclesiastical jurisdiction over Probate ceased in 1858, and these F.C.C. wills are now preserved in the Principal Probate Registry at Somerset House. They represent the wills of almost all people of substance in England, and most great men. Each will was copied into a folio and the original was stored. The manuscript copies of wills are bound in large folios, in order of date, the folio being named after the first testator in the year. The MSS. indices to each year entered each will, in order of date, under alphabetical order. The years date from Lady Day (25th March) to Lady Day, as did Church Registers up to the Reform of the Calendar. In counting the years of a monarch's reign the year dated from the actual day and month of his accession to the Throne.

The spelling of names and words often varies widely in the same will. The word "cosen" means nephew or niece, more often than not. (For example : 1615 F.C.C. 84 Rudd, Mrs. Malyn Palmer, widow of Sir Henry Palmer of Lambourne, "My cosin Malyn wife of Mr. E. H. one of the gentlemen of the King's Chappell" ; and 1621 P.C.C. 67 Dale. Edmond H. . . . . Esq. "Mrs. Malyn Palmer, my wife's Aunt.") Son-in-law, father or brother-in-law generally means stepson, stepfather or stepbrother.

It is unfortunate that the Marriage Settlements are unavailable ; they provided for the issue of the marriage and would shed more light on the wills if any had been preserved. A few wills recapitulate the terms of the Marriage Settlement, but this is rare. An Inquisition Post Mortem was held, not to discover the cause of death, but to determine who were the rightful heirs. Many of these are to be found at the Record Office. There was an I.P.M. to every tenant-in-chief who held lands from the crown. The British Record Society has printed indices to all wills in the P.C.C. 1383 to 1685, indexed as to name and place. I have taken all wills up to 1566 to places in Surrey, beginning with the letters "ST" recording names, place-names and the main substance of the will.

My thanks are due to Mrs. A. E. Rowan, of Belsize Road, who did the Latin ones for me.

Some of the wills are very long. I have tried to indicate what information would reward a study of the entire document, and, above all, to preserve everything that gives a clue to the personality of the man behind the will.

1471 P.C.C.2 Wattys
Sir Thomas COBHAM, Knight, STARBOURGH

Dated 2nd April 1466. To be buried in parish church of St Peter within my college of Lyngfeld. My standing cross with the fote of silver and gilt to remain in said college and a suit of vestments of blewe cloth of gold. To repairs of said church xx^{li}. To the church of S. Thomas the Apostle[1] in the Ryall of London for any dues by me to the parson and curat. To same church my gowne of crimson velvet upon velvet. To Merton Abbey a velvet gown with prilled gold. To the Prior of the House of Chanons at Donmowe co Essex my chalices at Starbourgh and myn old masse books. To parish church of Stonbrig co Kent my litill pairs organes standing within the chapell of my castell of Starborough. To Sir Gervoys of Clyston knight my sawter book with silver and gilt clasps which he claimeth to be his own. Gifts to poor within a mile about my castle of Starbourgh, xx^{d} to each householder having a wife, to marriage of poor maidens, and other gifts of charity in parishes of Cowden Chiddingston Lyngfeld Stonebrigge. To the most Rev. father in God my gracious Lord Thomas Cardinal and Archbishop of Canterbury and primate of all England a book called Crayell. To Elizabeth Codington my servant III^{li} VI^{s} VIII^{d}. To Elizabeth Cobham dwelling with John Gayneford III^{li} VI^{s} VIII^{d}. To my base son Reynold called Reynold Cobham silver a salte made like a woman a little primer book a cross of gold with the four evangelists garnished with pearls and stones. These goods to be put into the hands of John Donne the elder citizen and mercer of London until Reynold is age twenty. If Reynold die, executors to sell the jewels etc. and devote proceeds for the wealth of my soul and Reynold's soul and to charity. Residue to Anne Vere my most entirely beloved lady and wife. Executors Thomas ffrowch and Richard fford gent and wife Ann. My daughter Ann Cobham. If her mother die Ann to be under the governance and keeping astis the good advice and discretion of my said Lord Cardinall and of the right high and mighty princess and my good lady the Duchesse of Bokyngham[2] unto the time

---

[1] Tower Royal, at the eastern end of the Church of S. Thomas the Apostle across the present College Hill. The wine merchants of La Reole, near Bordeaux, settled here during the reign of Edward I.

[2] The Barony of Cobham was originally in the family of the Duke of Buckingham. In the fifteenth century the family lived at Starborough Castle, near Edenbridge, and they rebuilt at that time the Church of S. Peter and S. Paul at Lingfield. Reynold Cobham (d. 1440) married Eleanor Colepeper. Their second son Thomas married Anna, widow of Aubrey de Vere and daughter of Humphry Stafford, Duke of Buckingham. See her will, 1472. See Calendar of I.P.M. and other documents preserved in P.R.O., Vol. II, Henry VII, pp. 585/6, Nos. 920, 923, also 884. I.P.M. Thomas Cobham, Commission of Concealments, 26th February, 20 Henry VII.

that Anne come to her lawful age or marriage. In witnes whereof
to this my present testament I have sett my seal the day and year
above writyn.

This is the last wil of me Thomas Cobham of Starborough co
Surrey, Knyght made at London 26 March 1471. The manor
of pentlowe called pentlowhalle with the advowson of the church
of the same town co. Essex and a pece of land in the town of
Canndishe co Suffolk, with advowson of the church there and all
the lands & tenements with appurtenances called Symond Londes
in parish of Stowbrigge, co. Kent and of all my place and Inne
called Ypres Inne[1] in the Parish of S. Thomas the Apostle in ye
Ryall in ye Cittie of London that is to say first I wil and require
that all such persons as are enfeoffed with me or to my use of said
lands and manors suffer my right trusty friend Gerveis Cliston
squire and uncle unto Reynold my base son called Reynold
Cobham and Hugh Mathewe my servant by the oversight of
John Clopton squire, co Suffolk to have the rule and governance
of said lands till Raynold come to age twenty or marriage and then
by deed indented the estate shall be to him and his heirs for
evermore. And if Raynold die then the manors to be sold, and of
the proceeds I bequeath to Sir Gerveis of Cliston Knight one
hundred marks if he then be on life and to . . . Cornynestrm and
to his children one hundred marks ; to Gerveis Cliston squire
and to his children one hundred marks thereof. The residue of the
money to be distributed in releving of poor householders and
bedred people within seven miles next about my Castell of Starborough and other dedes of charitie. Further more my wife to have
and occupy my place called Ypres Inne at her pleasure during
an hoole year next since my decease. And if John Denham knight
Lord Denham and Dame Elizabeth his wife daughter and heir of
Water Fitzwater late Lord Fitzwater do pay to my said entirely
beloved Lady and wyf & myn Executors one hundred pounds
of lawful English money at the ende of the year next after my
decease then the said place and Inne to be unto Lord Denham
and Dame Elizabeth and their children, Remainder in default of
such heirs to the right heirs of Water ffitzwater. And if John Lord
Denham and Dame Elizabeth will not paie the said c^{li} then the
said Ypres Inne to be sold and the money disposed in alms to
poor people and in dedes of charity. In witnes thereof I put my
seal.

Probate 10th July 1471 to Executors.

1413 P.C.C.28 Marche (Latin will)
    Thomas SWYFT, STOCKWELL, Surrey

Dated 27th September 1413. To be buried in the church of
S. Mary Northlambhithe co. Surrey facing the altar of St. John.
To repairs of said church twenty pounds and to said altar of

---

[1] Ypres Inn was a mansion built by William of Ypres, a favourite of King
Stephen.

S. John a missal chalice and vestment etc. For my burial twenty marks. For the poor in said parish of Northlambhithe. For prayer for me and for souls of the faithful departed twenty markes. Thirteen torchbearers to follow my body three chaplains to be at the ceremony and to pray for my soul. Twenty shillings for the road which leads to the said church lying between the tenements of Peter Swyft and of John Archer. Twenty pounds for repairing the King's Highway which leads to Southlamehithe. All residue of goods and chattels and all debts owing paid I give to my Executors namely Peter Swyft John Sondford John Werying John Fox, to lay out for my soul and the souls of my parents.

Proved 3rd October 1413 by Executors Peter Swyft John Sondford John Clevynge John Fox.

Note.—Lambeth originally Lambhithe, *cf.* Queenhithe, Rotherhithe, Stebonhithe (now Stepney). The earliest record of Lambeth is a charter of King Edward the Confessor, dated 1062, confirming a grant of Lambe-hithe with all fields, pastures, meadows, woods and water thereto belonging to the Abbey of Waltham, Essex.

1509 P.C.C.24 Bennet
Rauf LYGH, of STOCKWELL, LONDON, LAMBETH

Dated 7th November 1st year of Henry VIII. My body to be conveyed to Lamehithe at expense of x^{li} there should not be above v^{li} spent at my funeral. I require my wife to cause three trentals to be sung for me one at the freers of Greenwich another at Charterhouse of London and a third at Syon. I bequeath to God and my broder all my children if my brother will have them desiring him of brotherhood to be good to them. Executrix my wife and to her I commit the rule of my children goods and land.

Probate Feb. 1st 1509-10 to Executrix.

Note.—See the recorded inscription on his tomb in the Legh Chapel at Lambeth, now destroyed: "Raufe Legh son of Raufe Leghe of Stockwell Esquire and brother to Sir John Leghe of Stockwell Knight which Raufe Legh deceased Nov 6th 1509."

Rauf Legh's children were John, Rauf, Isabel, Joyce, Margaret, the eldest son John being under age twenty-four in 1523.

The Legh Chapel of S. Nicholas at Lambeth Church, now destroyed. John Leigh of Ridge in Cheshire married Alice, daughter and heir of John Alcock. He bore arms "argent, a chevron sable with three cocks heads erased gules." The inscription on his brass in Lambeth is recorded as "John Lighe armiger quondam serviens ad arma cu Domino Rege duo decimo quinto Aprilis 1445." He had a son Roger who married Eleanor, daughter of Robert Leigh, one of the same family. Their son Roger married Eleanor, daughter of . . . Sutton, but died childless. John Leigh's third son, also named John Leigh "of the Rigge," Esquire, changed the Leigh coat of arms to "gules a crosse eng. engraved ar. within (a bordure) invected ar." He died 1453. His son Rauf (Ralph)

Leigh of Stockwell purchased the manors of Stockwell and Levehurst in 1461 and had a lease of the manor of Leigham in Streatham.
He was Knight of the Shire for Surrey in 1460. The manor of
Leigham was granted by Ela, wife of Jordan de Sackville, in
1152 to the Prior and Convent of Bermondsey. It was conveyed
to Henry Knight in 1534 and passed to Henry VIII in 1549.

A recorded inscription on a tomb in Lambeth Chapel was to
"Elizabeth late wife of Rauf Legh Esquire sometyme lord of the
Manors of Stockwell and Levehurst which Elizabeth was daughter
of Henry Langley of Richinge Co. Essex Esquire. The said
Elizabeth died August 2nd 1479 and the said Rauf was son of John
Legh of the Rigge Esquire in the Shyre of Cheshire which Rauf
died 22 August 1470 and is buried in the Church of Abbey of S^t
Maria at Winchester." On the same brass are shown four sons
and nine daughters to the said Rauf.

According to *Miscellanea Genealogica et Heraldica*, Vol. I,
pp. 163, 213-4, 246, another inscription read, "Rodolphus Leghe
generosus serviens et consanguinens Joh'is Leghe de Surrey
armiger qui obiit 1490." Also : "Raufe Legh son of Rauf Leghe
of Stockwell Esquire and brother to Sir John Leghe of Stockwell
Knight which Raufe Legh deceased Nov 6th 1509." *Miscellanea
Genealogica* has a pedigree which states that Ralph Leigh married
"Joyce daughter of Richard Colepeper who bare arms 'ar a bend
eng. g. with an annulet or'." There is no reference to any such
marriage in the will of Dame Isabel, who refers to the children of
Ralph Legh as her "cosens."

An inscription on a marble tomb ran : "Sir John Leghe Knight
of the Bath son of Rauf Legh Esq., Lord of the Manors of Stockwell and Levehurst and Isabel his wife daughter of Otwell Wurseley
which Sir John deceased Aug 28 1523."

Isabel Wurseley, of Stamworth, married (1) Richard Culpeper
of Aylesford, Kent, son of Sir William and grandson of Sir John
Culpeper. Their children were Thomas, who died young, and
daughters Margaret and Joyce. She married (2) Sir John Legh.
Margaret married William Cotton of Oxenhoath, Esquire, and
Joyce married Sir Edmund Howard. Her youngest child was
Katherine, fifth Queen of Henry VIII. The Culpeper arms were :
ar, a bend engrailed gu.

John Legh, son of Ralph (deceased 1509), was married by 1522
to Elizabeth, daughter of Sir Roger Darcy, deceased, by his wife
Elizabeth, daughter of Sir Henry Wentworth. Elizabeth's mother
married (2) Sir Thomas Wyndham, who died 1522, and whose
name is mentioned in Sir John Legh's will in the matter of the
marriage settlement. John Legh and Elizabeth had an only child
Anne, who married (1) Sir Thomas Paston, and (2) Edward
ffitzgarrett.

Ralph, younger brother of Sir John, married Margaret, daughter
of William Ireland, armiger, and died before 1563. Their son
John married Margery, daughter of William Sanders, and their

son, Sir John Leigh, Knight, married a daughter of Thomas West, brother to Lord de la Warr.

In the "glasse window" of the Chapel were shown the arms of Langley and Walden matched together, then Walden and Legh, and after, Legh and Culpeper.

The manor of Stockwell was conveyed to Henry VIII in 1547 by John Legh.

1523 P.C.C.15 Bodfield
Sir John LEGH, Knight of the Bath, STOCKWELL

Dated 16th June, 1523. To be buried in the Chapell by me late byelded in the Parish Church of Lameheth co Surrey. To mother church of S. Swithyn in Winchester vi^s and to the Gray freres in London whereof I am a brother, and the Chantry of Stockwell in parish of Lamehith. My new Stockwell Chapell to be repaired at need from revenues of the manor of Stokwell and Levehurst. My nevewe John Legh my brother Rauf Legh's son and heir to have manors as by indenture made by me and Sir Thomas Wyndham Knight late deceased and he therewith to hold him well contented for it is a c^{li} more than my father left me. My manor of Stokwell to my wife Dame Isabel for life and after her death to John Legh at age twenty four. If she die before then the manor to remain in Executors hands during interval. At death of wife Executors to hold all such lands etc. as my wife hath to the value of cc^{li} as my said wife holdeth in dower of the Dowment of her first husband until John Legh be age 24. If John die without lawful issue the remaynder to Rauf Legh brother to said John. Executors to take lands except those of the joynture of the wife of said John Legh, except manor of Effingham.

Failing Rauf remaynder in turn to Isabel Legh sister of John and Rauf & her lawful issue to Joyce Legh my neece and sister to said Isabel to Margaret Legh my neece another sister then failing these to Erasmus ffurde Dorothy Martyn Elizabeth Spilman Johane Illingworth. Failing all these and their heirs remaynder to my cosyn Roger Legh to Thomas Legh his brother to George Legh his brother to William Legh to Frances Langley my cosyn. To my nephew Rauf Legh my brother Rauf Legh's son my great cheyne and my cross of gold and a flat hope that was his fathers and to have lands at Padyngden Co Surrey and in parish of Abingworth otherwise Abyngrowe Valued at L^{li} ii^s ii^d 1 lb. wax a capon, etc at age twenty four. Also all those manors bought of Thomas Bareham and of John Holden and Anne his wife in Kent to John Legh. If he have no heirs then to Henry Howard son of Lord Edmond Howard and Dame Joyce his wife, with remaynder in turn if no heirs to Charles Howard George Howard Isobel Legh Joyce Legh Margaret Legh Erasmus fford Dorothy Martyn Elizabeth Spilman Johane Illingworth Roger Legh Thomas Legh George Legh William Legh Francis Langley his heirs. If the Howards trouble the Executors they are to have nothing. If any others make trouble the difficulty to be expounded and ordered by Sir Richard Broke Knight of Kings Bench John Rooper the Kings attorney John Spylman Serjeant at law and Roger Legh. My wife to have my park at Layham for life the parsonage of Epsom which I have in fferm of the Abbot and convent of Chertsey. My nephewe Rauf Legh to have X^li to find him at Clifford's Inn for three years and at the Temple XVI^li VI^s VIII^d yearly till age 24. John Legh to have my manor of Effingham. Annuities to servants William Parre XX^s Randall Goldsmyth XX^s to Francis Langley LXVI^s VIII^d. To Edmund Benet my horse keper X^s. To St Christpofer ye eld at Lamehith VII^s VIII^d. To parson of Clapham for tithes to parson of Batersey. William Woodward to be clerk to Executors. Overseers my cosyn John Gaynsford Knight of Crowhurst and my cosyn Erasmus fforde. Signature to date 12th June 15th Henry VIII Witness Rauf Legh Sir Richard Deane priest Francis Langley William Woodward Nicholas Hill William Hill John Savage and others.

List of lands with yearly values over the quit-rent

Manor of Padyngton XVIII^li VII^s XI^d 3 lbs wax a capon and a pounde of pepper.

Lands in Cranlegh Albery & Wonersh called Strodeland XL^s.

Manor of Westland in Ockley L^s VI^d.

Lands in Cranlegh Wonersh and Albery late Northowe LX^s.

Lands in Shyre which John Seymon hath to ferm VII^s V^d & 2 hennes.

Lands in Shyre late bought by William Sawyer XLVIII^s III^d.

Lands in Wotton which Thomas Beldhm and John Ulvan hath to ferm XLVIII^s.

Lands in Shalford Hastcombe Bramlegh which Robert Combes and John Michell hath to ferm XL^s.

Lands in Okleigh which John Shalford hath to ferm and Thomas Shalford XXIII^s V^d.

Lands in parish of Oxsted X^li VIII^s II^d.

Lands in West Landon and Merew late bought of William Leger XXVI^s VIII^d.

The manor of Effingham hannsarde XXXIX^s VI^d.

Manor of Samers in Asshested XLII^s II^d.

The sum of all the values of said rents L^li II^s I^d and three lbs wax a capon a pound of pepper two hens.

A codicil 26th August gives leave for part of the land to be used in marriage settlements.

Probate to Dame Isabel Legh relict, Executrix Dec 10th 1523.

See I.P.M. Chancery Series C142/40/12 (2) John Leigh, 16th Henry VIII.

1527 P.C.C.18 Porch

> Dame Isabel LEIGH late wife of Sir John LEIGH, STOCK-
> WELL

Dated 6th April 18th year of Henry VIII. To be buried in
the Chapel of St Nicholas where my husband lieth buried. To
the brotherhood of St Christopher in said Church and to repairs of
ornament in the chantry chapel of Stockwell. To my daughter
my Lady Howard wife of my lord Sir Edmunde Howarde knight
my best gold chain with a cross hanging upon the same my
gown of black velvett lined with crimson velvett and my gown of
chamlett furred with marterns my last wedding ring, jewellery
and plate (described). To my daughter Margaret Cotton wife of
William Cotton Esquire my collar of gold a harness of gold for a
girdle my gown of black velvett furred white also one of black
chamlett lined with bokera and black velvett, etc. To my daughter
Elizabeth Legh wife of my cosen John Leygh jewels. To my cosen
John Legh Esquire plate and all my goods in Leigham Park and
my yeares interest in the mores Londe and meadow in parish of
Batersey holden to ferme of the Abbot and Convent of Westminster
To my cosen Rauf Leigh goods plate a St Anthony Cross and my
ring of gold called hoopes. To Elizabeth Leigh if unmarried at my
departing a crosse of gold with the four Evangelists. To my
servant Margaret Metcalfe. To my cosens Joyce Stanney and
Joyce Carleton and goddaughter Joyce Welbeek xx^s apiece and
v^{li} to be divided equally between Margaret Welbeck[1] and the
children of my daughter Cotton and her husband. My said Lady
my daughter to have x^{li} to find Richard Lee and Agnes Lee if they
be living. To every wife in Stockwell an ell of linen cloth price
xii^d or else xii^d in money. To Humphrey Charrossez wife
vi^s viii^d to my nece Noks xx^s to my nece Welden xx^s To
Margaret Legh x^{li} silver, clothing and a playne mazer. To Charles
Howarde Henry George Margaret Catherine Howarde xx^s each
to Mary Howarde my goddaughter x^{li} To said Elizabeth Legh
wife to John Legh my long harness of gold with a pearl To
my sons Sir Edmund Howarde and William Cotton to pray for me
xx^{li}. To repairs of the Highway from Harreys field to the crosse
toward Lambhithe vi^{li}. All the Residue to my daughter Lady
Howarde upon condition that her husband redeem all lands the
inheritance of my daughter in co Kent from her father Richard
Colpeper and her brother Thomas Colpeper so that the lands
descend to her heirs according to the will of Sir John Colpeper
Knight. The said Lord Edmund and Joyce his wife shall find
sureties for true performance within a month after my decease
Executors my nephew Edward Lee clerk the Kings Almoziner
John Carleton gent John Legh Esquire   Witnesses my lord
Edmund Howard knight John Legh Esquire Rauf Legh gent.

---

[1] Joyce and Margaret Welbeck, daughters of William Welbeck or Welbek,
Citizen and Haberdasher in London.

Sir Richard dean preste John Carleton gent my lady Howarde Elizabeth Leigh Joan Kelycke.

Codicil 28 April 18th Henry VIII made one John Leigh Esquire of one Executor of my last will written with the hand of John Carleton being dated 11 April 1527 the which testament I wil shall stand in his full strength to be obeyed in every part except Thomas Argall be put out of said will and to be noon of my executor.

Probate 26th May 1527 to Edward Lee and John Carleton and John Legh Executors.

It seems clear that Thomas a Lee of Streatham, who died 1504 (see P.C.C.7 Holgrave), was one of the above family.

1565 P.C.C.3 Crymes
Sir John LEGH, Knight, of STOCKWELL, LONDON, LAMBETH

Dated 30th April 1563. To be buried in Parish Church of Lambeth in chappel made by my uncle Sir John Legh late of Stockwel knight deceased, or else in Parish church of S. Margaret Lothbury in the City of London where I do partly inhabit. A tombe at cost of xx^{li} to be made with my Image and arms to be graven in Lattyn and the similitude of the Cross of Jerusalem that is on my breaste cutt in my flesh. If I die more than sixty miles from London to be buried where convenient. For cost of funeral c^{li}. To poor xx^{li}. To Richard Blonte my servant fifty poundes of English money. To Thomas Rice my sisters son one hundred marks if the said Thomas be with me at howre of my decease. To my cosen Marie Marten x^{li} and to ffrances Martyn her sister x^{li}. To Sir George Hawarde knight c^{li} to my goddaughter my lord William Hawarde daughter c^{li} to Jane Arundell daughter of Sir Thomas Arundell knight one hundred marks. To children of my sister Joyce Staney deceased c^{li} to be divided among them at age 21 or marriage. To John Henry Arthur Lovelace and Elizabeth Lovelace children of John Leigh Esquire late deceased x^{li} apiece at 21 or marriage. To Richard Rice and Elynor Ryce children of my sister Margaret deceased c^{li} to be divided as above said. To Frances Leigh daughter of my brother Raffe Leghe c^{li}. To my son in lawe Edward ffitzgarrett my collar of golde with stories enameled and to him and my daughter the Ladie Agnes Paston his wife L^{li} worth of my plate. Item three hundereth pounds lawful English money to the daughters of the said Edward ffitzgarrett by my daughter Agnes Paston provided the said Edward ffitzgarrett shall find two sureties to be bound in the sum of six hundreth pound to my executors at the receipt of the said ccc^{li} that it shal be put in a stock for his daughters at age 21 or marriage. If the daughters die then to the sons of said Edward and Agnes. To Edward Paston the younger son of Sir Thomas Paston knight c^{li} to Katherine Paston his sister cc^{li}. To Mr. Whetill Esquire c^{li} Bequests and provision made for servants in Lothbury. The

Residue of my goods chattels plate ready money furniture apparel
to my nephew John Legh. Overseers of will Sir Nicholas Bacon
Knight Lord Keeper of the great seale of England, Lord Montague
Roger Manwoode Esquire. Executors Thomas Lovelace Esquire
Sir Thomas Cotton knight Thomas ffelton of Clerkenwell co
Mdx Esquire and my servante Richard Blonte. Elizabeth my
wife in recompence of her joynture which she had of certayn
manors in co Surrey shall be paid an annuity of XXXIII^{li} VI^s
VIII^d out of my manor of Hilton co. Dorset. An annuity of
VI^{li} XIII^s IV^d out of my manor of Hilton Dorset to Richard Blonte
if with me at time of my death. My nephew John Leghe to
grant to Thomas Rice if he be with me at time of my death an
annuity of XIII^{li} VI^s VIII^d out of the Manor of Co Williton co
Somerset. To Henry Rice brother of said Thomas an annuity of
X^{li} out of my manor of Hilton. To my nephewe John Legh son
and heir of my brother Raffe Legh deceased manors in countie of
Buckingham and Oxford late bought of Sir Frances Stowe Knight
and all lands. Witnesses John Birche John Jeffrey Thomas
Bradshawe, mercer, Nicholas Barham William Sleywright Richard
Bostocke Peter Baker and others.

March 8. 1563

Codicil One hundred pounds more to Dame Agnes Paston.
Her husband to have three of my best furred gowns all my furs
that be to make up. To Xtopher Lacelle Esquire C^{li}. To my cosen
Whetelle daughter dwelling with my lady of Pembroke the C^{li}
which Sir James Stompe knight deceased gave me in his will the
which some my sister Stompe must pay To my servants John
Dyckby X^{li} Jacob X^{li} Anthony V^{li} John Colly X^{li} to Harmon Johnson the horsekeeper V^{li}. And to Richard Blonte XIII^{li} V^s VIII^d
more. To my Lord Keper my collar of golde or fifty pounds. To
my Lord Montague my best hobbye or one of my best horses.
To Mr. Baker scryvenor VIII^{li}.

Probate 5th Feb. 1565-6 to Thomas Lovelace Richard Blonte,
Executors.

Note.—See Inquisition Post Mortem Sir John Legh, 20th
August, 1565, at Guildford. C142/141/26.

Before Edward Bray, milite, Edmund fforde Thomas Brown
William More armiger. The Jury are Ralph Ellingworth gent
Lawrence Ellyott Richard Myddleborowe Alain Colcoke Edmund
Cutton Chrystopher Brystowe. The manor of Boddeles and
Upgrove and messuage Lyon Inn in Guildford. On 7th March
5th Elizabeth, John Legh, by deed indented, granted to Thomas
Felton Roger Marwood and Richard Blont gent said manor and
messuage to the use of John Legh himself for life and after to
John son of Rauf Legh his brother deceased and his heirs for ever.
Failing issue to him, to Agnes Paston wife of Edward ffitzgarrett,
said Agnes is age 34 at death of her father. Failing issue to her,
then in turn, remainder to Thomas, Henry, Richard Rice, George
Stanney, Henry, Francis Baynton, Matthew Arundel, Charles

K

Arundel. Failing all these, to right heirs of John Legh. John Legh son of Rauf Legh entered into said manor.

1416 F.C.C.33 Marche. (Latin will)
>William CREYSER Esq., armiger. of STOKE D'ABERNON
Dated 17th October 1415.
To be buried in the chancel of the parish church of St Mary Stokedabernon, & bequest to building of said church. Bequests to Winchester Cathedral to the poor at my funeral to the preacher at Gildeford. To John Talworth.
Executors Sir Henry Hyde rector of parish church of Fecham, and William Smyth rector of Stokedabernon and my wife Edith. All residue to my said wife Edith.
Witnesses present Master Robert Levick and Henry Hampshire at Stokedabernon said day and year.
Probate 17 April 1416 to Edith, the widow of testator.
Note.—See Inquisition Post Mortem, 17th August, 6th Henry V. William Croyser Refer *S.A.C.*, Vol. X, pp. 283-287 inclusive. Daughter Ann, age 9 years plus, was his heir.
In 1404 William Croyser was Knight of the Shire of Surrey. William Creyser died Monday, 9th November, holding jointly with Edith his wife manors of Stoke D'abernon, Aldbury and Fetcham. I.P.M. 21 May, 14th Henry V, Edith Croyser. June 1st, 1418. Anne, next heir aged 13, married to Ingleran Bruyn, son of Sir Maurice Bruyn, Knight. Edith Croyser married (2) Sir Maurice Bruyn.
See brass of Lady Ann, daughter of William and Edith Croyser and wife of Sir Henry Norbury, Knight. She died 12th October, 1464.

1418 P.C.C.41 Marche. (Latin will)
>Edith BRUNE (BRUYN) formerly CROYSER, STOKE-
>DABERNON
Date 25th April 1418. Edith wife of Sir Maurice Bruyn Knight mentions "my manor of Stokedabernon." The mother church of Winchester, the church of Stokedabernon and the poor there and in Fechinam and Aldebury. My tenements in town of Stokedabernon and of Fechinam and Aldbury.
Executors Sir Maurice Bruyn knight, my husband, Sir Thomas Welton Sir John Mawry clerk, Sir John Bryunne, Master Robert Keton.
Examined in presence of witnesses William Wolsey John Clerk Willimo Langley of Bokenham diocese of Kent.

1431 P.C.C.14 Luffenham. (Latin will)
>Richard TYRRELL Esquire of STOKDABERNOUN
Dated 26th May 1431. To be buried in the church of Soppewell. I give ten marks for repairs there and to the nuns of the said church and to the Freres of Gilford for repairs of the church and especially the rode lofte of Stoke. The remainder of my goods I give to William Estfold, Mercer and Alderman of London

Dame Alionore Hull Roger **Husewyff** prest and to Amy my wife whom I make Executors of my testament to dispose for the profite and wel of my soul after their discretion.

Overseer Sir Nicholl Dixon, Clerk. Written at Stokdabernoun 26th May 1431 "with myn owen hand"

Proved 10th July 1431 by Executors named, and on 23rd September execution completed.

1464 F.C.C.5 Godyn and 8 Godyn. (Latin will)
    John RYPON of STOKE NEXT GULDEFORD

Dated 5th September 1464. To be buried in the Church of St. John Evangelist of Stoke. I leave to the mother church of Winton six pence. To Margaret my daughter ten marks sterling. I give to John Clerke of Stoke a russet cloak. The residue of all my goods to Agnes my wife she to be my executor. And I appoint John **Sturmyn** Executor with her.

Proved at **Lamehith** 14th September 1464 by the Executors named in the will. A full Inventory to be made of all and singular goods etc.

    P.C.C.8 Godyn. (Latin will)

Will of John Rypon of Stoke next Guildeforde 5th September 1464 (Identical with the will registered 5 Godyn).

1503 F.C.C.22 Blamyr
    William COMBES of STOKE nygh GULDEFORD, gent.

Dated 31st January 1500-01. To be buried before the Rood in Stoke Church if I happen to be there. To the High Altar of Stoke XIII^s IV^d for tithes. To the repairs of Trinity Church to S. Mary's Church and S. Nicholas church XX^d apiece. To the frdres of **Guldford** for a trental[1] to be done for me there XIII^s IV^d. After my departure LXVI^s VIII^d to be dealt to poor people in alms. Also I will that Anne my wife bring me conveniently to my long home. I will that my executor do lay a stone upon me within a yere after my departing and shall receive the profits of my lands besides my wifes joynture during nonage of my son William till the some of XL^{li} be fully received the which some of forty pounds I bequeath to my daughters every of them twenty marks and every of them to be others heir. I will that the overplus of said lands to be stored upon fynding of my children to schole and upon reparacon of lands. My brother Thomas shall have my team of oxen with the Weyne and harness thereto belonging and my best horse and the half occupying of the ferm of Stoke during my yeres. Also my brother Henry fifteen marks towards his lerninge and mete and drynke with my wife till he be provided of a master. My sister Julian to have in money at her departing to household LXVI^{li} VIII^d. Residue to wife Anne. Executors my wife Ann and Thomas Combez my brother Supervisor William Coope.

    Probate 11th April 1503 to Executors.

[1] A trentall is either masses for thirty days or a mass on the thirtieth day after decease.

1503 P.C.C.24 Blamyr

John WHELAR of STOKE next GULDEFORD

Dated 5th August 18th year of Henry VII. To be buried in chapel of our Lady in parish church of the blessed Trinity in Guldeford. To the mother church of Wynchester xII^d. To high altar of parish church of Trinity for tithes xx^d, and x^s. To parish church of the Blessed Lady at Guldford and S. Nicholas in Guldford xx^d. To house and church of freres preacher in Guldford xIII^s IIII^d. To parish church of Stoke next Guldford and parish churches of Worplesden Compton Shalford and Merowe. To my godchildren who are living fourpence. Residue to Isabell my wife and to John Chabeleyn, Executors. Isabell immediately after my death shall have to her and her heirs for ever all my lands tenements barns gardens etc in burgh of Gulford also all the lands with a barn set there-upon within burgh of Gulford which I late purchased of Robert Sandes. Witness Sir Richard Chapman preest Sir Thomas Gate preest, John Perkyn Thomas Greene William Baker and many others.

Probate 16th August 1503 to Executors.

See Register F at Canterbury.

1529 F.C.C.5 Jankyn

Thomas POLSTED the elder of STOKE next GULDE-FORD Surrey
HENLEY upon Thames Oxford

Dated 6th March 20th Henry VIII. To be buried in church of Stoke next Guldeford before the Rood there. To church of Holy Trinity in Guldeford xx^{li}. Prayers to be said for my soul and my father's and mother's soul and of Henry Elyott Robert Bekingham and Elizabeth his wife and for Laurence Harryson's soule for six year. An annual rent of xx^s to be granted out of the Londes called Craces as of all other lands in Guldford which were somtyme Henry Cowpers to such persons as Alice Cowper widow late wife of said Henry Cowper shall name to the intent that there be a yearly obite kept in parish church of S. Marie Guldford according to the will of Henry Cowper. Alice Cowper to occupy all the lands for her lifetime. To Margaret my daughter £50 at marriage if she marry with her mothers consent. Residue of goods to be divided in three parts among my wife Agnes and sons Thomas and Henry Polsted. My wife to have my lands in Stoke next Guldford and a wood called Swanmede for life and after her decease and the decease of Alice Cowper all lands to my son Thomas Polsted. Failing issue to him remaynder in turn to Henry Polsted Margaret Polsted Henry Polsted my brother John Polsted my brother and Thomas Jones of Wytley. My wife and two sons to have rule and guidance of Anthony Elmes to be well brought up in learning and all lands that were his fathers and mothers to said Anthony at age 21. My two sons to see the chantry priest at Henley his wage paid every year so that they sing for every yere yerely an obite to value of twenty pounds for the soules of Humfrey Elmes and Elizabeth his wife. To Blackfreres at Guldford. Executors, wife Agnes and sons Thomas and Henry Polsted & John Polsted Witnesses John Parkyns David Yngge John Coke John Polsted.

Probate 22 April 1529 to Executors.

Note.—See *S.A.C.*, Vol. II, p. 59, for pedigree of the family of Polsted. Also *S.A.C.*, Vol. XV, p. 37. "Henry Polsted gent citizen and merchant taylor of London died 1556, Dec. 25." Palimpsest brass at Sanderstead.

1556 P.C.C. Ketchyn
Henry POLSTED Esquire, ALBURY, Surrey

Dated 1st August 1555. Executors wife Alice William More Esquire and John Brace gent, and Richard Polsted my son to be an executor at age 21. Richard Polsted to have farm of Wonersh in Surrey and the farm of the parsonage of St. Osites co. Essex and my farm at Stoneham at age 21. If he die then to my daughter Jone wife to Thomas Sambourne, and her sons Henry and Hugh Beke to have Stoneham and Henry Perker and Brian Ansley the farms of both parsonages. My wife to take profits of my farm of Prailand and if Richard Polsted die, then after my wifes death to Henry Weston my servant. My wife to take profit of farm commonly called Lolesworth otherwise Spitalfields in Middlesex solong as she liveth unmarried. If she marry my overseers William More and John Brace to take profits towards bringing up of said Henry Beke until my son Richard be 21. If he die the farm to said Henry and failing him with remainder in turn to Hugh Beke or to their mother my daughter Samborne. To poor of Gilford and to the Spital there iiii^{li}. To my brother John Maynard.

I am not seized of any manors or land in capite. To wife Alice my manors of Albury and Wildwood and my house called Channtery House and lands of Shere and other lands in Alfold Shere and Albury for life and after to son Richard. Failing him to my uncle Henry Polsted for life with remainder to Thomas Polsted failing him to Francis Polsted his brother. To wife in satisfaction of her dower lands etc. in Pagham and Yaxton co Sussex being sometyme Chantry lands and also farme land called Byrkley and farm called leyth in psh of Shalford and woods etc. called Kingefold Southland and hobbis and lands in Ridgwyke co Sussex sometime also chantry lands my manor of Speldherst co Kent and advowson there and a messuage and storehouse in psh of Allhallows Berking London and after her to son Richard. To Anthonye Elmes Squier my nephew my manor called Bayliss in Sussex and lands in Wratlinge which were Elizabeth Elmes widow my sisters daughter and heir of . . . Pakker and mother of said Anthony which same Elizabeth left me in her will in the Prerogative Court. To my daughter Jone Samborne my barne and close in psh of S. Giles

Redinge Berks. If my son Richard die my parcel of land and wood in Billinghurst Sussex my copies wood called Tillinghokes in Shere to Ann the wife of Robert Clerk gent and remainder to Brian Ansley her son and Nicholas Ansley his brother remaynder to Henry Berde. My messuage called Horne meads and pasture called Watforde Close in Stoke and all my litel pightell there by Mongers house and land in Cranley to Elizabeth the wife of John Henning-wer for life. Julyan Both widow her son Cuthbert Blackden and her son John Both. Overseers John Carrell Wm More Esq John byrche John Agmondesham John Brace John Statham gent to have order and disposing of lands until son Richard be 21. John Gawdye Esq Sergeant at law Robert Kylwaye Richard Blackwell Richard Randall Sir Guy Wade Esquier to advise from time to time. Witness William More John Byrch John Brace gent.

Probate 15th May 1556 to relict Alice Polsted and John Brace.

Note.—See *S.A.C.*, Vol. XV, p. 132. Richard Polsted of Albury, Esquire, marriage to Elizabeth, first daughter of William More of Loseley, Esquire.

See wills : 1511 Dame Elizabeth Elmes, P.C.C.1 Fetiplace ; 1526 Elizabeth Elmes, Humphrey Elmes, P.C.C.11 Porch ; 1576 Richard Polsted, P.C.C.6 and 33 Carew.

Francis Polsted Albury, P.C.C.38 Langley.

1516 F.C.C.25 Holder

Gilbert STOUGHTON, CHALGROVE, Oxford, BEA-CONSFIELD, Bucks, STOUGHTON, Surrey

Date 7th April 1516. To be buried Beaconsfield Buckingham-shire. To Marion my wife the Manor of Stoughton in Suthery for life she making no waste. To my two daughters fourty pounds to be paid at marriage out of the rent of the manor of Stoughton and a ground called Aldham. To John my son the manor of Estbury. The freres of the place of Gilforth to have a yearly rent of ten pounds out of my ground calld Mowrtysley for ever-more. Executrix my wife Marion. Supervisors of will Master William Yong dwelling at Wytham in Berkshire and William Westbroke dwelling in Suthery. Witnesses Domino henrico Rither Thomas Halfarre Phillipo Purtey John Elyott.

Probate at Lamhithe 7th November 1516 to Marion, relict and Executrix.

Note.—Gilbert Stoughton, educated for the Bar, was Escheator of Surrey and Sussex in 1492 and 1493. He lived at Chalgrove in Oxford, where he died. See *History of Surrey*, by G. W. Brayley, pp. 444-5. See *S.A.C.*, Vol. XII, for the pedigree of Gilbert Stoughton, wife Marianna, daughter of Robert Beardsey of London. Eldest son Laurence and sons Anthony, John and George. See will of Laurence Stoughton, 1572, P.C.C.12 Daper, and of George, 1563, F.C.C.23 Chayre.

THE STAINED GLASS OF GUILDFORD GUILDHALL

BY

BERNARD RACKHAM, C.B., F.S.A.

I N a manuscript volume of the Borough records of Guildford,[1] on p. 26, is the following entry :—

> "*Item* that this yeare the Guildhall of the Towne of Guldeford was enlarged & made longer att the north ende And the Queenes Armes and the Armes of this Towne sett in the windowe att that north ende."

The entry (which has the title "The Guilhall [*sic*] enlarged" in the margin) is without a date, but the next following entry includes the date 26th May in the 31st year of Queen Elizabeth, and the last date preceding it is twenty days after the feast of St. Hilary, in the same year of her reign. We may therefore conclude that the lengthening of the Guildhall was carried out in the year 1589, when George Austen was Mayor.

Dr. G. C. Williamson quotes the entry, with some inaccuracies (notably "windows" for "windowe") and a wrong date, on p. 1 of his book on the Guildhall.[2] He goes on to say that "inasmuch as Queen Elizabeth's arms and the arms of the town do still appear at the north end of the Town Hall, it seems probable that this entry, on the Monday after Hilary, the 31st of Elizabeth (1588-89), refers to a part of the existing building.'

The present article is not concerned with the date of the existing structure as a whole, but with the three heraldic panels to be seen among plain leaded glass in the large window above the dais at the north end of the hall. They were taken down for safety during the war and have recently (1949) been replaced ; the opportunity was taken of studying and photographing the panels at close quarters.

It is curious that Dr. Williamson leaves it to be inferred that there are only two shields in the window and says nothing of a third ; nor does he seem to have perceived that, although one of the shields is charged with the Tudor royal arms as borne by Queen Elizabeth, the shield with the arms of Guildford is entirely different from this in style and technique, but accords with the third shield, which shows the arms not of Elizabeth but of Denmark, in reference undoubtedly to Anne of Denmark, Queen of James I. Several questions consequently arise which can only be answered conjecturally by a detailed examination of the three panels.

---

[1] *Guildford Court Book 28 Eliz.–27 Chas. II (1586–1675).*
[2] *The Guild Hall of Guildford and its* Treasures, Guildford, 1928.

The earliest of the three (Plate VII) is that with the royal arms, quarterly, France Modern and England, as borne by Elizabeth and her predecessors in the 15th and 16th centuries. The shield is badly damaged, but shows interesting technical features. The lilies of France, in golden-yellow glass, have been inserted in openings ground out of the blue pot-metal of the field. The technique has been obscured by repairing leads in the first quarter of the shield, but is seen unimpaired in the fourth ; this process, calling for a high degree of skill in the glazier, was first introduced into England in the 15th century. In the second and third quarters, also much damaged, the lions have been rendered by abrasion—that is, by grinding away the "flash" of the ruby glass so that only the "white" (colourless) sheet remains, which is then stained with silver-yellow to give the gold tincture of the charge. The shield is enclosed by the Garter, with motto in the Roman capitals introduced under the influence of Italian artists in the reign of Henry VIII. An irrelevant fleur-de-lis, probably from another royal shield now lost, has been inserted in the front of the crown which surmounts the whole. The interval between the shield and the Garter is filled with dark green glass coated with a thin smear of grey enamel through which a feathery diaper has been scratched, a feature seldom found in English glass-painting after the reign of Elizabeth. It is possible that this shield may be the Queen's arms inserted in the north window in 1588, as related in the town records, although the style and technique show little advance from that which already prevailed under Henry VIII. On this panel a name, *Richd Simmonds* (presumably that of a glazier who repaired it), and the date August 10th, 1885 (or perhaps 1835—it is not very clear) have been scratched with a diamond, as well as a name (*Castillis* ?) not easily legible.

The two other panels are much damaged, patched and jumbled, but seem originally to have been made both at the same time, presumably in the reign of James I if not also in the lifetime of Anne of Denmark, whose arms are displayed in one of them ; she died in 1619, six years before her husband. The technique is here widely different from that of the earlier panel, which is still essentially that of the mediæval glass-painter. We no longer find coloured "pot-metal" (*i.e.*, glass dyed throughout its substance by the admixture of a colouring oxide during the manufacture, whilst the glass is in a molten state in the furnace); instead, the necessary colours have been obtained by painting on plain white glass in enamel colours which are subsequently fixed on the surface of the glass by firing at a low temperature in a muffle. A drawback of this technique—conspicuously exemplified in these later panels —is that the enamels, particularly the blue, are liable to flake off as time passes, owing to faulty composition and a coefficient of expansion unequal to that of the glass itself.

The shield of the Queen (Plate VIII) is emblazoned as follows: A cross gules surmounted by another argent : in the first quarter or,

STAINED GLASS, GUILDFORD GUILDHALL.

On right of plate is a photostatic extract from the Borough records of Guildford:
"Item that this veare the Guildhall of the Towne of Guldeford was enlarged
and made longer att the north ende And the Queenes Armes and the Armes
of this Towne sett in the windowe att that north ende."

Facing p. 98

PLATE VIII

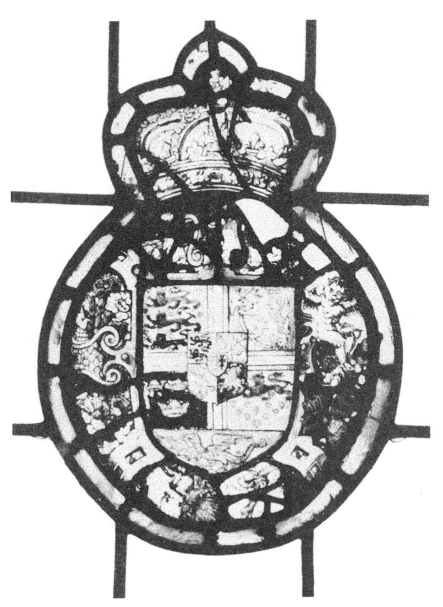

STAINED GLASS, GUILDFORD GUILDHALL.

semé of hearts proper three lions passant gardant azure armed gules crowned or (Denmark) ; in the second quarter gules, a lion rampant imperially crowned holding in its paws a battle-axe argent (Norway) ; in the third quarter azure, three crowns or (Sweden) ; in the fourth quarter or, ten hearts (four, three, two and one) proper and in chief a lion passant gardant azure (Gothland) ; in a compartment gules, at the base of the shield beneath the cross a wyvern tail nowed and wings expanded or (the Vandals). Over all an inescutcheon quarterly : 1 or, two lions passant gardant in pale azure (Sleswick) ; 2 gules, an inescutcheon argent three holly-leaves between three nails in triangle all proper (Holstein) ; 3 gules, a swan argent membered sable ducally gorged (Stormarn) ; 4 azure, a chevalier armed at all points brandishing his sword all proper upon a charger argent barded or (Dithmarschen) ; surtout-de-tout an inescutcheon of pretence party per pale or, two bars gules (Oldenburg) and azure, a cross paty fitchy or (Delmenhorst). It may be observed that the Holstein quarter is faultily rendered, through misunderstanding or lack of space.

The Danish shield is enclosed by scrollwork of the *ferronnerie* type which was developed by Antwerp designer-engravers about the middle of the 16th century, with flowers—carnations and marigolds can be recognized—in the intervals ; for this design blue and mauve enamels have been used, with yellow stain (combining with the blue to give the green of foliage) and a deep amber colour. To the right at the top (on the sinister side of the shield) this ornament has been broken away and replaced by a piece of contemporary glass painted with a cupid sitting on a scroll ; there are other defects below, at the base of the shield, where a bearded man's face and the waist and dimpled hand of a draped female figure have been inserted. The crown is complete though broken and shows in the curve of the arches, when compared with those of the Tudor crown, the impact of the incipient baroque style.

The third panel (Plate IX), of almond-shaped outline, with the arms of the town of Guildford, is more seriously damaged. The shield shows the customary sable field, the castle argent with its triple-towered middle tower, the two embattled flanking towers each with a spire surmounted by a ball, its port proper charged on the centre with a key and portcullised or, its two roses in fess or, its lion couchant gardant or on a mount vert before the port, and the two woolsacks in pale on each side of the castle ; the escutcheon quarterly France and England with which the middle tower should be charged has been omitted, doubtless owing to the great difficulty of rendering this complicated detail by glass-painter's technique, whilst the water which should occupy the base of the shield has been broken away. A curious feature of this version of the arms still remains, the luxuriant rushes growing on the mound, a flight of the designer's fancy not provided for in the official blazoning. Above the shield and on the upper half of its dexter side the panel retains its original framing design of *ferronnerie*, with cutwork scrolls, in the openings of which are set apples, grapes, gourds and other fruits. There can be little doubt that this panel was executed by the same painter and set up in the Guildhall at the same time as that with the arms of Queen Anne, that is, some time in or after 1603. In the place of the missing lower portions has been gathered a jumble of fragments of painted glass. Among these can be made out a fragment of a crown similar in the treatment of its cross and jewels to that of the Tudor panel. Other fragments, apart from several unsightly pieces of plain modern coloured glass, are enamel-painted with cut strapwork similar in style to the original work in the upper part of the panel, but brought from another source. To the left, just below the middle, in the same enamel technique, is the upper half of a naked boy with outstretched arms and a cartouche in front of him.

A careful examination of these inserted fragments seems to indicate that unless they were introduced from some other building—which is not very likely—they are remnants of stained glass which once occupied other windows in the Guildhall, perhaps those on the west side of the Court Room now filled with plain leaded panes. The presence of a second crown of 16th-century type, taken in conjunction with the recorded placing of Queen Elizabeth's arms in the north window of the room, perhaps implies that her arms may have been repeated, or those of her predecessors have had a place, either in one of the west windows of the room or in some window of that part of the building which was demolished to make way for the present façade, built in 1683. It is also evident from the records that there must have existed a panel with the town arms earlier than that still to be seen, which, as has been shown, can hardly be dated before the beginning of the 17th century. It is, of course, possible that the town shield put up in 1589 was damaged or destroyed soon after and the existing shield made to take its place. The presence among the fragments inserted in this panel of part of a crown similar to that surmounting the shield of Anne of Denmark makes it likely that there was at one time another royal shield in the windows of the Court Room and this may be supposed to have shown the arms of James I.

If it is asked why the arms of Denmark should find a place in the Guildhall it has to be said that no sufficient reason is to be found in the town records, which are silent as to any visit of the Queen Consort to Guildford; it is, however, likely that she was from time to time in the town, since she resided during the last three years of her life at Byfleet Manor, which was given to her in 1616, after the death of Henry, Prince of Wales.[1] There is no record of a visit to Guildford by James I before the death of Anne (1619). It may be noted that the arms of Denmark, together with those of the King and other members of his family, appear in the east window, dated as late as 1621, in the chapel of Abbot's

---

[1] *S.A.C.*, Vol. L, p. 101.

PLATE IX

StAIneD GlAss, GuIldford GuIldhAll.

Hospital, in the immediate neighbourhood of the Guildhall.[1] It need not therefore be argued that the Guildhall panel with the Danish arms must necessarily be dated before the death of the Queen. We have seen that the fragments of other panels used to make good the damages of those surviving comprise several similar in style and technique to that with the Danish shield, including part of a royal crown which may well be that of James I. It is recorded that on 27th July, 1622, "King James knighted at Guildford Sir Richard Weston and Sir Robert Spiller"[2]; the former, of Sutton Place, was "the great promoter of the plan for rendering the river Wey navigable from the Thames to Guildford, in putting which into execution he was the first to introduce into England the use of water-locks which he had seen in Flanders."[3] This may have been the occasion for embellishing the Guildhall with the royal arms, but it is more likely this would have been done in celebration of the charter granted to the town in the first year of James's reign in England ; the setting up of the town arms besides those of the King and Queen would have been appropriate to such an occasion. This charter appointed the Mayor of Guildford and others to be Justices of the Peace, in pursuance of an unfulfilled promise of Queen Elizabeth.

Thanks are due to our Member, Mr. C. E. Sexton, for placing at the disposal of the Society for reproduction photographs taken by him, which are the first ever made of the Guildhall glass.

---

[1] The authorship and origin of the Abbot's Hospital windows are discussed in the *Journal of the British Society of Master Glass-painters*, Vol. X (1947-1948), pp. 6-8 (Bernard Rackham, "The East Window of the Chapel of Trinity Hospital, Greenwich").

[2] James Nichols, *The Progresses, Processions and Magnificent Festivities of King James the First*, Vol. IV, London, 1828, p. 774.

[3] *ibid.*, p. 774, note.

AN EXPERIMENT IN LOCAL HISTORY

BY

JOHN H. HARVEY, F.S.A.

I N recent years the high cost of printing has rendered the publication of adequate parish histories impracticable except in cases where a substantial subsidy can be obtained. This state of affairs has undoubtedly discouraged many potential authors, and tends to discount the value of a great deal of private research. Where original documents are published, they are often produced in support of some thesis of broad interest, and are not indexed for the personal and local names which they contain. For example, no index is provided to the 1635 Survey of Laxton, Nottinghamshire, printed entire in the otherwise admirable treatise on *The Open Fields* by Dr. and Mrs. C. S. Orwin.[1]

In contradistinction to the historian and the field archæologist, the local topographer and still more the genealogist are interested in details rather than in broad outlines ; the individual house and the particular person are all-important to them. For their purposes the "perfect" publication of a parish would include a transcript of the registers up to 1837, copies or abstracts of all wills of residents, a summary of the Court Rolls including all personal and place-names, reproductions of the Tithe Map and of all earlier MS. maps, a collection of charters and deeds, and of such survey books or rentals as survive ; added to this should be an architectural account of all buildings, down to 1820 at least.

In Surrey possibly the nearest approach to this ideal has been made at Banstead, where the late Sir Henry Lambert produced an admirable parish history in two volumes, and the registers from 1547 to 1789 have been printed by the Parish Register Society. Another magnificent two-volume history, of Blechingley, by the late Mr. Uvedale Lambert, is not matched by printed registers, though the latter have been copied. So far as parish registers are concerned, efforts are being made by the Society of Genealogists to promote further transcription, and the success of the duplicated series of parish registers, collated with the Bishops' Transcripts, now in course of publication for Bedfordshire, gives ground for hope that other counties of moderate size, Surrey among them, may also be able to attain total publication of their registers within a relatively short period.

Comparable publication of other types of record is not to be hoped for, but it is here suggested that a series of "keys" to Surrey parish history should be compiled upon a uniform plan and

---

[1] Oxford U.P., 1938.

deposited in the collections of the Surrey Archæological Society. Each key would consist of two essential parts : a map or set of maps ; and a collection of index-cards. Upon the maps would be shown : ancient parish boundaries ; ancient and modern communications ; waterways ; quarries and marlpits ; commons ; the extent of former open fields ; manorial divisions ; land-tenures (freehold, copyhold or indenturehold) ; the sites of courts and fairs ; churches, chapels, and wayside crosses ; houses and the sites of former houses. In view of the work already done in connection with the listing and mapping of prehistoric and Roman sites by the Ancient Monuments Committee of the Surrey County Council, the period which it is suggested should be included is from Anglo-Saxon times up to approximately 1840—the date of the Tithe Maps.

The maps once made, the card-index could be built up gradually as time permitted. Each site marked upon the map would be provided with a card, on which would be marked the salient points connected with the history of the site, beginning with any geological or geophysical peculiarities, and continuing in chronological order of the known references. The source of each reference, and the whereabouts of the sources would also be noted, in accordance with a separate section of cards devoted to records and archives.

Since it is easier to refer to a concrete example than to prepare extensive and possibly misleading descriptions, a start has been made on the parishes of Great and Little Bookham. Two principal and two subsidiary plans record the basic information available. One plan (A) is mainly devoted to communications and inhabited sites ; another (B) to manors and land tenure. The subsidiary plans, on an enlarged scale, show the township of Bookham and the centre of the tithing of Preston respectively. For general maps the 6-inch and for details the 25-inch Ordnance Survey form suitable bases.

Little explanation is necessary ; the principal sources are a map and survey book of the manor of Great Bookham, made by Thomas Clay in 1614, and a map and reference book of the parish of Great Bookham, c. 1798 ; the former is at present in the custody of the National Trust ; the latter has been deposited at the Kingston-on-Thames Surrey County Record Office.[1] All houses which existed in 1614 have been numbered, from 1 to 85, and the few additional sites occupied by 1798 are distinguished on Map A by the addition of letters, e.g., 33A, 33B, etc. Beneath the explanation of symbols on Map A is a list of all the inhabited sites shown, with the following particulars, so far as they can at present be established : name of site in 1614 or earlier ; name of site in or about 1800 ; present or recent name ; the manor of which the tenement was held, and by what tenure ; date of the first known reference to the habitation ; and date or period of the building (if any) existing

---

[1] And photostat copies (full-size) at Guildford Muniment Room.

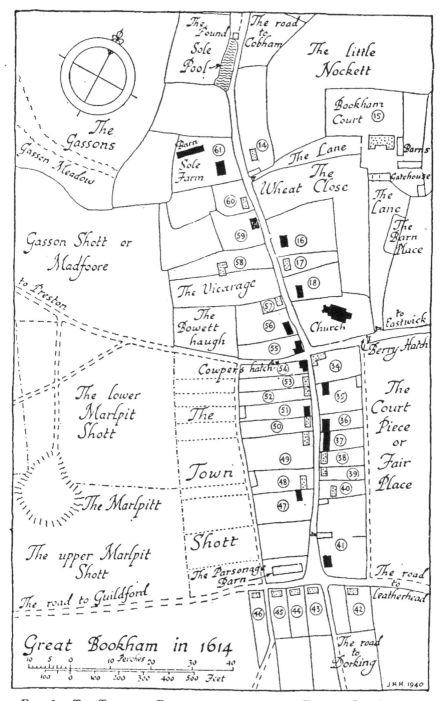

The Pound

Sole Pool

The road to Cobham

The little Nockett

Bookham Court ⑮

Barns

The Gassons

Gasson Meadow

Barn

Sole Farm

⑥① ⑭

The Lane

The Wheat Close

Gatehouse

The Lane

The Barn Place

Gasson Shott or Madfoore

⑥⓪

⑤⑨

⑯

⑰

to Preston

The Vicarage

⑤⑧

⑱

The Bowett haugh

⑤⑦

⑤⑥

⑤⑤

Church

to Eastwick

Berry Hatch

Cowper's hatch ⑤④

⑤③

㉞

The lower Marlpit Shott

The

⑤②

⑤①

⑤⓪

㉟

㊱

The Court Piece or Fair Place

Town

㊲

㊷

㊸

㊹

㊻

The Marlpitt

Shott

The upper Marlpit Shott

The Parsonage Barn

The road to Leatherhead

The road to Guildford

㊻ ㊺ ㊹ ㊸

㊷

Great Bookham in 1614

10 5   0   10 Perches 20   30   40
100   0   100   200 300 400 500 Feet

The road to Dorking

J.H.H. 1940

FIG. 1.—THE TOWN OF BOOKHAM, ADAPTED FROM THOMAS CLAY'S MAP.

Buildings which survive, wholly or in part, are shown solid black; other houses stippled; vanished barns and outbuildings in outline.

upon the site in 1945 ; where no building now exists, note of the approximate date of demolition is given.

The following specimens are included by way of explanation of the principles adopted in preparing index cards for Bookham. The following abbreviations are used :—

C   Chertsey Abbey Cartulary (P.R.O., E.164/25).

Ch   Chertsey Abbey Register (B.M., Lansdowne MS. 434).

Ct   Court Rolls & Books of Great Bookham (National Trust).

L   Little Bookham Court Rolls and Books (Messrs. Carter & Swallow).[1]

M   Map & Reference Book, c. 1798 (Surrey Record Office, Kingston).

P   Plan & Survey of 1614 (National Trust).

PCC Will in Prerogative Court of Canterbury (Somerset House).

S   Survey of Great Bookham, 1548 (P.R.O., E.36/168).

SW   Surrey Wills, Archdeaconry Court (Somerset House).

BOOKHAM, Great & Little   Common Wastes.

Lower or North Common on clay, between township and River Mole ; typical tree, Oak.

Upper or South Common on chalk, on ridge of North Downs, between township and summit ; typical tree, Beech.

For North Common, see Reports of the Ecological Survey of Bookham Common in *The London Naturalist* for 1942 (1943) and succeeding years. In the First Year's Report are Preliminary Observations and large-scale base-map by C.P. Castell, and Short History of the Common, with map, by J. H. Harvey.

The South Common is Suthwode, c.1200 (C) ; la Southwode, 1333 (Ch) ; South or Abbotts Wood, 1606 (Ct) ; described as the Upper or South Common of 448 acres 14 perches, 1614 (P) ; Ranmore Common (M).

BOOKHAM, Great   Roads—Main N.-S.

The first known main road through Bookham from N. to S. entered the parish at a ford in the Mole ¼ mile W. of Stoke D'Abernon Church, passed beside and to W. of tenements Nos. 2 & 3, crossed the N. Common partly on a made causeway (in 1523 Walter Hudson left 20d. "to the Causey towarde the Comyn there as most new is"—SW), thence climbed steadily between enclosures to the cross-roads at Great Bookham Church ; here it passes from the clay to gravel capping on the chalk, forming for the next ¼ mile the High Street of the town of Bookham (frequently refs. to the "Regia Strata"—C & Ch) and continues on the chalk as

---

[1] Now in the possession of Miss Green, Lady of the Manor; others at the County Record Office, Kingston.

Hole Hedge Way (*P*) past the early enclosures known as Vines (now Phœnice Farm), to descend sharply into the valley at Bagden (see tenement No. 80) ; at the bottom of the valley it turns eastward and leaves the parish, after which it forms for some distance the boundary between the parishes of Mickleham and Dorking, and ⅓ mile from Bookham boundary reaches West Humble Chapel (on S. of road) (see *S.A.C.*, XLVII, p.1*ff*.) ; the road which leads to "Dorkyng" is mentioned temp. Abbot Adam of Chertsey (1207-23) ; two King's highways extending towards Dorking occur in 1243, of which one is almost certainly this ; and this road is described as leading from "Coueham "(Cobham) to "Dorkynge" in 1342 (all *C*). For some later history see Roads—Cobham Road.

BOOKHAM, Great   Roads—Cobham Road.

At a date uncertain, earlier than the survey of 1614, the Mole was bridged a little to the E. of Stoke Manor House, and a new ford made for use in the dry season still higher upstream. The bridge is said to have been (re-)built by Sir Francis Vincent, 1757-75. (*V.C.H.*, iii, 457). A new brick bridge was built in 1805, still higher up the river, some ⅓ mile to E. of the original ford. This (made) road now leaves the parish at Mark Oak and proceeds to Leatherhead by way of Fetcham. The section of this road from a point roughly ¼ mile W. of Mark Oak to a point near tenements Nos. 63 and 64 (a distance of about 1 mile) has never been made up, and is not used by through traffic. From the S. end of this section onward the route followed is that of the original Main N.-S. Road through Bookham. In 1561 the homage and tenants of Great Bookham presented that Edmund Slyfield gen. had made a purpresture in the King's highway leading from Bookham to Stoke to the common hurt, and that he had made insult and affray upon John Longe and Richard Roger attempting to pass there with two cartloads of the Queen's timber. Slyfield was ordered to destroy his encroachment on the road (*Ct*). In 1776 the Surveyors of Highways were ordered to mend "the Road leading from Slyfield Mill to the Bridge by Sir Francis Vincent," but the parish was unwilling to make up the higher lying section of the road to Mark Oak ; in 1787 this section : "the Road from Sheep Bell House (tenement No. 7) to Mark Oak" was indicted by a Mr. Page, and by resolutions of 11 March 1787, 23 Feb. 1791, and 2 March 1792 the Vestry agreed to defend the case before the Assizes. (Great Bookham Vestry Minutes—Rectory.)

BOOKHAM, Great   Tenement No. 72.

Copyhold of the Manor of Little Bookham, known as Rolts, later the Half Moon Public House ; divided into two, became known as Half Moon Cottages after the house was de-licensed ; since 1935 forms a single house, Half Moon Cottage. In the 16th

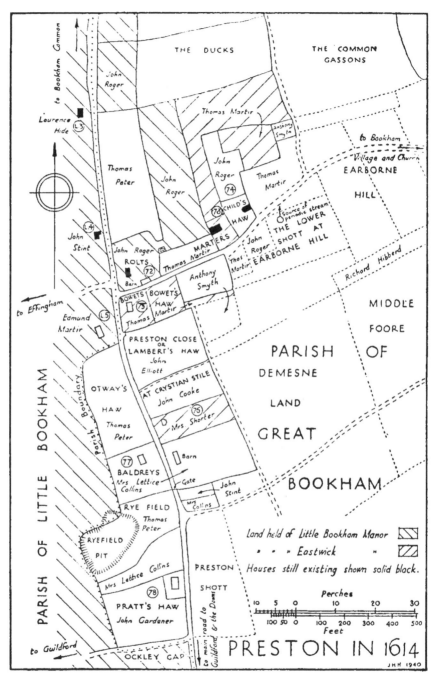

THE DUCKS

THE COMMON GASSONS

to Bookham Common

John Roger

Laurence Hide (L3)

Thomas Martir

Anthony Smyth

John Roger

Thomas Peter

John Roger

John Roger (74)

Thomas Martir

to Bookham

Village and Church

EARBORNE HILL

(73) CHILD'S HAW

Source of periodic stream

THE LOWER SHOTT AT EARBORNE HILL

John Stint (L4)

John Roger Martir

MARTERS

ROLTS (72)

Thomas Martir

Barn

Thos Martir

John Roger

Richard Hibberd

Anthony Smyth

to Effingham

Edmund Martir (L5)

BOWETS BOWETS HAW Martir (73) Thomas

MIDDLE FOORE

OF

PARISH

DEMESNE

LAND

GREAT

BOOKHAM

PRESTON CLOSE OR LAMBERT'S HAW John Elliott

AT CRYSTIAN STILE John Cooke

(76) Mrs Shorter

OTWAY'S HAW

Thomas Peter

(77) Barn

BALDREYS Mrs Lettice Collins

Gate

John Stint

Mrs Collins

PARISH OF LITTLE BOOKHAM

Parish Boundary

RYE FIELD Thomas Peter

RYEFIELD PIT

Mrs Lettice Collins

(78)

PRATT'S HAW John Gardener

PRESTON

SHOTT

to main road to Guildford & the Downs

Land held of Little Bookham Manor

" " Eastwick "

Houses still existing shown solid black.

Perches
10 5 0 10 20 30
100 50 0 100 200 300 400 500
Feet

PRESTON IN 1614

to Guildford

OCKLEY GAP

JHH 1940

FIG. 2.—THE ENCLOSURES AT PRESTON, SHOWING INTERMINGLING OF MANORS. This applied also to individual strips in the surrounding open field.

century held by John Rowlis (*L*) ; **1593** part of holding of John
Rogere of Preston (*S.A.C.*, XIX) ; **1614** held by John Roger (*P*) ;
1623 death of John Roger and his son of same name admitted
(*SW ; L*) ; **1634** surrendered to John Masseye ; rent 2 capons
(*L*) ; **1641** John "Macy" obtains licence to sublet ; **1650** dies ;
William Macey later admitted ; **1678** dies ; his daughter Agnes,
widow of —— Foxwell, admitted and surrenders to John Oakeshott, gent. ; **1697** held by him ; **1710** dies, son John Oakeshott
admitted ; *c.*1725 occupied by James Elliott ; **1723** reversion to
Thomas Wood ; **1735** John Oakeshott dies ; **1739** Thomas Wood
dies ; **1739** admission of William Wood ; **1772** dies ; Sarah Wood
his only child admitted ; **1786** death of Sarah Skinner, *née*
Wood ; her husband, William Wilson Skinner, admitted ; **1798**
dies ; his brother Thomas Skinner admitted ; *c.* 1798 described
as Half Moon Public House (*M*) ; **1800** in occupation of William
Edgeler ; **1838** Thomas Skinner dies ; William Willis admitted ;
1840 Willis surrenders to Joseph Bonsor Esq. of Polesden ; **1846**
Bonsor surrenders to Thomas Samuel Seawell ; in occupation of
William Quelch and John Cleveland ; **1852** T. S. Seawell dies ;
his son Thomas Augustus Seawell admitted ; **1894** T.A. Seawell
surrenders to Arthur Horace Bird Esq. ; **1895** enfranchised
(generally *L*).

Bookham, Great   Records—Manorial.
    These records, consisting of Court Rolls and other documents,
though known to Manning & Bray and to the compilers of the
V.C.H. had disappeared when the Guide to Surrey Manorial
Records was drawn up by Miss D. L. Powell in **1928**. They were
rediscovered in **1936** in the possession of the National Trust, to
whom they had passed with the Lower Common and Manorial
Rights in **1922**.
    These records include the following :—
Survey Book and Map, begun **1614**, by Thomas Clay (Transcript
of Book and copy of Map by J. H. Harvey in collections of S.A.S.)
Court Roll A—**1554-1617** (not complete ; large hiatus in Eliz.)
Book **1621-1642** ; Roll B—**1643-1660** ; Roll C—**1661-1679** ; Roll
D—**1680-1698** ; Book E—**1691-1706** with Index ; Book F—**1707-
1722** with Index ; Book G.—**1722-1739** with Index ; Book H—
1739-1784 with Index ; Book I—**1784-1823** with Index ; Book—
1825-1848 ; Book—**1845-1874** ; Book—**1875-1935** with separate
Index ; Minute Book containing Courts of Great Bookham—
1737-1770 ; Fetcham—**1737-1770** ; Cannon Court—**1767-1790** ;
Book—**1707-1800** with Index ; Draft Books—**1606-1615** ; **1707-
1710** ; **1709-1723** ; **1801-1812** ; **1812-1817** ; **1818-1821** ; **1822-
1828** ; **1829-1831** ; **1833-1847** ; Minute Books—**1708-1715** ; **1812-
1819** ; **1831-1848** ; several bundles of 18th and 19th century
deeds ; Book of Copyhold Lands in the Manors of Fetcham and
Cannon Court—**1787**. At the end of the Book of **1621-1642** are

minutes of four Courts of the Manor of Eastwick, held in **1626**, **1628**, **1631**, and **1634**.   Abstracts of these and extracts from some of the earlier Great Bookham Courts are contained in a typescript entitled *Materials for the History of Great Bookham* deposited in the collections of the S.A.S. Certain of the documents have now been deposited at the County Record Office, Kingston-upon-Thames.

Note.—Copies of the 6-inch scale plans of Bookham (*A & B*), here referred to, can be consulted at Castle Arch, Guildford.

OLD HOUSES IN EPSOM, EWELL AND CUDDINGTON

BY

CLOUDESLEY S. WILLIS, F.S.A.

THE situation of Epsom and Ewell lying among trees in fresh country rising to the North Downs has attracted residents since Stuart times. The larger houses which they built were for the most part in the great Georgian tradition. When they were lived in they were ample and pleasant, and, although some are only preserved by other uses being found for them, they still give pleasure as treasuries of English building crafts and design. Their "true intent is all for your delight."[1]

It was time that some attempt, though inadequate, should be made to describe them, and in the years preceding the Second World War these notes were made.

EPSOM.

Until the 17th century Epsom was a quiet village round its church, of which only the 15th-century tower remains. It was Ebesham in Domesday Book and afterwards Ebbisham. The manor was held by the Abbey of Chertsey and later by Richard Evelyn, brother of the diarist. The common fields lay on the south.

A thin brick found during alterations at the Spread Eagle is incised PW 1609.

The discovery of water with medicinal properties at Epsom Wells early in the 17th century made Epsom fashionable. Parkhurst, Lord of the Manor, built Assembly Rooms and planted an avenue. Persons of quality and citizens of London flocked to Epsom, which became a watering-place ; and houses and inns built for their accommodation probably gave the High Street its form. Charles II and his Queen visited the Wells and were entertained by the Earl of Berkeley at his house, Durdans. Samuel Pepys came and found the town so full of people that he was forced to find lodgings at Ashtead. When he stayed at the King's Head he noted that Nell Gwyn lodged next door. Queen Anne was a visitor ; and as late as 1754 the neighbouring gentry assembled for public breakfasts at the Old Wells. Soon afterwards the vogue for Bath and Tunbridge Wells prevailed and Epsom was no longer a fashionable place of resort.

Charles II granted to Mrs. Evelyn, the Lady of the Manor, the

---

[1] Quince's words—himself an English carpenter.

110

right to hold a weekly market and two fairs, and a Court of *Pie Poudre* was also granted.

Horse-racing on Banstead Downs, which included Epsom Downs, had been popular from Stuart times. But the institution of The Oaks in 1779 and The Derby in 1780 made Epsom famous.

Until recent years Parliament rose on Derby Day.

Two houses of about the time of Charles II in Church Street have been destroyed and are noted in *Surrey Archæological Collections*, Vol. XLV, p. 154.

Two of the best-known Epsom mansions were much altered in the 19th century. At Woodcote House, the home of the Northeys, the principal reception rooms were then built ; and the late Lord Rosebery transformed Durdans by turning the house back to front.

A picture of upper middle-class life in such a town as Epsom about the year 1816 may be found in Jane Austen's *Emma*. The draper's shop at whose door Emma Woodhouse stood and looked out, "the shop first in size and fashion in the place," would have been Bailey's famous establishment at Waterloo House. The mileage to other places, carefully given in the book, all agree with Epsom. For her *Highbury* read *Epsom*. And it is probable that Jane Austen had Epsom in mind.

PITT PLACE, CHURCH STREET.

The name of Pitt Place, taken from the statesman, suggests that it was first named from its situation with lawns and cedars in a great chalk pit.

There was originally here a low-ceilinged Georgian farm-house, to which the notorious Thomas, Lord Lyttleton, added a mansion, thus complicating the plan. The date of this addition, 1770, is cast on the fire-bell. On the north side is the farm-house of two storeys, refronted in plain George III brickwork with a projecting wing, the new kitchen forming the other wing. The east front of the mansion was of stone, since cemented, with round-headed windows below and square above. A colonnade with a pediment, and columns brought from Nash's Regent Street opens on to the lawn ; on the other side of the house is a pleasant old conservatory with small panes.

The house was afterwards lived in by Mr. Fitzherbert, whose widow became the morganatic wife of George IV. It was at her wish that a semicircular bay was thrown out from an upper room, in which the door has enriched architraves and panels and the ceiling a plaster cornice with leaf ornament.

The drawing-room is a stately room. The centre of the ceiling is an oval patera, framed in rococo ornament ; and the walls are covered with painted canvas in early Victorian taste. In the centre hangs a fine glass chandelier. There is a Palladian over-door and the architraves have leaf and ribbon ornament ; the dado-rail and skirting are carved. The dining-room possesses a panelled ceiling with modillion cornice, and a classic marble chimney-piece.

The room in which Lord Lyttleton died, after an apparition had warned him that he would die in three days, is known as the Ghost Room. It is decorated in the Chinese taste with carved and painted woodwork, and there is a wooden chimney-piece of Louis Quinze pattern with marble slips. The room is divided by a screen to form a small theatre. Another bedroom and a dressing-room have carved wooden chimney-pieces and marble slips.

In the house are two carved stone caryatides in Elizabethan dress, said to have come from the destroyed palace of Nonsuch, and now used as the jambs of a bedroom mantel-piece. A pair of seated lions on the piers of the stable gates are of Tudor date and are also from Nonsuch.

There are in the garden a well-house, an ice-house, and a badger-house built of flint, with a compartment open at the top so that people might look down and see the badgers worried by dogs.

Pitt Place is now the residence of Major W. H. Bagshaw.

Ebbisham House, Church Street.

This is a remarkably interesting and somewhat puzzling house, as, although it is of one build and almost untouched, it possesses early 18th-century features as well as others in Restoration taste. The conclusion is that it was built about the reign of Queen Anne, when there was some overlapping of styles.

It is a square building, and an early example of the use of stock bricks, and consists of three storeys, with a parapet, slightly relieved by brick string-courses and a cornice with dentils. To this a northern addition was made in the third quarter of the 19th century. There is a walled fore-court and a walled garden behind. The wooden front porch has rusticated pilasters and a pediment, and the garden doorway has trusses. The sash windows have outside frames and the original sash-bars have been preserved on the second floor.

There is a fine panelled hall with a bracketed cornice and a high Palladian stone chimney-piece. An archway leads to a staircase of early 18th-century design which has low risers with brackets on their ends, grouped balusters of round and spiral patterns, breaks in the handrail and a dado on the wall to agree. The south ground-floor room, once two rooms, is divided by an elliptical arch ; the walls are panelled and a deep wooden moulded cornice is carried round a projecting moulded beam. There is a flat marble fireplace lining with flattened arch and fluted key-stone—a form characteristic of the Restoration period.[1] Another chimney-piece of wood with thin swags was inserted towards the end of the 18th century when the two rooms were made one.

---

[1] cf. Shuffery, *The English Fireplace.*

PLATE X

[*Photo : H. L. Edwards*

(A) WOODCOTE END, EPSOM. PORTICO.

[*Photo : F. Woods*

(B) HYLANDS HOUSE, EPSOM. FRONT ELEVATION.

[*Facing p.* 112

[Photo: F. Woods]

(B) ASHLEY HOUSE, EPSOM. CANOPY AT CROSSING OF
PASSAGES.

[Facing p. 113

[Photo: H. L. Edwards]

(A) WHITMORE'S, EPSOM. DOORWAY.

The first-floor landing is panelled and the doors have six raised panels. The drawing-room on this floor has panelling with a cornice and a beam similar to those in the room below, and two veined statuary marble chimney-pieces of the same Restoration pattern. It has also a panelled and windowed closet. A back room on this floor has panelling and a chimney-piece like those in the drawing-room. Two bedrooms on the second floor are also panelled and fitted with chimney-pieces of a similar design, but in stone.

There is chalk masonry in the cellar, and the cellar staircase has a solid string and tapered balusters of late 17th-century character.

PARKHURST, CHURCH STREET.

Parkhurst is an early Georgian house, built of pleasant light red brick, standing on the west side of Church Street facing south. It is of three storeys with a basement and dormer windows to the garret. There is a parapet to the roof, below which a moulded brick cornice runs round the house. The imposing front doorway stands on a flight of semicircular stone steps and has a wooden segmental pediment supported on carved trusses.

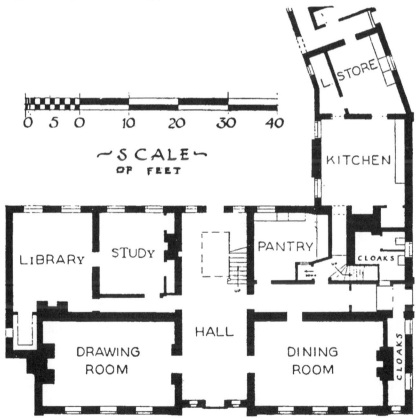

FIG. 1.—THE CEDARS, EPSOM: GROUND FLOOR PLAN
By courtesy of the Corporation of Epsom and Ewell.

About a hundred years later an angular wing to the west was added which contains the drawing-room. There is also a low extension on the east. A new staircase and sashes with reveals were fitted about the same time. In front of the house is a lawn bordered by apple trees, and there are extensive kitchen gardens. The stabling has been adapted as a garage and dwelling.

The Cedars, Church Street.

This is a George II house enclosed within walls in a garden and fore-court. Two cedar trees stand on the roadside in front. There are stables adjoining (Fig. 1).

The front, facing north-east, is two storeys high, with a parapet and the middle compartment carried up as an attic storey. It is built of stock bricks with red brick dressings. The porch has a pediment supported by trusses and on it are the arms of the builder.[1] The garden elevation has camber-headed windows and a heavy porch with fluted pilasters and a pediment.

The spacious hall has a moulded plaster cornice and is paved with stone and black lozenges. It contains the staircase, which is of wood with low risers, turned balusters and a moulded hand-rail ; the half-landing is carried over the garden door as a gallery. On the ground-floor south front is a handsome room decorated with plaster panelled walls with enriched mouldings, cornice and a panelled ceiling with rococo ornament. The wooden chimney-piece has carved drops on the jambs and a pediment on the shelf ; the overmantel is arranged to take a picture. The doorway has reeded pilaster jambs, trusses and a cornice ; over it are the arms of Mysters. The door has six raised panels ; and there are sash windows and box shutters. The joinery throughout the house is good and pleasant work, and there is some original door-furniture with drop handles. The north front room is more plainly treated. The south back room has a plaster cornice and a heavy panelled ceiling with gadroons, and medallions containing the heads of the Four Seasons. The north back room has a panelled ceiling, and well-designed architraves, and cupboard doors and dado with raised panels.

In the kitchen, which probably formed part of a late 17th-century house, are moulded beams, and Dutch tiles covering the walls ; the fireplace and two flanking arches have a heavy mould-ing carried round their heads.

Two bedrooms north and south front are treated with dados and acanthus cornices. Two bedrooms on the garden front have the walls covered with raised panelling with wooden moulded cornices and dados.

In the 19th century a young ladies' school was kept here by Miss Esdaile ; she was a friend of Dr. Robert Moffat, and Dr.

---

[1] Mysters of Charterhouse Square, London, Lord Mayor of London. In-formation of Rev. E. E. Dorling, F.S.A.

David Livingstone married Mary Moffat from The Cedars. It is now the property of the Corporation of Epsom and Ewell.

RICHMOND HOUSE, CHURCH STREET.

It appears that there was a house of Stuart date standing on the site, which, in the early years of the 19th century, was remodelled, extended to the north and refaced in stucco in the manner of the Greek revival. The house is of two storeys with well-proportioned sash windows ; the front is treated with Doric pilasters, entablature, and a pediment with a window to light an attic. The end compartments break back and there is a porch carried on Doric columns. The back elevation has coupled pilasters, a rectangular doorway and round-headed windows to the upper floor. Changes in the decorations have since been made by successive owners, and a drawing-room has been thrown out at the back. The 19th-century staircase had square wooden balusters and a mahogany handrail ; and the kitchen at this period was in the basement. The north front room has a plaster cornice with Greek honeysuckle and a reeded vein-marble chimney-piece with roundels at the corners ; there are several similar ones in the house. The south front room has a chimney-piece with moulded jambs, trusses and coloured marble panels. There are also in this house a marble chimney-piece with arched frieze and key-stone, some Dutch tiles and several oak eight-panel doors— and all may well have belonged to a house of the Restoration period.

The garden is walled, and the front garden is divided from the road by cast-iron railings with spear-heads of classic pattern. On the south side is a pleasant range of red brick stabling. The late Mrs. Eggar, who occupied Richmond House until about 1925, is believed to have been the last person to keep a horse and carriage in Epsom.

THE VICARAGE, 18 CHURCH STREET.

The Vicarage, facing east in Church Street, was built late in the 17th century. It is of red brick in two storeys with garret and cellar and has a bold tiled roof with dormer windows and a wooden cornice with modillions. The middle compartment of the front breaks forward and has stone quoins at the angles, and under the first-floor windows there is a brick string-course which, on the end compartments, is moulded.

Considerable alterations have been made to the house from time to time ; and in the 18th century sashes and much new joinery were supplied. The original staircase remains from the ground floor to the garret ; it has a solid string, wide moulded handrail and turned balusters. The pleasant drawing-room at the back is fitted with a chimney-piece of marble or stone of reeded pattern with baskets of flowers at the angles, and a door with sunk panels and hollow mouldings. The front south room is plainly panelled in pine with a dado, and there is a reeded marble chimney-piece. On the first-floor landing the architraves of the doors are reeded with rosettes at the corners.

THE HIGH STREET.

Epsom High Street appears to have been laid out in the second half of the 17th century when company came to drink the waters at Epsom Wells; and many of its buildings are of that date, although altered and refronted since.

The New Inn, number 147 High Street, was built for the accommodation of those visitors and, although there are now shop-fronts and the ground floor has been lowered, and one-half is in a sad state of dilapidation, its noble mass standing on a raised pavement dominates the wide street. It is a red brick building with stone quoins and a plinth, and the bold hipped roof has dormer windows and a wooden eaves-cornice with modillions. The middle compartment of the front breaks forward and is finished with a pediment pierced by an oval window. The back of the building is plainer. The arrises of some of the sash-window openings are worked with a bead and quirk. The cellar is entered from the yard. On the first floor the assembly room runs nearly the length of the house; it has a deep wooden moulded cornice and moulded beams, and is lighted by a row of windows. The staircase which led to the assembly room had a solid string, fluted taper newel, and alternate twisted and taper balusters. It has now been destroyed. An open area in the middle of the building was entered through archways at either end, so that coaches might drive up to the door. The premises afterwards became Bailey's drapery shop, named Waterloo House. Mr. Gordon Home's *Epsom* gives a sketch plan of the assembly room and first floor and a drawing of the staircase. C. J. Swete, in *A Hand-book of Epsom*, dates the building 1706.

Number 127, occupied by Messrs. Harsant and Lee, chemists, seems to be a timber-built house hung with tiles to which a brick face with sash windows and a shop-front were added in the 18th century (Plate XII). It is a double shop-front of polygonal shape with small panes; the fan-light over the door has been removed. The inner windows of the high stall-boards are painted in enamel with flowers. The fittings of the shop are substantially of the period; and with its bottles and drawers and show bottles in the window this is a chemist's shop of a type that is becoming rare.

On the opposite side of the street is a small stuccoed house kept by Mr. Sheath, baker, with a pleasant little bow shop-window.

THE KING'S HEAD HOTEL.

Early in the 18th century the front of this ancient inn was rebuilt with two wings, with windows, projecting towards the street. The space between the wings was open to the sky. Later this space was enclosed to form a hall and a floor was inserted above. But corn dealers continued to meet their customers in the same place, the hall, on market days.

ASHLEY HOUSE.

This house, which stands on the west side of Ashley Road, is dated on a lead rain-water head 1769, with the initials I.R. Excepting the front elevation and porch, there is little that suggests the fashionable Adam style of this date ; and the house generally is in the taste of some twenty years earlier (Fig. 2).

It consists of three storeys and a basement. The front is faced with stock bricks with stone dressings, and there are modillions on the cornice and the pediment which cuts the parapet. The porch stands on stone steps and is carried on columns and pilasters and the frieze has round pateræ and flutes. The other elevations are in red brick with parapets. The garden front has a plinth, a cornice with modillions and stone dressings ; the outer compartments break forward and are finished with pediments ; there is a wooden porch with Ionic capitals and a pediment. The north end

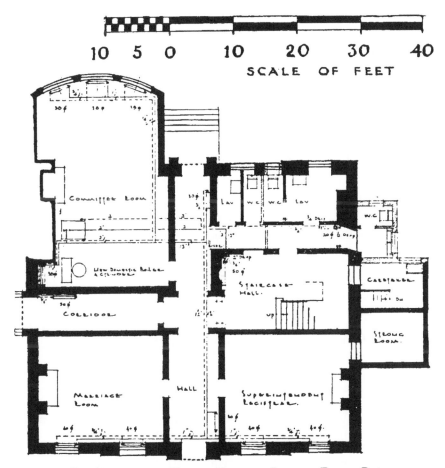

FIG. 2.—ASHLEY HOUSE, EPSOM : GROUND FLOOR PLAN.
By courtesy of the Surrey County Council.

of the house is boldly treated with an arch beneath a broken pediment and containing a Venetian window.

There is a charming room—south-east, ground floor—richly and elegantly decorated in the taste of the middle of the 18th century. The walls are treated with plaster panels with enriched bolection mouldings and masks ; at the top and bottom of the panels are arabesques springing from shells, and between the panels are rich drops of flowers and fruit of excellent workmanship. The doorway has a fluted architrave and a cornice overdoor. There is a plaster cornice, a wooden chair-rail, and a high carved and composition chimney-piece with marble slips. The floor is packed underneath with rubble for sound-proofing. The ground-floor north-east room is similar, but more plainly treated. All the ceilings are plain plaster. The principal rooms have mahogany doors with six raised panels and mortice locks. There are sash windows throughout the house and, usually, box-shutters.

In the south-west room the bay and decorations are modern. The passage-way through the house leading to the garden entrance has panelled plastered walls and a cornice. Originally it had a black and white stone pavement. The crossing of this passage with another is skilfully treated with a vaulted canopy carried on four columns and pilasters and marking the access to the staircase hall, which is panelled and niched and lighted by the Venetian window (Plate XI). The wooden staircase has turned and fluted balusters and a mahogany hand-rail with breaks to the ramps, and it is moulded under the treads with brackets on the ends. This stair-case is entirely supported from the walls between the floors.

On the second floor is a room panelled in pine with a good wooden chimney-piece.

There is a carriage-sweep, and the front railings and gates are of wrought iron with square vertical bars and globular cast-iron vases. The garden formerly extended behind the houses in the High Street and contained an avenue of lime trees.

Mr. D. A. Burl states that the house was built by John Riley the younger on the site of a former messuage in the possession of Lord Baltimore. It was afterwards owned by John Braithwaite, Mary Ashley, spinster, after whom the house was named, and George White, clerk to many local public bodies. It is now the property of the Surrey County Council and used as offices.

HOUSES IN SOUTH STREET.

In this street, formerly known as New Inn Lane, there are several smaller houses of interest. On the east side The Shrubbery is a brick building of two storeys, a semi-basement and an attic, with a wooden eaves-cornice and modillions to the roof. It is of late 17th-century date and has been a good deal added to and altered. The wooden front doorway, with Corinthian pilasters, is approached by stone steps having wrought-iron ramps with twisted newels of the period. The garden doorway has somewhat confused mouldings and seems to be the work of a joiner accustomed to work in an earlier style. The hall is treated with elliptical arches and key-blocks. The south front room is similarly decorated and has an alcove with shelves for china. The staircase has a solid string and slender vase-shaped balusters. There are fine panelling, wooden cornices and raised panel doors in the house.

Mead House, on the same side of the street, overlooking the common fields, now Rosebery Park, is also of the late 17th century. It has a similar staircase with vase balusters of more robust form. The front door, which has trusses and panels with a small bead, was inserted about a hundred years later.

The house number 26 South Street was built, late in the 17th century, in three storeys with a brick front and ends and weatherboarded back ; some of the sash-windows have their wide sash-bars. About the end of the 18th century a shop was thrown out in the front garden and provided with a double shop-front with deep bows and many panes. The lower flight of the staircase has turned balusters of early 18th century shape, but those on the upper flight are contemporary with the building. Some beams showing under the ceilings and an interior doorway with arch and key-stone are also of the earlier period. Here was the cock-pit.

THE HYLANDS.

The Hylands is the eastern one of a group of three 18th-century houses in Dorking Road. It stands in a fore-court enclosed by wrought-iron railings, with vases, abutting on brick piers carrying stone vases, and an iron gate with an overthrow.[1] It is flanked on east and west by two stable yards and buildings. Behind is a walled garden with old yew trees spaced apart in the taste of Queen Caroline (Fig. 3).

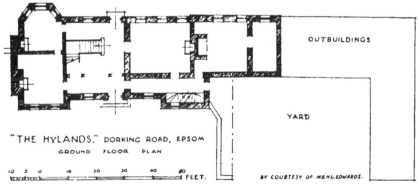

"THE HYLANDS." DORKING ROAD, EPSOM
GROUND FLOOR PLAN

OUTBUILDINGS

YARD

10 5 0 10 20 30 40 50 FEET.   BY COURTESY OF MR.H.L.EDWARDS.

FIG. 3.—THE HYLANDS, EPSOM : GROUND FLOOR PLAN.

[1] The railings and gates of this and other houses in the Borough, some of which have been removed for scrap, are described in *Surrey Archæological Collections*, Vol. XLVIII, p. 8.

Originally there was here a house of late 17th-century building, of which the kitchen wing still exists. In the second quarter of the 18th century the house was reconstructed and extended to the east. This later building is of red brick in two storeys and a garret. The end compartments of the front elevation break forward, and there is a rusticated doorway with a pediment. The older part has a modillion cornice. The back elevation corresponds, but the sash-frames of the older part are flush.

The entrance hall extends the full depth of the house and is stone paved; wooden galleries carried on columns and arches run round three sides ; and the staircase in the middle is in two flights with tapered balusters, wide hand-rails with breaks and carved brackets on the ends of the treads (Plate XIII). The lower rooms have plastered walls. In the ground-floor west back room, part of the older house, is an early 19th-century grate with trusses to the hobs. Several chimney-pieces from a late 17th-century house have been made use of in the new building ; that in the ground floor room east is of ogee section in veined marble ; the room above has a similar one and an 18th-century hob-grate. The west back bedroom, 17th century, has its original flat chimney-piece with a fluted key-stone and in it an 18th-century hob-grate. The dressing-room adjoining is panelled in pine with bolection mouldings, and has a similar chimney-piece to the last and an original sash-window with bars of 1¾ inches wide.

The kitchen, which is on a lower level than the later house, possesses an arched panelled chimney-piece intended for a roasting range, a moulded wooden cornice and a charcoal hot-plate faced with Dutch tiles. The back staircase in this part of the house has a solid string, deep moulded hand-rail and spiral balusters. In the wash-house adjoining is an old pastry oven with its furnace.

HYLANDS HOUSE.

This is the central house of a group of three, facing north-north-west in Dorking Road, until lately named respectively Hylands, The Hylands and Hylands House. It is a gracious house in form and colour, and stands back with a circular drive enclosed by wrought-iron railings with vases, and brick walls pierced by garden doorways, and over the doorways are stone vases. In front a row of pollarded lime trees border the road leading up to Epsom Common.

It is an early Georgian house, three storeys high with an attic above, which has been re-roofed, and it is built of red brick with yellow brick dressings. The front breaks back at the ends and it has two angular bays carried up two storeys ; there is a cut brick cornice below a parapet and below the second-floor windows a string-course which is carried round the bays as a cornice. The bold wooden doorway has fluted Corinthian pilasters and an entablature carved with modillions and foliage ; over this is a round-headed window. The frames of the sash-windows are slightly recessed (Plate X). The garden front corresponds, but with one bay only, and the window-frames are flush with the wall ; the wooden doorway has an entablature supported on trusses.

In the entrance-hall there is a heavy moulded plaster cornice, and an arch marking the division from the inner hall, which contains the main staircase. This wooden staircase has an open string and carved brackets on the ends of the treads decorated with rosettes ; it has twisted balusters and a moulded oak handrail with breaks in the ramps ; on the staircase wall is a panelled dado

The west ground-floor front room contains a moulded marble chimney-surround without a shelf, a glazed china-cupboard, box shutters with raised panels and a heavy moulded cornice. The east front room is similar with foliage on the plaster cornice. The drawing-room on the first floor extends the full depth of the house and is lighted from a bay at each end. There is a quantity of joinery of later dates in the house ; and there is evidence that the principal rooms were panelled in pine, but that this has been removed except in the dining-room.

On the third floor are bedrooms fitted with inside shutters that slide back on the face of the wall ; and there is a marble chimney-piece without shelf and a late 18th-century hob-grate with a pierced fret.

At the end of the last century Hylands House was occupied by the Hon. Sir Thomas T. Bucknill ; it is now in the possession of Mr. Cecil Millar.

WHITMORE'S.

This house, formerly known as Hylands, is the western one of three on the south side of Dorking Road. Its date is early 18th century. It is built of brick in two storeys and a garret with dormer windows. There is a moulded brick cornice and a string-course runs round the house. The handsome wooden doorway has Corinthian pilasters and entablature and the enriched architrave is fancifully turned up over the freize ; it has an eight-panel door and stands on elliptical stone steps. (Plate XI).

The hall is spacious and L-shaped, the shorter arm leading to the garden door ; it is paved with stone and black insets. The walls are panelled in pine with a bold moulded cornice, and the ceiling is panelled with plaster bolection mouldings. The staircase well and landing are decorated in the same way. The drawing-room has a plaster cornice with a leaf pattern and the dining-room one of floral design. The bedrooms on the first floor are panelled and have wooden cornices, some having raised panel doors and window seats. The principal staircase is modern, but the back staircase has contemporary turned balusters. Some pieces of wall-paper of the period, of floral design printed in black, are in the house. At the end of the 19th century bay windows were added at the back and the dormer windows altered.

The garden has brick walls ; and there are pleasantly coloured stable buildings of red brick and Reigate stone.

WOODCOTE END.

A group of buildings of various dates forming a country house of remarkable interest standing, with a large lawn and paddock, on the north-east side of Woodcote Road (Fig. 4).

Quite at the end of the 17th century there was built here a small house with unusually good decorations. The front is of red brick with a brick cornice and moulded string-course and the original windows with heavy sash-bars. The entrance is paved with stone and black squares. The ground floor of what remains of this house is occupied by a fine kitchen, the walls of which are lined with Dutch tiles finished with a wooden cornice ; it has a moulded beam and six-panel doors. The original oven and charcoal hot-plate, and a long working bench for the cook under the windows, are preserved. The range opening has a flat moulded arch with key-stone and pilasters. The upper part of this building has two rooms with panelling, cornices and dados and doors with six raised panels.

About 1760 a house abutting on the south-east side was erected ; it is of red brick in two storeys with a garret and parapet. The entrance is through an elliptical portico standing on stone steps (Plate X). This admits to a stone paved hall of elliptical plan with a niche and a fluted and coved cornice. The architraves of the doors follow the sweep of the plan, but the doors themselves are flat and of mahogany with six raised panels. On the south is a charming room of octagonal form with three windows and a dummy

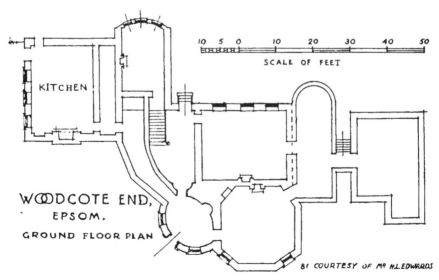

FIG. 4.—WOODCOTE END, EPSOM : GROUND FLOOR PLAN.

window. The walls are plastered and panelled, with a dado and decoration of the ceiling is a scalloped patera and oval compartments with ewers. The wooden mantel-piece has a frieze with carved swags and pilasters with foliage springing from vases. A room on the garden has a ceiling panelled round the cornice with rosettes in squares and in the centre a square panel with scrolls. There is a carved wooden chimney-piece with pateræ and swags. The planning of some of the rooms is circular. The staircase has carved brackets on the ends of the treads and fluted balusters of delicate form (Plate XIII). The bedrooms have doors with six raised panels fitted with beads.

About 1790 the original house was extended into the garden with a semicircular bay, thus providing a room on the ground floor with a wide bay-window, and doors with beaded panels and fluted architraves with rosettes at the corners. The room above corresponds and has the original door furniture with drop handles.

The red brick stabling to the east provides a pleasing wing to the forecourt. The stable is treated with two guaged brick niches of good workmanship, round pateræ and a pediment ; the coach-house also has a pediment. Between the fore-court and the road are wrought-iron railings and gates with cast-iron posts and vases. In the garden, between brick piers, is an early 18th-century wicket gate of wrought-iron with side panels, pilasters and overthrow and the cipher J.P.; the opening is 4 feet 1 inch wide, perhaps to allow the passage of sedan-chairs.

The house was occupied by the Rev. Martin Madan, B.A. (1726–1790), an Anglican clergyman of Methodist views. In 1780 he published *Thelyphthora* advocating polygamy, which raised a storm of indignation ; and he retired to Epsom, where he is said to have been burnt in effigy. He was a cousin of William Cowper, the poet. The footpath between garden walls skirting the property is known as Madan's Walk.

WOODCOTE HOTEL, CHALK LANE.

Behind the stucco front that it shows to the south-west is a very interesting house formerly called Woodcote Place. It was originally built of red brick in three storeys and a cellar in the reign of Charles II. The hall is panelled ; and there is a small panelled room at the north back with bolection mouldings and wooden cornice. Opposite the front door is the staircase well, which has a richly undercut plaster ceiling panelled with a circular wreath, and a floral cornice with cherubs' heads and two shields of arms[1] and dated 1681. In the middle of the 18th century a new staircase with open string, carved brackets on the ends of the treads and turned balusters was put in, and a Venetian window inserted to light the staircase. At the same time north and south wings were

---

[1] One shows a chevron between two demi lions, the other three ragged staves. Neither has an indication of tinctures, and it is impossible to identify the owners. Information of the Rev. E. E. Dorling, F.S.A.

M

built on to the house. That on the south side contains a pleasant parlour on the ground floor. The north wing is occupied to its full height by a Palladian drawing-room which has round-headed windows, lofty doors of eight panels, and overdoors having cornices with cushion friezes decorated with C scroll ornament. Above the main cornice of the room rises a coved ceiling panelled in the centre with a vine wreath, the spandrels being treated with rococo ornament. The original chimney-piece of marble with trusses has been painted.

The carriage sweep in front is enclosed by Georgian wrought-iron railings and gates with cast-iron vases.

WOODCOTE GROVE, CHALK LANE.

Hanging in the hall at Woodcote Grove is a portrait of Charles II with an inscription stating that it was painted by Lely by order of the King and presented to J. Diston, founder and builder of the house where the portrait was hung about 1680, and to which it has returned.

This gives an approximate date for the house. It was formerly known as Mount Distou, there being a mount that is part of the layout of the gardens. There is a large paddock. The estate is partly walled, with panelled stone piers to the main entrance gates and arches to the flanking side gates.

The house is of two storeys on a semi-basement, of brick, with rubbed brick dressings, a plinth and string-course. The enriched wooden cornice with modillions runs round the house and the front has a pediment to correspond. The attic is lighted by dormer windows with alternate circular and angular pediments, at front and back, which are somewhat crowded together. The front door, standing on stone steps, has fluted Corinthian columns and an entablature ; at the back a door with steps opens to the garden. The sash windows at the back have outside frames, those in front are recessed.

Woodcote Grove has undergone extensive alterations from time to time ; the architraves of the doors and windows in the hall are carved with egg and tongue, probably done in the time of George II; and about 1895 wings north and south were added by the late Lord Rosebery, when use was made of some mahogany doors brought from the upper floor. The dining-room floor is said to be inlaid with tulip wood.

The hall is paved with vein marble, and it has a similar chimney-piece with columns and black and white jambs and frieze. The staircase, which is screened by a Doric colonnade with an entablature and elliptical arches, is of stone with a wrought-iron scrolled balustrade and a ribbed barrel ceiling. The library is lined with raised panelling of pine with a wooden cornice and doors and box shutters to agree ; in it are two rococo carved wood chimney-pieces with shoulders, and marble slips of mid-18th-century date.

A concealed door in the library is arranged to look like rows of books.

Three of the bedrooms are panelled in a similar style, and one has an original flat chimney-piece of marble and an 18th-century hob-grate. The service staircase is spiral and of stone. The attic passage and rooms are panelled.

In the cellar, which is below the basement, is a brick tunnel leading to the garden. Another tunnel runs from the road under the carriage drive, so that tradesmen calling at the kitchen door are not visible from the house.

EWELL.

The name of Ewell signifies the place of springs or wells of water. These springs which supply the Hogsmill river have brought men here since the Mesolithic period. It was an important Roman settlement ; and in 1934 Mr. A. W. G. Lowther, F.S.A., found by excavation that Stane Street, the Roman road from Regnum (Chichester) to Londinium, passed through Ewell. At the south end of the High Street is an extensive Saxon burial-ground.

Ewell was a royal manor in the time of Edward the Confessor. Henry II granted the manor to the Prior and Convent of Merton. The principal common field lay to the south. The parish was enclosed in 1803.

In the Middle Ages Ewell was one of four Deaneries into which Surrey was divided. James I granted to Henry Lloyd, Lord of the Manor, a licence to hold a weekly market. There were two fairs, that held on 29th October was one of the largest sheep fairs in England. There were two flour mills driven by water—one is still working ; and gun-powder was made here until about 1875.

Samuel Pepys visited Ewell, which he spelt Yowell—as, indeed, it was often pronounced until lately. Mrs. Jordan, the mistress of the Duke of Clarence, afterwards King William IV, lived in a house in Church Street that has been pulled down.

The pleasant situation of Ewell within driving distance of London made it a place chosen to live in by business men, including three Lord Mayors.

The late Sir Edward F. Coates, Bart., was the last to drive to London daily from Tayles Hill in his mail phaeton, drawn by a pair of horses, Major, the coachman, with folded arms, sitting in the dickey behind.

There were some fifteen farms in the parish at the end of the last century. But after the First World War three of the largest landowners sold their land, which was soon covered with roads and houses.

The house wrongly named The Manor House in Cheam Road was demolished in 1934 and houses in a road called Staneway were built on the land. It was the home of the Lemprieres, friends of

John Everett Millais (afterwards Sir John). Ewell Grove, which stood opposite, was the residence of Sir John Rae Reid, Bart., Governor of the Bank of England. It is described in *Surrey Archæological Collections*, Vol. XLV, p. 155. It was destroyed and the site is marked by a road named Portway.

Mr. Hobman, the uncle of William Holman Hunt, lived in Rectory Farm House, which was in the garden of the Rectory (Glyn House). Hunt painted his pictures "The Hireling Shepherd" and "The Light of the World" on the Hogsmill river at Ewell ; and his friend Millais found the background for "Ophelia in the stream," now in the National Gallery, on our river.

Two mansions in Ewell, Tayles Hill, built in the first half of the 19th century, and Ewell House, late 17th century, but much altered since, have been converted into flats. At the latter house the wooden canopy and trusses of the front door and wrought-iron hand-rail of the steps remain. Some Jacobean panelling is preserved in the house.

Bourne Hall.

When James Edwards, about **1789**, was preparing his road book he noticed this house as "the seat of Philip Rowden, Esq. It had been erected about **19** years." The estate passed to Thomas Hercey Barritt, who named it Garbrand Hall and enclosed the grounds with a brick wall. A lithograph and plan, dated **1829** apparently issued at a sale, shows the place much as it is now, excepting the addition of a lodge. It has now been renamed Bourne Hall.

The house stands on a lawn beyond a lake formed by the springs that supply the Hogsmill river. It is of two storeys and a semi-basement with angular bays at the ends, a hipped roof and, above the centre compartment, a pediment that cuts the parapet. The front door is enclosed in a semi-circular Ionic peristyle approached by encircling stone steps, with wrought-iron ramps which are continued along the balconies of the ground-floor windows. Pavilions have been added at either end ; one is a conservatory. The back elevation has an Ionic porch. On the ground floor are two cross corridors with plastered panelled walls ; the plan is similar to that of Ashley House, Epsom. The intersection is treated with a groined vault on arches, clustered pilasters and columns. The part forming the entrance hall has a ceiling of alternate bays of groined vaults and moulded barrel vaults ; the architraves of the doorways have trusses. Beyond the crossing is the back staircase, which has turned balusters. The cross corridor to the left is a second hall in which is a statuary marble chimney-piece with green slips and a carved panel of Hebe and the eagle. The continuation to the right contains the main wooden well staircase moulded under the treads and furnished with wrought-iron scroll balusters and a mahogany hand-rail ; the walls are panelled and have a dado and scroll frieze. The south front room has a statuary marble chimney-piece with trusses and coloured panels ; the door architraves are reeded with rosettes at the mitres ; the panels of the doors and the box shutters have small beads laid on ; and the windows have deep bottom sashes and long panes. The similar north room has a cornice with brackets and panelled walls in plaster.

By the lake stands a pretty Ionic bathing temple with a lead cupola roof. The stable buildings are of brick panelled with arches ; the clock bell-cot has lately been removed. The dairy and brew-house, built before 1829, and now a dwelling, is castellated and cemented ; glazed in the windows are the arms of Barritt. The entrance archway from the road is stuccoed and flanked by two griffins; standing on top is an heraldic talbot and below arms on a shell for Barritt ; an old sketch shows the side arches as alcoves containing figures with guard-rails. The property, except the dairy and its surroundings, is owned by the Corporation of Epsom and Ewell.

FITZNELLS.

This is a picturesque house of the early 17th century standing by the Upper mill-pond.

The west front has three gables with barge-boards, now replaced by plain boards. In the middle of the 19th century a south wing was added to the earlier house. There is no trace of a hall arrangement. But under the present roof there are heavy roof trusses of three bays, perhaps 16th century, of which the principals have been removed and the cambered tie-beams alone serve their proper purpose ; while the king-posts and braces, with signs of plaster partitions, have been allowed to remain. One beam is worked with a hollow and square moulding. The chambers on the floor beneath are divided by plastered partitions below the beams. There is a number of chamfered and stopped beams in the house. In the scullery is a re-used cambered and moulded oak beam of about 1500 supporting the opening of a massive 17th-century brick chimney-stack. There is chalk masonry in the cellar walls.

The house appears to have been built as a farm-house or small manor house by the Hordes, who were an armorial family holding the manor of Fitznells ; one of their 16th-century brasses is in Ewell church. The manor was held earlier in the 16th century by the Iwarbys and one of their brasses also remains.

HOUSES IN HIGH STREET, EWELL.

A square brick-built house of the early 19th century, number 7 High Street, has two shop windows of bow shape of which that to the south is original.

The house number 9, actually two houses, had sash windows with some box shutters and a front doorway inserted about the end of the 18th century, when the whole was refronted. The shop-front was added in 1838 when the shop floor was lowered. The north or shop portion of this house consists of a timber and plaster structure standing on a cellar built of flint and chalk. The building is of four bays, each 8 feet 6 inches long and of 12 feet 9 inches span, with a roof of cambered tie-beams, arch braces, collars and queen-posts. One of the principals has been filled with a plaster partition. There are remains of two unglazed windows, one with diagonal wooden bars, the other with slots for inside shutters. The date is probably early 16th century. The upper floor has chamfered mitre-stop joists 13 inches apart ; and if this floor is not part of the original work it was inserted soon afterwards. Whatever stood to the south of this building was replaced about the end of the 17th century by a three-storey dwelling-house. This later building contains beams below ceiling level, some of them reused 16th-century oak beams of great size. The passage through, formerly paved with bricks, is enclosed with late 17th-century and late 18th-century panelling. Two of the bedrooms have each a large and a small closet, plank doors with moulded stiles and rails laid on to form two panels and locks with drop handles. There are a pair of Jacobean cockscomb hinges on a later cupboard door. An old smith's workshop formed from a barn and stables, now demolished, is recorded in *Surrey Archæological Collections*, Vol. XLVIII, p. 159.

The houses were at one time the Queen Anne Inn and are now occupied by Mr John O. Willis.

The houses numbered 11 to 15, of half-timbered construction, have deep roofs, overhanging upper storeys and casement windows, and their doorsteps project on the footpath. They are of early 17th-century date and their picturesque appearance gives the street character.

Barclays Bank, number 31, is a timber-framed building of two storeys with two gables, of the late 16th century. At the end of the 18th century a bowed double shop-front was added ; the fascias are treated with reeded fillets and there is a similar window on the return end of the building. The house gives an air to the view up the street.

Number 24 High Street was a corn merchant's, and before that a homestead of which the farmyard remains and, until lately, a barn of four bays. At the end of the 18th century the house was extended to the street, leaving the original front-door at the back of the shop, and an angular double shop-front with heavy sash-bars and a front-door were put in (Plate XII). The adjoining house, number 22, was also brought out 10 feet as the brackets of the overhanging storey remain to show. This house is faced with hanging tiles imitating bricks.

Spring House, Spring Street.

A Georgian house *circa* 1735, with many original features. It stands on the south side of Spring Street facing north. The front elevation has a large angular bay, a parapet and a fine entrance

PLATE XII

[Photo : F. Woods

(A) NUMBER 127, HIGH STREET, EPSOM. SHOP-FRONT.

[Photo : F. Woods

(B) NUMBER 24, HIGH STREET, EWELL. SHOP-FRONT AND DOORWAY.

[Facing p. 128

PLATE XIII

[*Photo: H. L. Edwards*

(A) WOODCOTE END, EPSOM. STAIRCASE.

[*Photo: H. L. Edwards*

(B) THE HYLANDS, EPSOM. STAIRCASE.

[*Facing p.* 129

door with Doric columns and pediment. The walls are timber framed and covered with hanging tiles in imitation of brickwork. Several windows are original with wide sash-bars. The back elevation is plain with good windows.

Internally there is a good staircase with excellent moulded balusters and hand-rail. There is also much early woodwork remaining. Most of the doors are original with raised panels and fine reeded architraves with rosettes at the corners. The window architraves are of similar design. The dado rails in the ground-floor rooms have been removed. The house was occupied by Sir John Stokes, d. 1902. About that time the columns in the hall were removed.

The study and one bedroom have original wood fireplace surrounds. Several rooms have good moulded plaster cornices. There is an original hob-grate in a bedroom. Two bedrooms on the second floor have Jacobean scratch-moulded panelled doors (removed and adapted from an earlier building) and H hinges to the cupboards. There is also a quantity of Jacobean panelling in the kitchen.

Two early Fire Insurance badges remain on the front wall. There is a walled garden behind the house and one of the walls is coped with tiles.

CHESSINGTON HOUSE, SPRING STREET.

Late in the 17th century this house was built, and perhaps was occupied by some substantial yeoman who had his farmyard adjoining and holdings in the common fields.

The house, which outside resembles the contemporary building at Woodcote End, Epsom, is of two storeys, with attic and cellar, and is built of 2½-inch red bricks, ornamented with moulded cornice, plinth and string-course. It appears that there was a back-addition which has since been extended ; and that alterations were made early in the 19th century, while about 1888 the house was enlarged east and west on both floors. The sashes have outside frames and some old sash-bars remain. The handsome wooden porch has three-quarter Doric columns and a broken entablature with pediment and arched doorway.

The staircase, which is uniform up to the top floor, is framed with a solid string, turned tapered balusters, breaks in the hand-rail and double newel on the first floor. The north-east lower room has a plaster cornice of egg and tongue pattern, and still has its stone or marble chimney-piece with flat arch and key-stone of Restoration type. The south-west room has a moulded plaster cornice ; and a room in the back-addition has a marble chimney-piece of late 18th-century style. The bedrooms have moulded plaster cornices ; and stone or wooden chimney-pieces all of the period of the house.

In the middle of the 19th century the house was inhabited by Mrs. Cutler, one of a family of farmers and maltsters in Ewell. It is now the property of A. W. Nicholls, Esq.

HOUSES IN CHURCH STREET, EWELL.

At the corner of Church Street and High Street is a building containing the Watch House and Engine House with those names inscribed over the doors. It is built of timber with a square front of stone and brick which has been covered with Roman cement, and the two doorways are contained under an arch. The Watch House has two iron-barred windows and a bench for the prisoner. In the other compartment was the 18th-century fire engine. When built it had a gable and a turret with a vane dated 1786.

In the Ewell Award of 1803 there are mentioned two houses lately erected here. They are doubtless Roslyn, number 2, and Ballard's Garden, number 4, on the south side of the street. Both are timber-framed buildings with sashes and their fronts are hung with tiles imitating bricks. Number 4 was a butcher's shop, kept in the 19th century by the Charmans, members of an old Ewell family.

Number 6, Tabards, and number 8, Malt End Cottage, were originally one timber-framed house, probably built in the 17th century, and made into two houses late in the 18th when an attic storey was added and the fronts were hung with the tiles like brickwork, probably made at Ewell Brickyard. Sashes were inserted and front entrances provided with six-panelled doors, fan-lights and pedimental canopies supported on trusses. At number 8 the staircase of the period of the alterations has square balusters and round newels. In the back ground-floor room is a moulded veined marble chimney-piece of the late 17th century. In a front bedroom is a chamfered oak beam with a thumb stop. A quantity of oak Elizabethan panelling has been removed from the staircase to the Malt House. The passage through the house has late 18th-century deal panelling. Mr. Cutler, a maltster, lived here. His malt-house adjoining was converted into a museum of musical instruments by the late Miss M. H. Glyn.

Well House, number 10, was built as two houses at the end of the 17th century, which about 1910 were converted into one house. They are brick built in three storeys, and the sash windows have brackets under the cills, the upper floor back has casements. The rusticated arched front doorways between pilasters have flush panelled doors with beads and pierced wooden fan-lights and are grouped under a portico supported on Doric columns on stone steps. There are contemporary wrought-iron railings in front of each house. The rooms on the ground floor front were flat panelled in deal and have moulded wooden cornices and moulded beams below the ceilings. But the panelling of the northern of these rooms has been removed. The back door reused has six raised panels outside and flush panels and beads inside. The remaining staircase has a square newel from the ground to the upper floor, solid string, moulded hand-rail and turned balusters.

Well House was the home of the late Sir Arthur R. Glyn, Bart., and his sister Miss Margaret H. Glyn.

Ewell Castle.

In Church Street, behind a wall pierced by doorways and the stable gates, with lime trees and guard-posts on the pavement, is the house built in "Tudor style" by Thomas Calverley in 1814, replacing an Elizabethan house. It is crenellated and covered with warm-coloured Roman cement. The main feature is a tower with a six-light window and a niche. The entrance under the tower is approached by a covered way and porch with four-centred arches. There are wings to north and south, a gabled cross wing to north containing the kitchen, and an extension to south which is modern. The base of the tower is the hall, which has a corbelled ribbed plaster vault ; in it is the stone staircase which has "Gothic" cast-iron balusters and mahogany hand-rail. The garden door is opposite the entrance and an inner hall runs to the right. The reception rooms have been much altered by decoration ; that on the back south has an original door panelled in Gothic style outside and Classic inside. The back elevation is flat, relieved by two turret-buttresses, and has sash windows. The end of the kitchen cross-wing has a bell-cot and a gable with a large pointed window. There is a formal garden, a paddock and a lake of recent construction. The house is used for a boys' school by the owners, Messrs. Budgell.

CUDDINGTON.

The Prior and Convent of Merton were the improprietors of the church of Cuddington. The manor was granted by King John to William de St. Michael ; and in 1337 it was held by Lawrence who used the surnames of St. Michael or Codington. The family assumed the name of their manor as their own names.

In 1538 Richard Codington, Esq., and Elizabeth, his wife, conveyed the manor of Codington to King Henry VIII, receiving in exchange the manor of Ixworth in Suffolk. Henry destroyed the village and church of Cuddington and built there his unrivalled Palace of Nonsuch. There were two parks—the Little Park, in which the palace stood, part of the park being in Ewell parish, and the Great Park, which lay to the west of the present London Road.

The property formed part of the jointure of Queen Henrietta Maria, and at her death Charles II bestowed it on Barbara, Duchess of Cleveland. She pulled down the house, sold the materials, much of which was used in the construction of houses then being built in Epsom and Ewell, and converted the land into farms. For long after it was said that Cuddington was a parish without a church, a public-house or a blacksmith's shop.

In 1780 the land east of the London Road was bought by Samuel Farmer, and thereafter the estate became in part farms and in part an English park, still singularly lovely.

THE DOWER HOUSE, CHEAM ROAD.

Nonsuch Park estate, being the property of Samuel Farmer, was in course of improvement ; and The Dower House, which was long known as Harefield, appears to have been built about 1800. It is a red brick structure and consists of three storeys and a basement. The front parapet has a balustrade. Two Venetian windows give character to the front elevation, which is faced with white bricks. The central front door opens into a passage leading to a hall that contains the staircase. The south front room has a classic leaf cornice and a marble chimney-piece with moulded jambs and frieze and rosettes at the corners. The architraves of the windows of this and the corresponding room have sunk mouldings and square leaf ornaments at the angles, and the door panels have small fitted mouldings. There are several contemporary marble chimney-pieces in the house; and a pretty hob-grate with pierced steel fret is some years older than the house.

The kitchen and offices were originally in the basement, but afterwards a kitchen annexe was built.

There is a small well-designed stable building and a lodge near the road. The house stands pleasantly among trees in some paddocks.

NONSUCH PARK HOUSE.

The mansion was built by Samuel Farmer in 1802–1806 from designs by Sir Jeffrey Wyattville. It was enlarged about forty years later. The principal rooms are in a "Tudor" style building, of two storeys, rendered in Roman cement. The original house, built by Joseph Thompson, 1731, was adapted as the kitchen wing of the new building, and includes two pine panelled rooms. There is a Sun Fire Office badge over the kitchen door.

The entrance porch of the house is at the base of a square tower with the arms of Farmer and of England quartering France in the spandrels of the four-centred arch. The building is crenellated, and the turrets at the corners of the main block and of the tower serve as chimneys. There is a bell-cot and weather-vane on the roof. Planted against the front is a vaulted colonnade of four bays. There are large brick vaulted cellars. Built on to the kitchen are red brick stables of about the date of the main building. There is a detached octagonal brick larder with eaves of three feet projection.

From the hall the ante-room is reached, in which is the garden entrance, with French windows, opposite the front door. To the right of the ante-room is an octagonal drawing-room treated with lightness and grace in the "Gothic" taste with plaster and colour and an armorial frieze to the cornice. The black and gold marble "Gothic" chimney-piece is an example of several in the house ; the register-grate is contemporary. Leading out of this is the King's Room, and in the window is a panel of late 16th-century German stained glass representing Saint Andrew and donors.

There are also in the house several small panels of early 17th-century German and 19th-century stained glass. The dining-room has a fine wooden panelled and ribbed ceiling ; the "Tudor" bosses and the square flowers on the cornice appear to be of plaster. There are panelled two-leaf doors 10 feet 6 inches high and mullioned windows fitted with sashes in the reception rooms. The library has a plaster ceiling with pendants. A passage from the hall leads to the kitchen wing, and contains the stone main staircase, which is lighted by a mullioned eight-light window. The balustrade is of cast-iron, fitted with a $2\frac{1}{4}$-inch mahogany hand-rail and, on the landing, a lantern, all in supposed "Gothic" style.

The boudoir and principal bedrooms have sash windows, "Gothic" panelled doors, plaster cornices and chimney-pieces as already described. There are lazy-bolts to the doors, and crank-bells throughout the house.

At the sale of the furniture of the Hon. Mrs. Colborne, the last private owner, a disregarded picture was merely catalogued as "portrait of a gentleman." It was sold for the surprising sum of £10,300. It is actually a portrait by Frans Hals (1580–1666) and is now in the Gallery at Haarlem.

The pleasure gardens are to the north and east with cedar trees and specimen lilacs, and on the wide lawn is an old chalk-pit sown with grass. The garden wall incorporates a wall of chequer-work in flint, chalk and freestone of Tudor date ; on it is growing a wistaria of great age and size.

At both ends of the Park avenue were lodges in "Tudor" style. Only the Red Gate lodge remains. In the walled kitchen garden is the gardener's house of the early 19th century.

In the wall of the porch of the mansion is an inscribed stone dated 1543, said to have been over the entrance of the former Nonsuch Palace.

A canal, known as Diana's Ditch, with its brick discharging culvert, is probably part of the layout of the palace of Nonsuch ; and a chalk and brick retaining wall in Cherry Orchard Farm, adjoining the park, formed the base of the high wall of the palace gardens.

The park and the house are public property and were formally opened on 29th September, 1937. They are managed by a join committee of the Boroughs of Epsom and Ewell and Sutton and Cheam.

The author thanks the owners and tenants who allowed him to see their houses. He also thanks Mr. E. A. R. Rahbula, M.C., F.S.A., and Mr. C. D. Hawley, F.R.I.B.A., for information. Thanks and acknowledgments are also due to Mr. H. L. Edwards, F.A.I., for photographs and plans, and to the Surrey County Council and the Corporation of Epsom and Ewell for plans.

THE GROTTO, OATLANDS PARK
c. 1778-1948

BY

J. W. LINDUS FORGE, A.R.I.B.A.

BY the middle of the 18th century, England was in the grip of a rigid Palladianism. The brief flowering of her Baroque was over, and the soil which lay obediently heavy on Vanburgh had proved even less kindly to the rococo. For the landowner who wished to rebuild or "improve" his country seat, there was no alternative to an impeccably Vitruvian portico, flanked by sash-windows as rigidly marshalled as Frederick the Great's giant grenadiers.

The result was inevitable : the stronger the emotional strait-waistcoat, the more determined the struggle to escape. The terraces and the topiary were the first to go, when Kent "leaped the fence and found that all Nature was a garden," and although the new landscaped parks were at first decorously sprinkled with correctly classical temples, more unorthodox structures soon began to lurk amid the undergrowth. At Pains Hill, Hamilton erected a Gothic Pavilion, a "Turkish Tent," a log hermitage (complete with unwashed hermit), a thatched bath-house and, most significant of all, a Grotto.

It is John Evelyn who is reputed to have first introduced the grotto into the English landscape, but these curious structures only became really popular when they brought a welcome touch of fantasy into the age of reason, their surrealist architecture a gesture of defiance to a culture governed by the five orders and the heroic couplet. North Surrey, with examples at Pains Hill, Claremont and St. Anne's Hill, is particularly rich in these conceits, but the finest of them all, at Oatlands Park near Weybridge, was wantonly destroyed in January, 1948, so that this article is, alas, at once a description and an obituary.

The Estate of Oatlands, with its memories of "Bluff King Hal" and Elizabeth, was acquired in 1747 by Henry Pelham Clinton, ninth Earl of Lincoln and subsequently Duke of Newcastle-under-Lyne. The new owner immediately started to "landscape" the grounds, originally laid out by his brother seventeen years before, and this date has thus been repeatedly quoted by county histories and guides as that of the building of the Grotto "by an Italian and his two sons," a labour variously estimated as requiring "seven," "twenty" or even "forty" years to complete. Nor was this statement, whose source is unknown, ever questioned until Mr. Marcus Whiffen, in an article published in *The Architectural*

Review, pointed out that the building is not mentioned by Bishop Pococke (1757), Charles Lyttleton (1758), or even the compiler of *The Description of England and Wales* (1770), all of whom visited Oatlands and are careful to refer to grottoes in other parts of the Kingdom.

The clue to the real builders is given by Joseph Farington in his diary entry of 30th October, 1793 :

> ". . . The whole was put together by a man of the name of Lane and his son. They were common masons by trade, and lived at Westbury in Wiltshire. They were constantly employed six years about it. . . ."

If Manning and Bray are correct in their statement that Oatlands Grotto was constructed by the same men who built Charles Hamilton's still extant grotto at Pains Hill, it is, as Mr. Whiffen points out, "not rash to identify the elder of Farington's Lanes of Westbury with . . . Josiah Lane of Tisbury," who, according to John Britton (*Autobiography*), carried out the masonry of the cascade *à la Poussin* to Hamilton's design at Bowood. As the grotto at Pains Hill was finished by 1770, that at Oatlands was presumably constructed between this date and 1788 when that connoisseur of the unusual and the grotesque, Horace Walpole, wrote to the Countess of Ossory (9th July) :

> ". . . I am to go thither to-morrow to see The Grotto, which I have neglected doing hitherto though . . . much within my reach . . ."

—a visit which was, perhaps, anticipated too eagerly, as it was followed by :

> "Thursday.
> "Woe is me ! I don't know whether it is that I am grown old and cross, but I have been disappointed. Oatlands, that my memory had taken into its head as the centre of Paradise, is not half so Elysian as I used to think. . . ."

The death of Newcastle in the same year was followed in 1790 by the purchase of Oatlands by the Duke of York. There is a vivid picture of that impecunious, unconventional household in the pages of Charles Greville, whose diary chronicles fairly regular visits until 1820, when the death of the Duchess was followed by the sale of the estate to the "Golden Ball"—the immensely wealthy dandy, Edward Hughes Ball Hughes. Later in the century the Grotto was carefully repaired and maintained by Mr. Justice Swinfen Eady, who laid out the formal garden which is now incorporated in the grounds of Oatlands Park Hotel.

The Grotto was constructed on a core of red brick, and it is curious to observe that even here the Georgian passion for symmetry was not to be denied, for the irregular chambers and serpentine corridors were cunningly compressed into a double-storeyed central block, flanked by two lower wings each ending in

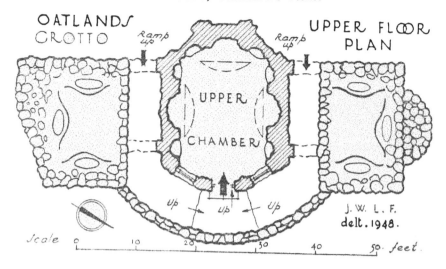

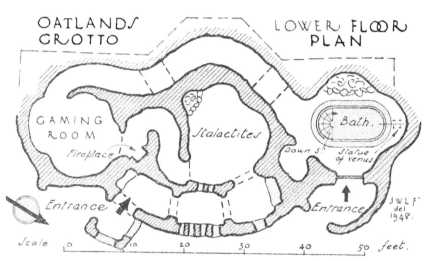

FIG. I.   PLANS OF UPPER AND LOWER FLOORS.

an apse. As the building was constructed against a steep slope, the lower floor was entered at the level of the ground at its foot and the upper by ascending two gentle ramps which united in a terrace before the doorway.

Beneath the terrace the ground sweeps round to form a natural basin, and here a little lake was constructed, fed with water by a pipe from St. George's Hill and bright with darting gold-fish. The whole composition, which now we can only see in prints, must have been very charming on a summer's day, when the surrounding trees and the grey stone-work were reflected in the clear surface ; but in 1838 the construction of the cutting for the London and Southampton railway interrupted the water supply

PLATE XIV

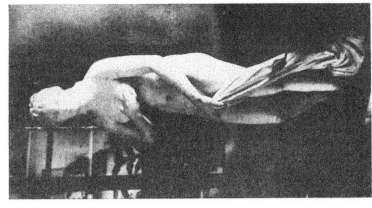

(B)   THE BATH ROOM : THE
STATUE OF VENUS.

Facing p. 136

(A)   THE HERMITAGE.

PLATE XV

[From a print in the Author's collection

(A) THE GROTTO FROM THE SOUTH-EAST. PRINT C. 1793.

[Specially taken for the Society by Mr. Maurice B. Cookson

(B) THE GROTTO FROM THE NORTH-WEST.

[Facing p. 137

and a thick coppice replaces what the jaundiced Walpole rather rudely terms "a basin of dirty water." Lining the shores of the lake and the neighbouring paths are the tombs of over sixty pet dogs, which together with numerous parrots and monkeys, consoled the loneliness of the Duchess in the absence of her warrior lord : a taste appreciated by Queen Victoria who, when she visited the Grotto in 1871, suggested that the little cemetery be rescued from decay and restored.

Externally the building was faced with a much-pitted stone which the guide-books are unanimous in terming "Tufa," a volcanic rock which would presumably have had to be specially imported from Italy or Iceland. Sir Arthur Russell, however, who has made a special study of the geology of artificial grottoes, informs the author that these facings are almost certainly, as far as can be judged from photographs, of a much weathered limestone, which confirms Farington's note that they "came from Bath and Cirencester." It was certainly most effective in the two cyclopean arches which guarded the foot of the twin ramps, while the pock-marked wall-surfaces were diversified by blind windows and string-courses of dressed stone, giant ammonites and specimens of "brain" coral.

In *The Chronicles of Oatlands*, published by James North in 1875, we have a description of the Grotto at a time when the statuary and furnishings were still largely intact. Skirting the shore of the lake and entering through a grille in the south-east corner, the curious traveller would find himself at one end of a wide corridor, running in a gentle curve round the east side of the central block and divided by arches into three bays, each with an elaborately patterned roof of satin spar (selenite), red calcite and a blue vitreous material. By 1947, the dust of a century and a half had dimmed the original gaudiness, and the "arms of Cecil, with quarterings, encircled by the Garter and motto," which glowed in stained glass from one of the narrow windows overlooking the lake, had vanished along with "some good wood carvings, a figure of Venus reclining in statuary marble and a statue by Torrigiano."

At the end of this corridor, an arch on the left hand gave on to the central chamber, which was at once the most impressive and the most beautiful. The ceiling was a solid mass of stalactites, varying in length from three or four inches to as many feet, very naturally grouped and each constructed on a conical fan of laths, anchored to the brick vault at the top and covered with glistening spar imbedded in mortar. Two concealed *yeux-de-boeuf* in the roof gave just sufficient light to enhance the mystery of these bright daggers stabbing downwards through the gloom without betraying the extent of the "cavern," which was only fourteen feet across, or revealing the entrance to the little passage whose stygian windings led further into the labyrinth.

Groping his way between the spar-encrusted walls, the visitor would suddenly find the passage widen to reveal, of all incongruities in a grotto, a fireplace complete with dog-grate. Nor was a cheerful blaze probably unwelcome, for these lofty semi-subterranean halls and corridors could strike chill on all but the hottest days, and after an hour or so the occupants felt in cordial agreement with Dr. Johnson's verdict on such whimsies. "A very pleasant place," the Sage thundered, "for Toads !"

Beyond lay the gaming den which was the scene of those gambling parties which appealed rather more strongly to the Duke than to the local tradesmen, parties which were apt to be cut short by those unreasonable and mercenary spirits stopping all supplies until their accounts were settled. The high vault, ornamented with bold star patterns and zigzags worked in spar, must often have echoed to the stentorian mirth of the Royal host, who took a simple delight in bawdy stories, while he and his cronies lolled on magnificent cushions, "worked by the Duchess's own hand."

From this second chamber, a corridor wound round the back of the stalactite hall to a corresponding room in the opposite wing of the building. Here was a truly noble bath, 10 feet 9 inches long and 5 feet wide and deep, whose waters Charles Greville found on 4th August, 1818, "as clear as crystal and as cold as ice." As in the gaming room, light entered through three round windows in the roof, whose cast-iron frames were probably not original as they closely resemble those used in the mills of the early 19th century ; while should he so desire, the bather could enter directly through a door from the shore of the lake, instead of traversing the rooms and corridors we have described. The walls were entirely lined with small shells, set inside-out into the plaster and punctuated at intervals with giant cowries, while room was found somewhere for a "terra-cotta of the infant Hercules," "a dug-out canoe from the South-Sea Islands," and "a stuffed alligator." Here too was the glory of the Grotto, a 2nd-century copy of the Venus de Medici who presided over the head of the bath, and of all the building's treasures alone survives, brooding over the newspapers in the Public Library, and until recently kept shrouded in a dust-sheet lest her near nudity corrupt the morals of the simple towns-folk.

The upper chamber, as we have seen, was approached by two ramps studded with horses' teeth (said to have been collected, for some obscure reason, from the field of Waterloo), and crossed by a few shallow steps which scarcely warranted Walpole's gibe ". . . and which never happened to a grotto before, lives up one pair of stairs." This room, the largest (22 feet 9 inches by 18 feet) and least uninhabitable in the building, was the favourite retreat of the Duchess of York while her husband was busy, if legend speaks true, marching his men to the top of the hill and marching them down again. Here great candelabras swung from the lofty

PLATE XVI

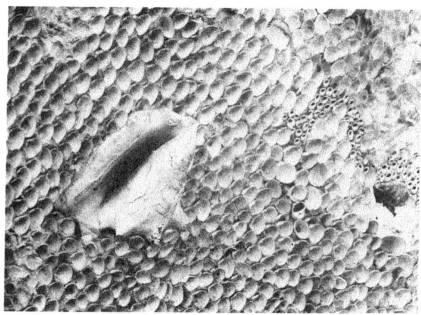

Taken by Messrs. Brian and Norman Westwood and reproduced by their permission

(A) SHELL-WORK ON THE WALL OF THE BATH ROOM.

Taken by Messrs. Brian and Norman Westwood and reproduced by their permission

(B) PANEL IN COLOURED SPARS, ROOF OF ENTRANCE PASSAGE.

[Facing p. 138

PLATE XVII

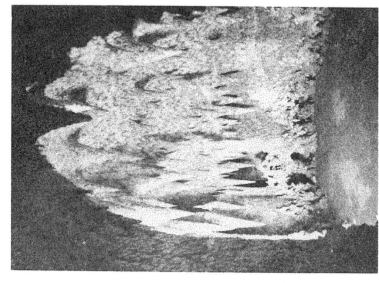

[Taken by Mr. Herbert Felton and reproduced by permission
of the Architectural Press

(B) THE CENTRAL CHAMBER.

[Specially taken for the Society by Mr. Maurice B. Cookson

(A) SPAR DECORATION IN THE APSE OF THE
GAMING ROOM

ceiling, their hundred tiny flames reflected a thousand times from the mirrors on the walls, and striking fire from the gleaming crystals of satin spar which hung pendant in stalactites from the roof and framed windows rich with the gules and azure, argent and or of heraldic glass. No Drury Lane transformation scene can have exceeded the splendour of this "pleasure dome" on a gala night, such a night as occurred in 1815 when the Grotto knew its greatest hour and four kings sat down to dine with the heroes of Waterloo.

After this it is something of an anti-climax to read that the room contained, besides "Chinese furniture" and stools most horridly contrived from giant shells, a "Roman battle-axe from Coway stakes," "an ivory model of a man-o-war," the skull of "Eclipse" ("first and the rest nowhere"—now preserved in Weybridge Museum), and a brace or two of stuffed lizards.

This opportunity may also be taken for mourning the destruction of "The Hermitage," a cottage *ornée* which stood not far from the Grotto and which vanished unhonoured and unsung some time between the wars. A hall and porch with fantastically steeply pitched roofs and windows enriched with lurid stained glass, and a more orthodox two-storeyed block, flanked a large but unsubstantial tower, forming a picturesque group which, when the author knew it as a boy, was as ivy-clad and ruinous as any romantic might desire. Within, according to our guide of 1875, were once "a terra-cotta of the struggling satyr," "a Roman cinerarium from Pompeii," formerly at Strawberry Hill, and a "seat formed of . . . white marble from the Mausoleum of Akbar . . . at Agra" [*sic*]. This last item more probably came from Agra Fort, where Lord William Bentinck ruthlessly pulled down magnificent specimens of Mogul architecture, selling the marble to contractors and shipping a few selected pieces home to the Prince Regent.

Unfortunately, the Grotto stood quite close to a road open to the public and, during the recent war, when fences remained unrepaired and gates were left unguarded, it became the prey of hooligans. Whether the culprits were soldiers, boys from a nearby "approved" school or just local "toughs" is uncertain and now immaterial. Doors and windows were forced, barbed-wire barriers severed and the delicate ornament of the upper room made a target for missiles, so that by the end of 1947 it had been completely ruined and bore all the appearance of damage from high-explosive rather than the hand of man. This fate, incidentally, is one that was nearly shared by two other historic monuments in the same district, Byfleet Manor and Waynflete's Tower, Esher, both of which were only rescued by occupation from the attacks of individuals also actuated by a maniacal urge for destruction, and who were apparently prepared to labour indefatigably with crowbar and wire-cutters to accomplish their perverted ends.

In the face of these repeated attacks the directors of North Hotels decided to demolish the building rather than spend any

N

more on its maintenance. This decision was the more regrettable
since, even if a good case might have been made out for the
destruction of the upper storey, by now a practically featureless
shell, the lower chambers were very little damaged and might
have been made reasonably secure by the blocking-up of the
window openings, pending consultation with interested bodies and
a public appeal for a restoration fund.

On the grounds that certain portions of the building were
unsafe and forgetting an old undertaking to inform Surrey County
Council before taking any such action, Walton and Weybridge
U.D.C. recommended to the Ministry of Works that a licence be
granted for the demolition. Getting wind of the affair, the Georgian
Group made strenuous efforts to halt the work of destruction, a few
interested residents endeavoured to overcome the usual local
apathy in such matters, and some questions were asked in Parliament which elicited from the Minister the reply that, until the
preparation of the necessary schedules required under the Town
and Country Planning Act, he regretted that he could take no
action in the matter. All that could be done, therefore, was to
make as complete a record as possible of the building during the
few remaining weeks of its existence. Through the courtesy of the
directors of North Hotels and with the co-operation of their
architect, Mr. R. Mountford Pigott, F.R.I.B.A., the author was
enabled to prepare a plan based on a measured survey, and to
arrange for Mr. Cookson, of the University of London Institute of
Archæology, to take a series of photographs which were later
supplemented by others taken by Messrs. Brian and Norman
Westwood, AA.R.I.B.A.

And so the picks crashed into the meticulously fitted shell-work,
and the exquisitely contrived stalactites plunged down to impale
themselves in the growing heap of rubble. The brick core, however,
put up an unexpectedly stout resistance and a pneumatic drill had
to be summoned before it could be levelled to the ground. Now all
that remains of this quaint and in some respects lovely essay in
architectural fantasy are a few stalactites, some specimens of
shell-work, an iron window-frame and several other pitiful fragments which Mrs. Grenside, the Assistant Curator, has rescued for
inclusion in the Collections at Weybridge Museum.

NOTES

A Macehead of Igneous Rock from Ranmore.—This half macehead was found about 1929 by Mr. F. E. Edmunds, of the Geological Survey, on Ranmore Common. When first found it was thought to be of sandstone. However, the implement was sliced by Dr. Dunham, Petrographer to the Survey. His report is as follows :

"ENQ. 953. The rock is a quartz porphyrite or quartz microdiorite, composed of oligoclase crystals up to 0.6 mm. long, heavily sericitised, lath-shaped hornblende and abundant interstitial quartz. A little micropegmatite is present and some epidote.

"Although I have not been able to match it exactly so far, I think it is very probable that this is from the Pre-Cambrian intrusive rocks of the Leicester district."—K. C. DUNHAM."

The measurements of this interesting half mace are :— Diameter over all, 3.5 in. ; thickness, 1.3 in. ; aperture, 1.05 and 1.6 in. at surface. It is now on temporary loan to the Guildford Museum pending the formation of a Dorking Museum. W. F. R.

A Diorite Axe from Kingston.—Mr. H. Cross, F.L.A., reports the following recent addition to the Kingston Museum.

"The undermentioned implement was given to Alderman Finny by the Borough Surveyor for inclusion with other specimens in the Museum.

"Celt : diorite, oblique edge ; Neolithic : length 6 in., width at edge 2⅞ in. and thickness 1⅜ in. Found during excavations at Cambridge Gardens Flats, Cambridge Road, Kingston in February, 1949."

It should be noted that this axe has not been sliced. W. F. R.

A Polished Flint Axe from Titsey.—This axe is in very good condition ; it was found lying on loose soil in a grass field about half a mile south of the Pilgrim's Way and about one quarter of a mile inside the county boundary between Titsey and Westerham (Grid Ref. 51/524549). The soil had obviously been dug from an adjoining drainage ditch which had recently been cleaned out to a depth of 18 in. A diligent search failed to reveal any other objects of interest in the field or in the ditch excepting a few flakes of flint.

The axe is 17.2 cm. in length and tapers from a width of 6 cm. at one end to 3.2 cm. at the other ; its maximum width is 3 cm. It weighs 13 oz. This Neolithic implement is now in the possession of Mr. J. E. Pater of Croydon, to whom we are indebted for the preceding information. W. F. R.

Three Stone Axes from Ashtead.—These three implements were found, ten or twelve years ago, during the making of the garden of a house on the Stag Leys estate, which lies on the south side of the main road between Ashtead and Leatherhead. The site is at the foot of the northern slope of the North Downs, and consists of a chalk subsoil with about a foot of soil covering it. (Map Reference : Surrey, Sheet XVIII S.E., O.S. 6 in. map, 173572).

All three implements are of the same type of hard, grey to brown-grey, rock, which has still to be submitted for petrological examination, when it is hoped that it will be possible to state whence it has been derived.

Nos. 1 and 2 are chipped and unpolished ; No. 3, a broken fragment, has part of four polished faces surviving. including the cutting edge. The butt of No. 2 is missing, and this implement has, at some date, been subjected to fire.

All three are foreign to the area in which they were found, and are "imports." As, however, they were found during the breaking-up of undisturbed downland, they are likely to have brought here in prehistoric (? Neolithic) times.

A. W. G. LOWTHER.

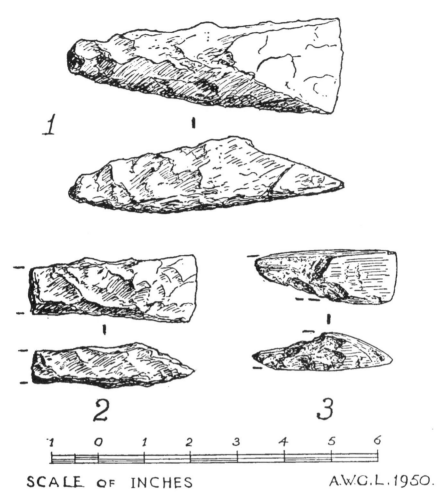

1

2   *3*

1   0   1   2   3   4   5   6

SCALE of INCHES   A.W.G.L.1950.

STONE AXES FROM ASHTEAD.

A Neolithic Flint Mine at East Horsley.—The site is on the 400-ft. contour at M.R. 097516 on Nat. Grid Sheet 170 and is on the edge of a narrow strip of woodland to the west of a dry tributary valley of the River Mole.

It was discovered on 10th June, 1949, and consists of a hollow with two saucer-shaped depressions with flint flakes scattered on the surface.

By permission of Mr. B. A. France, an excavation was commenced on the eastern depression. This is some 18 ft. in diameter, and the western half was opened to a depth of 12 ft. It revealed a stairway cut in the chalk to a depth of 9 ft., at the eastern half of the excavation. See Plate XVIII.

At the bottom of the stair, which cuts through three seams of flint nodules, there is a small platform 6 ft. by 4 ft. The shaft then drops to 12 ft., ending on a thick floor of flint.

The shaft has been disturbed from the west by 14th-century quarrying for flint, as shown by a fragment of bronze belt buckle at 8 ft. in the chalk infilling and identified by A. W. G. Lowther.

The eastern half of the shaft, which appears to have portions undisturbed, will be opened next season.

Trial trenches, 30 ft. north of the shaft, have uncovered an occupation floor on the chalk, varying in depth from 14 to 19 in. below the surface.

Some 715 complete flakes, 14 scrapers, 6 rough choppers, 40 cores and coroids as well as an adze, a pick, a Campigny-type flake axe, a backed knife, 2 fabricators, a flake from a polished axe and 2 polishers of carstone have been obtained.

All the flints are patinated from smoky blue to white, and the majority are in mint condition. In one place a patch containing about 300 flakes and fragments indicated a knappers' site.

At the north and east edge of the occupation floor is a rough wall, 2 ft. wide at the base and 1 ft. high, built of nodules and lumps of flint. It is in a large arc 27 ft. long, and overlies flint flakes and also has them banked up against it, which appears to indicate that it was built during the mining period. It was possibly used as a support for branches to form a windbreak. No signs of postholes have been found.

Of the 715 flakes, 10 are core rejuvenation and 91 end in a hinge fracture. This large proportion of hinge fractures has been noted at Grimes Graves and elsewhere, and gives rise to the typical stepped cores of the mining period.

As the majority of the flakes are rough dressings, I think the area was not permanently occupied but only visited when more supplies of flint were required.

It is of interest to note that a 14th-century silver button, with seven raised wavy lines on its face, was obtained 6 in. above the top of the flint floor.

K. R. U. TODD.

[We regret to record the death of Commander K. R. U. Todd while this note was in proof.—ED.].

Cast Bronze Ornament, of Late Bronze Age date, from St. Catherine's Hill, Guildford.—This object, recently obtained for Guildford Museum by Miss Dance, Archivist and Curator, is of particular interest by reason of the

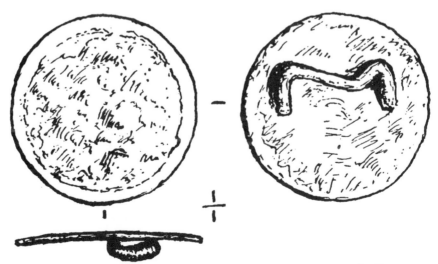

ORNAMENT OF LATE BRONZE AGE DATE FROM ST. CATHERINE'S HILL, GUILDFORD.

practically identical, but slightly larger, example (also in Guildford Museum) which was found at Farnham and is figured and described in the Farnham volume of *S.A.C.* (pp. 178-9, Fig. 74, Pl. xviii). Both examples have, as regards the disk and the loop at the back, been cast in one piece. While the Farnham specimen still has some remains of an ornamental, openwork, bronze binding round its edge, though none of this remains on the Guildford specimen, there are indications in the corrosion round its edge that it once had a similar binding.

The Farnham disk was found in an urn (of the period of transition from the Late Bronze Age to the Early Iron Age) with a cremation burial. Probably both of them once had some ornamentation covering the central area of the disk, but of this no trace now remains.

A. W. G. LOWTHER.

Iron Age Pottery from St. George's Hill Camp, Weybridge.—The following note arises from the presentation to this Society, by Mr. Tarrant, of a small collection of potsherds found, some years ago, during building operations at the above site. (Mr. Tarrant informs me that this pottery was recovered by his father, and that the pieces presented are all that now remains of a more extensive collection).

With the pottery here described were a few pieces of Roman ware (large jars, with combed-lattice ornamentation bands), but as the latter is still labelled "Found 1 ft. 6 in. below ground. Close to Keeper's Cottage," it is clear that this Roman pottery is from a separate site (the Keeper's Cottage in question being about half a mile away from the camp) and has nothing to do with the main group. The Roman ware consists of pieces of Late Antonine jars (of about A.D. 200) similar to vessels found at Farnham, in which area they were most likely made.

The pottery from the site of the camp appears to have been found between 1912 and 1914, and it seems likely that it was discovered during, or just prior to, the erection of one or other of the two houses erected inside the camp (in its south-west area) before the latter became a scheduled site. With the pottery were several pieces of iron-stone cinder, evidence of iron-working such as is common to Iron Age sites, and as that found in the earliest and subsequent levels at Purberry Shot, Ewell (*S.A.C.*, L).

On being cleaned and assembled (as far as was possible), the pottery, apart from a few indeterminate sherds, proved to represent five or six vessels (Figs. 1-6) of which two (Nos. 1 and 3) are typical vessels of Iron Age A date, and paralleled exactly by vessels from Caesar's Camp, Wimbledon (*Arch. Journal*, CII, p. 18, Fig. 3), and Leigh Hill, Cobham (*op. cit.*, Fig. 4), and which can be dated circa A.D. 300. The remainder comprised pieces of vessels of native Belgic types of ware, and of much later date—possibly circa 75-50 B.C. or later.

In view of the absence of any detailed excavations at this site (such as those at Oldbury, Kent, carried out by Prof. J. B. Ward-Perkins), this small group of pottery is of considerable importance and suggests a sequence of events similar to that which has, by excavation, been proved to have taken place at other of the larger Iron Age camps. This sequence consisted of an original Iron Age A camp, of simple outline and with single bank and ditch defences and which were later (and under the threat of Roman invasion) superseded by more elaborate, multiple defences, erected by the Belgic inhabitants of this later period.

Whether this was actually the case at St. George's Hill has still to be proved, and it is to be hoped that this site will, one day, be the scene of such large-scale scientific excavations as its importance undoubtedly warrants, and which, now that the whole of the un-built-on remainder of the earthwork is a scheduled national monument, is possible of being done.

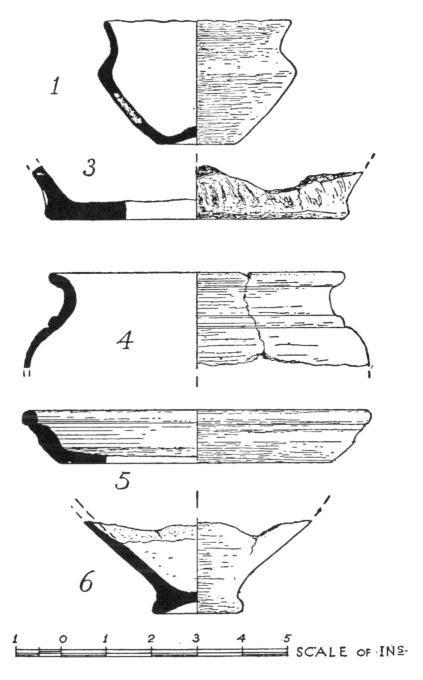

IRON AGE POTTERY FROM ST. GEORGE'S HILL CAMP, WEYBRIDGE.

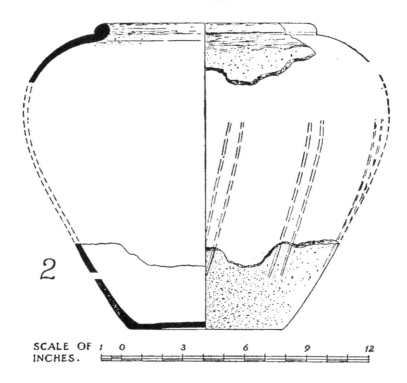

SCALE OF *1* 0   3   6   9   12
INCHES.

IRON AGE POTTERY FROM ST. GEORGE'S HILL CAMP, WEYBRIDGE.

Description of the pottery.—1. Small cup, shouldered and with out-bent rim, of hand-made ware. Of brown-grey paste, containing small white (? calcite) particles. It has a surfacing coat of red-coloured clay, applied to its outer surface and burnished originally to a high polish, some of which remains. The small base has been pushed up from below, forming a "boss," or "omphalos" inside the vessel. This cup is of exactly the same ware, shape and finish as the bowl *A*5 (Fig. 3, *op. cit.*) found at Caesar's Camp, Wimbledon. Date—Iron Age A, of the 3rd century B.C.

3. Part of the base of a coarse, hand-made pot; probably a "situlate" pot similar to *A*1, etc., from Caesar's Camp, Wimbledon, with the ware of which this fragment is in complete agreement. There has been some attempt to make a rough "foot-ring" round the edge of the base, by pressing out the clay with the fingers. Date—as last.

2. Base, and part of the upper part, of a large "bead-rim" jar. Made (as also Nos. 4-6) on a "turn-table" wheel, it is of a coarse, somewhat gritted grey ware. The rim, and a band immediately below, have been burnished and a burnished wavy line is at the bottom of this band. The lower part preserves traces of ornamentation ; sufficient to show that the body of the vessel had a series of burnished, slanting lines, arranged in pairs. This pot is very closely paralleled, both as regards its ware and its ornamentation, by the vessels found at Farnham and published in *A Survey of the Prehistory of the* Farnham *District*, pp. 209-213, Figs. 89-92. The rim, however, is turned inwards more sharply than is the case with the Farnham vessels, and both in this respect and as regards its actual shape (so far as this can be deduced) this jar is a more direct prototype, or forerunner, of the bead-rim vessels of

the Roman (Claudian and Flavian) period, of which the later examples were wheel-made in a hard, grey ware, but having only a single girth-groove by way of ornamentation.

4. Upper part of a typical cordoned Belgic pot of brownish-grey ware and with slight traces of external burnishing. (It is possible that No. 6 is the base of this vessel, but, as it may not be, it is here figured separately).

5. Dish, of Belgic type, of brown-grey ware. (Two pieces which, joined, form about a third of the complete dish.)

6. Small pedestal base, of similar ware to No. 4, to which it may have belonged. (Its outer surface is, in part, of a more brown-red colour than that of No. 4, but it appears that this may be due to irregular firing when the vessel was originally made.)

A. W. G. Lowther.

Stane Street.—Stane Street, connecting Chichester with London, has long been recognized as a Roman road. It has proved to be one of outstanding interest, attracting to it several of our best-known workers and at least one of our leading authors, Hilaire Belloc, whose chief contribution to its study, *The Stane Street*, while being unreliable in some aspects, is nevertheless most enjoyable reading. Of recent years alignments have been carefully laid down and in this respect there is no one more competent than Mr. I. D. Margary, who has given us recently his extremely important book, *Roman Ways in the Weald*. Mr. Margary has here dealt with Stane Street very adequately, but more than one problem remains still to be solved.

The stretch with which we are here concerned is the continuation of the Pebble Lane straight towards Ewell, which until recent years had caused considerable confusion of thought. S. E. Winbolt, in his book *With a Spade on Stane Street*, cleared much of this confusion, but suggested that further digging was required before the supposed line of the road became engulfed with housing and other developments. Following up this advice in October, 1948, by kind permission of the Superintending Bailiff of Horton Estate Farm, a section was cut at National Grid reference 51/1957/623 034 (6 in. quarter sheet, Surrey 18, S.E.) by Messrs. J. Fox, W. T. Millar, and G. W. Ridyard. This portion of the road runs close to Thirty Acres Barn between the Pebble Lane straight, which ends at National Grid reference 51/1956/474 740 on Surrey 18, S.E., and the section cut at Woodcote Park (see *Roman Ways in the Weald*, by I. D. Margary, p. 71), National Grid reference 51/2059/703 110 on Surrey 19, S.W., where the road was found in good condition, measuring some 21 ft. wide and 10 in. thick. Excavation was carried out at a position which was found by extending the line of the agger, which is plainly visible at the side of Pebble Lane, for 330 metres from the point where the road bends, in the direction of the excavated portion at Woodcote Park.

Fig. 1 shows a half-section of the road completely excavated. No attempt has been made to generalize any layer—the section was fully surveyed horizontally and vertically and gives as true a representation of what was apparent to the eye as it is possible to give. Full excavation of the complete width was carried out down to the surface of the second layer, which was 15 ft. 8 in. wide. Below this only one half of the road was fully excavated—it is therefore only possible to give horizontal measurements from the crown of the road to the outside from layer 2 downwards. There is no attempt at discussion of the varying effects on successive layers caused by incessant use of the road. It is hoped that Fig. 1, which carries full measurements, will be self-explanatory.

A trench, 32 ft. long, 3 ft. wide and 4½ ft. deep for half its width, was cut and the construction of the road was as follows :—

Layer 1.—Beneath 6 in. of top soil was a layer, 4 in. to 6 in. thick, of large flints varying from 3 in. to 6 in. in diameter lying in sandy soil. Towards the crown of the road they had been to some extent scattered by ploughing.

Crown

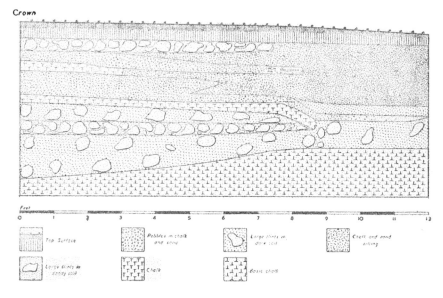

FIG 1. SECTION OF ROAD.

Layer 2.—The second layer was 15 ft. 8 in. wide with a thickness varying from 3 in. to 6 in. It consisted of pebbles of $\frac{1}{2}$ in. to $1\frac{1}{2}$ in. diameter packed in a mixture of powdered chalk and sand.

Layer 3.—The third layer was of rammed or rolled chalk 3 in. thick ; 3 ft. from the crown of the road the chalk layer altered in texture to a composition of powdered chalk and sand with small pebbles. Thickening gradually, this extended for a further 4 ft., at which point the pebbles began to thin out until at $8\frac{1}{2}$ ft. from the crown they appeared only intermittently.

Layer 4.—The composition of layer 4 was exactly similar to that of layer 2. For the first $5\frac{1}{2}$ ft. from the crown of the road it was 8 in. thick. From there on it decreased abruptly in thickness to $2\frac{1}{2}$ in., the layer finally ending at 12 ft.

Layer 5.—This extended just over $8\frac{1}{2}$ ft. from the crown and was an exceptionally fine layer of chalk 2 in. to 3 in. thick. It would not be exact to say that it was rammed. It had all the appearance of having been flattened with a heavy roller.

Layer 6.—This was composed of large flints, from 3 in. to 6 in. in diameter, embedded in a dark soil. It can be conveniently subdivided into three portions :—

(a) Was 6 in. thick at the crown, decreasing to 4 in. at 8 ft., where it ended. The flints were widely spaced.

(b) Was 5 in. thick at the crown, decreasing to 3 in. at $8\frac{1}{2}$ ft., where it ended. The flints were tightly packed.

(c) Was the lowest layer of all and rested on the basic chalk. It was 16 in. thick at the crown of the road, decreasing gradually to 6 in. at 8 ft. 8 in., where it thickened abruptly to 10 in. From there on it supported layer 4 to its end at 12 ft. from the crown. It was of similar texture to 6 (a).

Wedged between layers 1 and 2, which at 7 ft. from the crown were 5 in. apart, was a filling of the powdered chalk and sand composition described

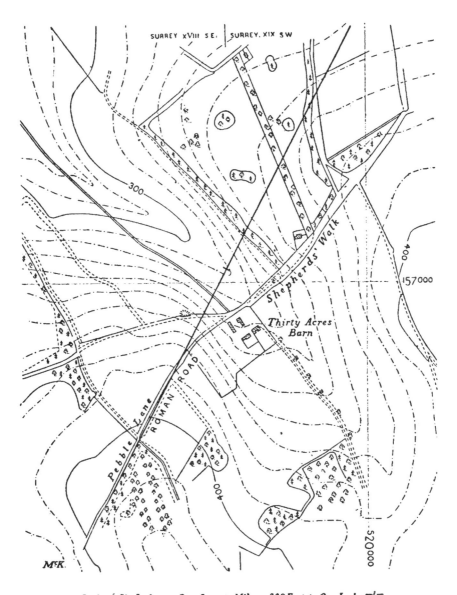

Scale : *Six Inches to One Statute Mile or 880 Feet to One Inch* - $\frac{1}{10560}$

1000 Feet   500   0   1000   2000

0   ¼   Mile ½

[*This map is reproduced from the Ordnance Survey Map, with the sanction of the Controller of H.M. Stationery Office.*

Fig. 2. A Plan of Stane Street Section.

in layers 2 and 3. This had inserted itself to within 2 ft. 6 in. from the crown, where layer 1 rested immediately on layer 2. At the outer edge of layers 1 and 2, at 8 ft. 4 in. from the crown, this filling connected with the "petered out" remains of layer 3, forming itself into a complete mass of powdered chalk and sand 21 in. thick. This extended downward from immediately beneath the top-soil to a short layer of dark soil and sand, 3 in. thick, which rested on the extreme edge of layer 4. From the 8 ft. 4 in. point the texture of this 21 in. thick layer altered in so far as there was a thinning out of the small pebbles. At 9½ ft. from the crown the pebbles were no longer visible, and the layer which continued to the edge of the trench had the appearance of containing a mixture of sand and chalk in the proportion of ten of sand to one of chalk. This layer, which for the purpose of further explanation will include both the wedge between layers 1 and 2 and that portion of layer 3 which commenced where the chalk ended, was laminated horizontally from top to bottom, the laminæ varying in thickness from ⅛ in. to ½ in. and each being separated from its neighbour by a wafer-thin layer of iron panning. There is no other explanation for this lamination than that the layer had formed itself naturally and in the following way :

The section cut was sited deliberately at the bottom of a coomb which slopes downwards from south-east to north-west (Fig. 2). The form lines show us that if there were sufficient rainfall—and this we may reasonably assume—a proportion of water would flow down the coomb from the south-east and, with the road at the point of excavation forming an effective dam, would collect, leaving in subsidence the silt that was washed down on the surface of the road. It is noticeable that the layer begins to form on the first road surface, rising and encroaching gradually towards the centre. Probably the first re-surfacing was carried out not so much because the road surface was going into disrepair (although it had started to crumble at its eastern side through the constant effect of the water) as in an effort to save it from being completely overrun by water, which in a wet season would cause erosion on the west side. In due course it must have become apparent that even this new surface, although structurally sound, was in danger (Fig. 1 shows just how far the residue of successive wet seasons had encroached towards the road's centre), so a second and final re-surfacing took place.

Layers 4, 5 and 6 comprised the road in its original form. A re-surfacing, made up of layers 2 and 3, took place at a later date, and finally came the last surface, layer 1, where it may be noted that for the first time no attempt at camber is apparent.

It is regrettable that the time at the excavators' disposal—a few days only between the lifting of a potato crop and the planting of winter corn—did not permit of fuller excavation.

The ditches, if they exist at all at this part of the road, did not come within the scope of the trench. Finds therefore were limited and consisted of a few scraps of Roman tile, a 1st-century linch-pin, and a small piece of metal which has been described by A. W. G. Lowther as a "securing wedge," used where nowadays one would normally use a split pin. This appeared to be complete in itself. The piece of metal came from layer 4, the linch-pin from layer 2 : both are shown in situ in Fig. 1. Mr. Lowther has illustrated these two metal objects at Fig. 3.

On the 5th December, 1948, the investigation was carried a step further, when the road was again "found" in a field centred on National Grid reference 51/1957/97 63 Surrey 6 in. quarter sheet 19, S.W.

The field had four "guide furrows" cut across it in preparation for full ploughing. Where these furrows crossed the supposed line of the road they raised themselves as much as 9 in., the four "bumps" lining up where, by measurement, the road was estimated to run. In so far as it is desirable to prove the existence of Stane Street at this point nothing further need be done.

In conclusion, although there are still several unsolved problems regarding one of our most interesting Roman roads, the theory held by several of our

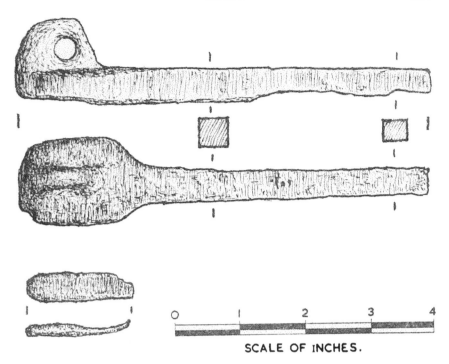

SCALE OF INCHES.

FIG. 3. LINCH PIN AND METAL OBJECT RECOVERED FROM ROAD.

leading authorities that it extends in a straight line from Pebble Lane across this previously unprobed stretch may now be accepted as absolute fact.

J. Fox.

Saxon Spearhead from Cheam.—This relic was found in 1941 by Mr. North of 3, Shrubland Grove, North Cheam, at a depth of about 3 ft. in clay, while constructing an ornamental fish pond. No associated finds were noted. The site is now sealed in by the fish pond and crazy paving.

The site stands upon a hillock some 300 yds. north-west of the London Road (Stane Street) at North Cheam and some 70 yds. to the rear of the Drill Inn on Cheam Common Road (Sheet 170, 1 in. O S. 1945 Ed., 235652).

Mr. Lowther points out that the proximity of the find to Stane Street may possibly suggest a Saxon burial of the period of skirmishes between Saxons and Danes as the latter retreated to their ships near London following their overwhelming defeat by Ethelwulf A.D. 851. Several Saxon interments have already been noted between Ashtead and Ewell in the vicinity of Stane Street.[1]

---

[1] These finds of skeletons are five in number, viz. :

(a) In the grounds of the "Goblin" factory, adjoining the pre-Roman trackway "Green Lane," south of the Leatherhead-Ashtead Road (6 in. O.S. Surrey, XVIII, S.E.). In 1927 a large pit was found, extending about 6 ft. into the chalk and containing skeletons of bodies thrown into it. No associated finds were recovered but the condition of the bones suggested that they were either of the "Dark Age" period or of mid-late Saxon date.

(b) S.E. of Ashtead Park (1910) in a triangular piece of ground, planted with larch trees, just S. of the line of Stane Street.

(c) Epsom (1929) in allotments near the N. end of College Road.—A. W. G. L.

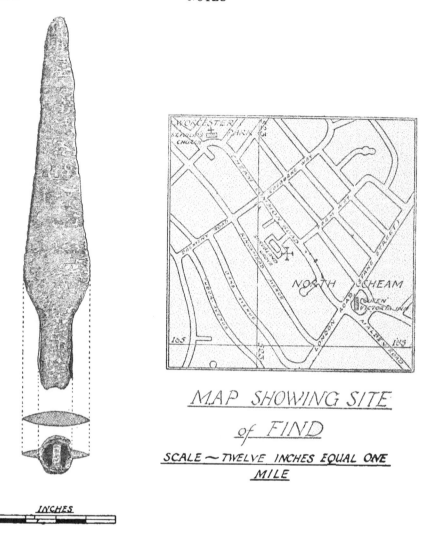

MAP SHOWING SITE of FIND

SCALE — TWELVE INCHES EQUAL ONE MILE

INCHES

SAXON SPEARHEAD, CHEAM

The actual burial here, however, was probably ploughed out in the Middle Ages.

The spearhead is described by Mr. Lowther thus :

"The spearhead is of the smooth faced, open socketed type, the socket being in two halves connected by an iron rivet which passed through the wooden shaft. It is 12 in. long and 2¼ in. wide at the widest part of the blade. It appears to resemble spearheads which can be dated as mid-Saxon rather than those of the early Saxon period."

L. W. CARPENTER.

A Saxon Pot from Thursley.—During 1947 various objects of archæological interest were rescued from builders' trenches in Thursley by the late Mr. W. Featherby, a local resident who proved himself a valuable observer on several occasions : I am much indebted to him for allowing me to publish these finds

PLATE XVIII

Photo by courtesy of J. P. May, Surrey County Journal

(A) NEOLITHIC FLINT MINE, EAST HORSLEY.
(See p. 142)

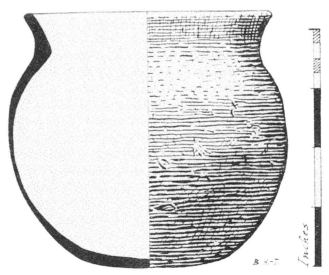

(B) A SAXON POT FROM THURSLEY.
(See p. 153)

[Facing p. 152

PLATE XIX

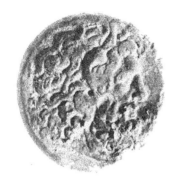

(A) Coin of Ptolemy IV (same size), Lingfield.

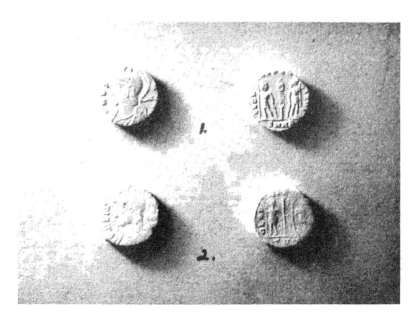

(B) Coin of Constantine from Ewell.
(*See p. 153*)

[*Facing p.* 153

and for his kindness in conducting me about the Thursley district to see its various antiquities.

The material recovered from the building site includes mesolithic primary flakes and cores, pottery fragments of 16th-17th century dates, and, most important, the greater part of the Pagan Saxon pot here figured.

This pot was found at a depth of about two feet in the centre of the foundations for the new house-block nearest to the police constable's house, *i.e.*, the most southerly of the new buildings (map reference : 6 in. O.S. Surrey, Sheet XXXVII N.E., 11 mm. from the bottom inner margin and 81 mm. from the right inner margin). Mr. Featherby observed no significant soil features, with the exception of a thick layer of charcoal, at about -36 in., in the face of a cutting a few yards north of the find-spot. He kindly drew my attention to this, but it was impossible to interpret the layer without much digging (which the building operations did not permit), the only visible section of the deposit being about 3 ft. long, the remainder running under an unexcavated bank. Extensive probing with a trowel did not reveal objects of any kind. There were slight indications that the charcoal lay at the bottom of a shallow pit, but most of the overlying soil formed part of a plough-bank which covered the old ground surface. This argues against a very recent date for the layer, but it might well be the remains of a 16th or 17th century bonfire, for Mr. Featherby has shown me a number of sherds of this date from trenches near by.

The pot is small, hand-made, of a dark brown colour and leathery surface, thin-walled and easily-crumbled ; it is, in fact, in no way unusual of its kind. Its most interesting feature is the presence on several parts of its exterior of impressions made by accidental contact with cereal grains. Professor Zeuner, of the Institute of Archæology, kindly undertook to have the impressions examined in order to confirm my identification of them, and brought them to the notice of Dr. Percival of Reading, who reported that they were made by grains of barley. Saxon vessels of this kind commonly bear upon their surfaces traces of plant fragments which were incorporated in the clay before firing, and a wide re-examination of such pots already in our museums (as has previously been urged particularly for prehistoric pottery) might produce interesting material.

Brian Hope-Taylor.

Coin of Ptolemy IV found near Lingfield.—A bronze coin was recently found in my kitchen garden at Chartham Park, Lingfield, during ordinary cultivation digging. It is a large coin, in excellent preservation, 39 mm. in diameter, 5 mm thick, and weighing 2½ oz. Mr. B. W. Pearce, F.S.A., kindly submitted it for me to the British Museum for identification and they report that it is of Ptolemy IV, Philopator, 220-204 B.C. The reverse shows an eagle on a thunderbolt with the letters DI between its legs, and the inscription "Ptolemaios Basileus," both in Greek characters. The obverse has a large head representing Jupiter Ammon, quite a striking design of flowing curls and profile. The find-spot was in a remote corner of the garden near the garage, where rubbish bonfires were often made both during and since the war. The likelihood that the coin may be a soldier's curio thrown out with other rubbish during their occupation seems a very probable explanation of its presence there.

I. D. Margary.

An unusual coin of Constantine (A.D. 306-337) found at Ewell.—This coin, originally given to me by Mr. Willis, with several others from Ewell (which were formerly in the possession of his father), has, on account of its numismatic interest, been presented to the British Museum, and the following note (and illustration) has kindly been prepared by Mr. R. A. G. Carson of the Department of Coins and Medals :

"The coin (Fig. 2) which has been kindly presented to the British Museum by Mr. Lowther, and which is reported to have been found, circa 1860-70, at Ewell, is described as follows : *Obv*. Bust of Roma, helmeted, draped. t.—legend VRBIS [ROMA]. *Rev*. Two soldiers standing, facing, holding spear and leaning on shield ; between them, a standard—legend GLOR [IA EXERCITVS] ; in ex. TR[?P].

The spelling on the obverse legend is an unusual variation of the normal VRBS (*v*. Fig. 1) *cf*. Cohen, "Monnaies frappées sous l'Empire romain," VII, p. 327, No. 2. The blundered legend, and the general style of the coin, suggest that it is a barbarous imitation, and that, despite the mint signature TRP, it is not an issue of the regular mint of Trèves."

                                                       A. W. G. LOWTHER."

Compton Church : The Oratory.—Anyone visiting Compton Church for the first time is startled at seeing the parish altar overshadowed by the chapel built above it. It is said there is nothing quite like it at home or abroad, and many suggestions, unsupported by evidence, structural or historical, have been made to explain its original use. My own belief is that this upper chapel originally was the oratory of an anchorite in priest's orders, where he could say Mass daily and the other offices of the Church, and whose cell exists today outside the south wall of the chancel.

During the seven and a half centuries that have passed since the cell and oratory were built much of the structural detail has been lost, but I believe that sufficient evidence remains to prove my suggestion to be true.

It is certain that Compton had its anchorites, but how early and how long is uncertain ; there are no records. The first cell we have knowledge of was outside the north wall of the short Saxon chancel. Remains of it found in 1930, are a cove in the wall outside, 40 inches high and about the same in width, with a semi-circular head and, a few inches above its base, a rectangular opening 12 inches by 8 inches in height and width passing through the chancel wall at a right-angle. Through this opening the anchorite had the altar in full view when lying on the floor of his cell, but after the lengthening of the chancel, before 1180, the altar was moved farther eastward and could no longer be seen from the cell—the cell had become obsolete.

It was established by Mr. P. M. Johnston that the upper chapel was built about 1185, some years after the alterations to the nave and chancel were completed, and the structural evidence supports the view that a new cell was built at the same time outside the south wall of the chancel, where it is now seen.

The new cell is very small, 6 feet 8 inches by 4 feet 4 inches in length and width. There is evidence that it had an upper floor where the anchorite slept. In the south wall of the cell there is a small window with semi-circular head apparently of 12th-century date. It is 32 inches by 8 inches in height and width, and has an inside splay of 18 inches. The rebate outside for a shutter is partly filled in. In the same wall is a blocked doorway with pointed head and without mouldings or decoration. It is old and is built up with old masonry. It is said by Lady Boston to be of early 14th-century date. It opened outward apparently because the ladder to the oratory door prevented it opening inwards to the cell. Through the north wall of the cell there is an opening giving a full view of the parish altar, and farther west is the doorway from the chancel into the cell, with pointed head and without mouldings or ornament to give a clue to its date. It should be noticed that its western jamb is built on the circular moulded base of an early nook shaft—similar to the bases of nook shafts seen near by in the abutment of the vault supporting the oratory. It can hardly be doubted that it is a surviving relic of the original 1185 doorway to the cell.

The only known entrance to the upper chapel or oratory is the one now in use to which there is a modern stair from the cell. It has a pointed head and is without mouldings or decoration. Originally it also would be of 1185 date.

There was an altar in the oratory and in the south wall is an early pillar piscina found years ago plastered over in an early blocked window.

The occupation of the cell by an anchorite, whether in orders or not, continued possibly until the early years of the 14th century. Lady Boston records in her Guide to the church, edition 1933, page 19, that in 1311 a chantry for the repose of the soul of Henry de Guildford and others was founded in the church, and the oratory was taken over for use as the chantry chapel, and the blocked doorway in the south wall of the cell was provided for the use of the chaplain.

The three doorways to the cell, the oratory and to the modern vestry resemble architecturally the chaplain's entrance to the Chantry Chapel, and when it was built they apparently were rebuilt to the same design.

The alteration of the Saxon church was made at two periods separated by a few years. The cost must have been heavy, which I think suggests that it was borne chiefly by one benefactor who was interested that it should be completed as one scheme which included the oratory. Compton therefore has its beautiful church and an anchorite's cell and oratory without rival.

ABOUT ANCHORITES AND ANCRESSES.

To have an anchorite in one's church seems to have been a matter of pride in the Middle Ages. When the incumbent and patron of the benefice had decided on a suitable person, application was made to the bishop for his approval, which he gave only after inquiries and particularly to ascertain that provision for maintenance was certainly made. The bishop or his deputy took the office of inclusion. The candidate passed ceremonially through the door from chancel to cell, and the door was closed on the chancel side and almost never built up. Inclusion was for life. The bishop was guardian to enclosed persons.

The cell was generally outside the chancel north wall, small and single, but might have extra rooms for a servant or disciple, and an anchorite priest had an oratory as at Compton.

On the chancel side beside the door of entrance there was a window with shutter giving a view of the altar; through it the anchorite received Holy Communion. At the back of the cell was a small window giving light, and for the service of food, and a small window barred and curtained through which the occupant conversed with the outside world.

Food was very restricted ; there was fuel for warmth and oil for light. Life was spent in prayer and meditation and rigorous discomfort with some alleviations.

REFERENCES.

Hermits and Anchorites, by R. Mary Clay. Antiquary Books.

Compton Church, with plan, by J. L. André. *Surrey Archæological Collections,* Vol. XII.

Victoria County History, with plan, by P. M. Johnston.

Guide to Compton Church, by Lady Boston. Ed. 1933.

Ancren Riwle : Camden Society.

J. H. GIBSON.

Pepys and Guildford.—With reference to the note entitled "Pepys and Brabœuf Manor" on p. 167 of *S.A.C.*, Vol. L, it is desirable, in the interests of historical accuracy, to point out that the inn at Guildford mentioned explicitly or inferentially in all three passages from Arthur Bryant's books on Pepys to which references are given in the note is not, as there implied, the still-existing Angel but the Red Lion ; the latter formerly stood on the North

O

side of High Street, immediately west of the present Market Street. There seems to be no evidence to support the statement that Pepys "frequently stayed at the Angel," or even that he ever did so. His uncle's residence (Brabœuf) is not mentioned in the Diary by name, although this is presumably "the house" spoken of as "dull" when Pepys walked to see his aunt "at Katherine Hill."

B. R.

St. George's Church, Crowhurst.—Recent work for the restoration of the church after the unfortunate fire has disclosed an unsuspected holy water stoup in the porch. The find was kindly reported to the Society by the Vicar, the Rev. P. W. Low, who showed me what had been found. The stoup is hollowed out of a single block of local sandstone set into the east wall of the porch close to the church door. The front edge of the bowl is broken away but the rest of it is in good condition. No doubt the heat of the fire (which had been lit by a madman in the porch and burnt fiercely there) was responsible for loosening the overlying filling and thus disclosing the stoup.

I. D. MARGARY.

A Scold's Bridle or Brank.—In the parish church at Walton-on-Thames, near the west door, enclosed in a small wooden cabinet, is a scold's bridle or brank. It consists of an iron frame to enclose the head of a scolding woman. It was formerly fitted with a flat piece of metal which entered the mouth, and, by keeping down the tongue, acted as a gag. The brank is much corroded and the tongue worn away. An inscription, no longer visible, reads, "Chester presents Walton with a bridle to curb women's tongues that talk too idle."

The story is that a man named Chester "who had lost an estate through the instrumentality of a lying, gossiping, woman" presented the brank to the church. In view, however, of the fact that branks are common in the north-west of England (there are four or five in Chester Museum and some at Shrewsbury), it may be that the reference is to the city of Chester and not to a person. The fact that John Bradshaw, a Cheshire man, was appointed Chief Justice in 1642, and is said to have lived at the Old Manor House of Walton Leigh, suggests the connection and the possible identity of the donor.

J. R. WARBURTON.

A 1792 Dorking Bequest—The Wheatsheaf Hog.—By her will dated 16th May, 1792, Sarah Philps of Dorking, Widow, bequeathed :—

> "The great Hog stuffed and the Machine and Picture thereof and thereunto belonging To hold to him my said son John Philps his Executors Administrators and Assigns to and for his own use and benefit."

The deceased was the widow of Thomas Philps, who died in 1780 and was the proprietor of the Wheatsheaf Inn, High Street, Dorking, and was famous for rearing large hogs. The hog in question, according to Timbs's *Picturesque Promenade Round Dorking* (1822), weighed 104 stone or 832 lb., its length was 12 feet, girth 8 feet, height 18 hands. A broken leg caused it to be killed before reaching maturity—had the animal survived it was estimated that it would have weighed nearly 200 stone. The hog was dressed and stuffed and exhibited to the public upon payment of a charge of 2d. per head. Timbs adds : "This prodigy may be considered as well worthy of the inspection of Agriculturists."

Documentary evidence shows the Philps family to have been residents and traders in Dorking since 1623, and they are variously described as Yeomen, Fellmongers, Woolstaplers, Innkeepers, Victuallers and Hatters and Tailors. They owned at one time considerable property in the High Street, including the Wheatsheaf Inn and neighbouring premises. The male members of the family were active in local affairs and upon eleven occasions were elected Churchwardens.

The last member of the family resident in Dorking, Miss Clara Philps, died on the 19th May, 1949, when a connection of over 320 years came to an end.

E. L. SELLICK.

REVIEWS AND NOTICES

ROMAN WAYS IN THE WEALD. By I. D. Margary, M.A., F.S A. Phœnix House, Ltd. 25s.

This important work, and one upon which the author is to be heartily congratulated, made its appearance just too late to receive mention in our last volume. It is compact, clearly written, well illustrated with maps and plates (and with strip-maps covering the whole length of each road discussed), and embodies a wealth of information—the result of years of study by one who has for long been recognized as a leading authority on the subject of Roman roads, especially those in south-east England.

For Surrey archæologists the main interest in this work is twofold. Firstly, covered by Chapters 1 to 4, which constitute a concise text-book on Roman roads, their engineering, construction and purpose, and on methods of field-work in discovering, investigating and recording; secondly, Chapter 5, "Stane Street," is a detailed and up-to-date account of the main Roman road in Surrey, and which, thanks largely to the excavations of the late S. E. Winbolt and to his book (*With a Spade on Stane Street*), is especially familiar to members of this Society.

Stane Street is in a somewhat different category from most of the other roads dealt with in this book in that it had no connection with the Wealden iron-working sites and was more in the nature of an "arterial road" in that it formed the most direct link between London and Chichester. Of the road itself, Mr. Margary has little to add as regards its alignment, as this was firmly established by work carried out in recent years. As regards the still unverified portion through Epsom, he favours an alignment slightly more to the north of the Pebble Lane alignment, carrying it close to the south-east corner of the present Epsom Church of St. Martin. The "old hedgerow" which is taken to establish his alteration one hesitates to accept unless supported by evidence of early maps, in view of the present built-up nature of the area and the fact that it has undergone very considerable alterations in the last two centuries. Anyhow the deviation is so slight as to be of little consequence.

As regards the Rowhook—Farley Heath branch off Stane Street, one must admit to some disappointment that Mr. Margary's work has not extended our knowledge as to the course of this route beyond Farley Heath, or in fact beyond Velley's Hollow, some distance from the Temple site with its adjoining clearly defined trackway heading for the North Downs. He does, however, suggest a possible route for this extension, and one that seems to the writer to be most probable (and which is, in fact, supported by certain finds of Roman material at points along its course).

As regards the suggestion (page 76) that the fourth and last posting station may have been situated at Merton, a rather better case can be made out for siting this at Ewell, even though it makes the final stage a few miles longer. At Ewell there was clearly a small town, or settlement, with a considerable number of occupants, as is shown not only by the large quantity of pottery, coins and general occupation debris covering a wide area (mostly beneath the present village), but also by the grid-plan layout of Roman roads, portions of which have been found at various points beneath Ewell and of which an extension, dated circa A.D. 200, has recently been found on the Poyles Hill—Purberry Shot estates to the west of the village. (Roman building debris, and some remains of foundations, have been found from time to time at several sites at Ewell, but mostly in situations where no excavations could be undertaken.)

It therefore seems more probable that the fourth posting station was somewhere at or near this point, and a point on the level ground immediately north of Ewell, where the road makes its first deviation from the London—Chichester alignment (and where, incidentally, much Roman pottery and other material has been found) seems most likely.

The only other Roman way passing through Surrey with which Mr. Margary deals is that from London to Brighton (Chapter 6). This, as is stated (p. 93), "passes through the iron-working district of the Weald and was, no doubt, much used in transporting its products to London and the coast, but primarily it was planned as one of a series of roads to connect the rich corn-growing area of the South Downs with London and the rest of Britain." This may well be so, but there is much reason to suspect that a "pre-Roman" trackway already existed along the line of this road, and was used to transport the products of the Sussex iron-working sites (which excavations have shown to have been in full production during the decade prior to the Roman conquest) to the Belgic settlements in Surrey and north of the Thames (Verulamium and Camulodunum). Also in Roman times it is clear that the North Downs were mainly given up to farming and corn production, and this road, as well as Stane Street, would have served for the transport of this market produce to London.

This book, with its wealth of information and excellent maps and illustrations, is indispensable to all interested in the subject of Roman Britain, and to members of this Society in particular. Its clear presentation of all the known facts makes it of value, and entertaining reading, as much to the expert as to the beginner, and it will form the foundation of all future research into the Roman occupation of south-east England.

A. W. G. L.

A PEEP AT CHIPSTEAD'S PAST. By F. J. Randell Creasy. The Hillside Press, Whyteleafe, Surrey.

This little booklet of sixteen pages, the author modestly declares in an introductory note, "has no pretensions to being a parish history of the orthodox kind." That may be so, but nevertheless by diligent delving in the mines of information at the Public Record Office, the British Museum and Croydon Reference Library, by searching such publications as the Surrey volumes of the Victoria County Histories, and those of our Surrey Archæological Society and the Surrey Record Society, to mention only a few of the many books examined, and by consulting almost everyone who had some knowledge of Chipstead's past, he has produced a most interesting and pleasantly written story of the village and its setting, from far-off prehistoric times until 1947, when this little volume was first published.

The price is half a crown, and the author generously gives all the proceeds towards the maintenance of the parish church of St. Margaret's.

A. T. S.

PUBLICATIONS OF

THE SURREY ARCHÆOLOGICAL SOCIETY.

BLECHINGLY. No. 1 of the Local History Series. A Short History by Uvedale H. H. Lambert.

Size 8vo (uniform with Surrey Archæological Collections). Bound in stiff paper. 48 pages, 9 illustrations, geological section, church plan, and a folding map. Indexed. Price to Members of the Society, 3s. 6d. ; to non-members, 5s. net, post free. Obtainable from Surrey Archæological Society, Castle Arch, Guildford.

RESEARCH PAPER NO. 1 : A STUDY OF PATTERNS ON ROMAN FLUE-TILES AND THEIR DISTRIBUTION. By A. W. G. Lowther, F.S.A.

Size crown quarto. 35 pages. Frontispiece, 19 illustrations. Obtainable from Surrey Archæological Society, Castle Arch, Guildford. Price to Members, 2s. 6d. ; to non-members, 5s. Postage 3d.

RESEARCH PAPER NO. 2 : A MESOLITHIC SURVEY OF THE WEST SURREY GREENSAND. By W. F. Rankine, F.S.A.Scot.

Size crown quarto. 52 pages, frontispiece, 17 illustrations. Indexed. Synopsis : I. Introductory ; II. Occupation of the Greensand ; III. The Mesolithic Flint Industry ; IV. West Surrey Mesolithic Sites ; V. Transect Digging ; VI. Appendices. Price to Members, 2s. 6d. ; to non-members, 5s. Postage 3d. Obtainable from Surrey Archæological Society, Castle Arch, Guildford.

INDEX

Abinger (Abingworth, Abyngrowe), 87

Paddington (Padyngden, Padyngton), manor of, in, 87, 88

Abingworth or Abyngrowe, see Abinger

Adams, R. G., xiv

Addington church, visited, ix

Agmondesham, John, 96

Albury (Albery, Aldbury), 88

manor of, 92

manor belonging to Henry Polstead in, 95

Alcock, John, his daughter Alice (Leigh), 85

Aldbury, see Albury

Aldham, 96

Alfold, lands in, 95

Wildwood manor in, 95

Alice Holt Forest (Hants), pottery industries, 50, 55, 56, 81

Anne, Queen, at Epsom, 110

Anne of Denmark, Queen of James I, arms of, in Guildhall, Guildford, 97 ; her residence in Surrey, 100

Ansley, Brian, 95, 96

Nicholas, 96

Archer, John, 85

Argall, Thomas, 90

Artington, St. Catherine's Hill in, 156; bronze ornament found at, 143

Arundel, Charles, 91

Matthew, 91

Sir Thomas, his daughter Jane, 90

Ashtead (Asshested), 110

pottery from, 14, 22

manor of Samers in, 88

three stone axes from, 141

Atkinson, R. L., C.B.E., F.S.A., xv

Austen, George, Mayor of Guildford, 97

Bacon, Sir Nicholas, 91

Bagden, see Bookham, Great

Bagshaw, Major W. H., 112

Baker, Mr., scrivenor, 91

David, 29

Peter, 91

William, 94

Balfour-Browne, Mrs. F. L., 54

Banstead Common, investigations of earthworks on, 63-64 ; Mylenfield Windmill on, 63

Bareham, Thomas, 87

Barham, Nicholas, 91

Barnes, Mr., 59

Barritt, Thomas Hercey, 126

Barrow Green Estate Co., viii

Batersey, see Battersea

Battersea (Batersey), land in, 89

parson of, bequest to, 88

Bayliss, manor of (Sussex), 95

Baynton, Francis, 91

Henry, 91

Baynards Park, see Cranleigh

Beaconsfield (Bucks), 96

Beardsey, Robert, 96

Beke, Henry, 95

Hugh, 95

Bekingham, Robert, and his wife Elizabeth, 94

Beldhm, Thomas, 88

Belloc, Hilaire, 147

Benet, Edmund, 88

Benger, R. B., xv

Bentinck, Lord William, 139

Berde, Henry, 96

Berkeley, George, 1st Earl of Berkeley, 110

Berkshire, see Reading

Bermondsey, Prior and Convent of, 86

Berry, Michael, 59, 65

Billinghurst (Sussex), 96

Billinghurst, Dr. W. B., xiii, xv

Bingley, Lady, xiv

Birche, John, 91

Bird, Arthur Horace, of Great Bookham, 108

Blackden, Cuthbert, 96

Blackwell, Richard, 96

Blonte, Richard, 90, 91

Boddeles (Bodley) manor, see Lambeth

Bokenham, dioc., Kent, 92

Bonsor, Joseph, of Polesden, 108

Bookham, Great, manorial records, 108

maps of, 103 ;

places in, Bagden, 106 ; Common Wastes in, 105 ; manor of Eastwick, 108 ; Mark Oak, 106 ; Phoenice Farm (Vines), 106 ; Rolts, afterwards Half Moon Public House and Half Moon Cottage, 106 ; Sheep Bell House, 106 ; Slyfield Mill, 106

Preston, tithing of, 103, 107

roads : Cobham Road, 106 ; Hole Hedge Way, 106 ; main, 105

Bookham, Little, Common Wastes in, 105

Bostocke, Richard, 91

Boston, Lady, 154, 155

Both, John, 96

Julyan, widow, 96

Bourchier, Thomas, Archbishop of Canterbury, bequest to, 83
Box, Donovan, 29
Brace, John, 95, 96
Bradshaw, John, of Cheshire, Chief Justice, 156
Thomas, mercer, 91
Bramley (Bramlegh), 88
Bray, F. E., xv
Edward, 91
Bridgewater, G. V., xv
Broke, Sir Richard, Knight of King's Bench, 88
Bronze brooch from Romano-British cemetery at Haslemere, 6
pin from Roman villa at Walton-on-the-Hill, 78
Bronze Age, late, ornaments found at St. Catherine's Hill and Farnham, 143, 144
Brooch, bronze, from Romano-British cemetery at Haslemere, 6
Brown, Thomas, 91
Bruyn (Bryunne) : Edith, see Creyser
Ingleran, 92
Sir John, 92
Sir Maurice, 92
Bryan, T. A., xiv
Brystowe, Christopher, 91
Bryunne, see Bruyn
Buckingham (Bokyngham), Duchess of, 83
Duke of, see Stafford
Buckinghamshire, see Beaconsfield
Bucknill, Hon. Sir Thomas T., 121
Burder, E. R., xv
Burl, D. A., 118
Byfleet, pottery from, 20
manor, residence of Anne of Denmark, 100
Byrche, John, 96
Byrkley, farm land, 95

Calverley, Thomas, 131
Camulodunum (Colchester) (Essex), pottery from, 18
Canndishe (?), Co. Suffolk, 84
Canterbury, Archbishop of (Thomas Bourchier), bequest to, 83
Prerogative Court of, some Surrey wills in, 82-96
Carleton, John, gent, 89, 90
Joyce, 89
Carpenter, L. W., xi
loans from to Museum, xiii
on a Saxon spearhead from Cheam, 151-152
Carrell, John, 96

Carson, R. A. G., 153
Castell, C. P., 105
Chabeleyn, John, bequest, to 94
Chalgrove (Oxon.), 96
Chandler, Mr., xiii
Chapman, Sir Roger, priest, 94
Charles II, King, at Epsom, 110
Charlwood parish registers, transcript of, viii
Charmans family, of Ewell, 130
Charrossez, Humphrey, 89
Charterhouse, see Godalming
Cheam, Lumley Chapel visited, ix
Park Lane, old houses in, ix
Saxon spearhead from, 151
Chertsey, Abbot and Convent of, 88 ; and Epsom manor, 110
church, visited, ix
Cheshire, see Ridge
Chester (Cheshire), 156
Chichester (Sussex), places in, visited by Society, ix
Chiddingston(e) (Kent), 83
Chipstead, Peep at Chipstead's Past, 158
Christie, Miss M., xv
Clandon, West (? West Landon), 88
Clapham, parson, bequest to, 88
Claremont, see Esher
Clark, Anthony J., on 4th-century Romano-British pottery kilns at Overwey, Tilford, 29-56
F., 29
Clay, Thomas, 103, 108
Clerk, John, 92
Robert, his wife Ann, 96
Clerke, John, of Stoke-next-Guildford, 93
Cleveland, Barbara, Duchess of, 131
John, of Great Bookham, 108
Clevynge, John, 85
Clinton, Henry Pelham, ninth Earl of Lincoln, and Duke of Newcastle-under-Lyne, his ownership of Oatlands Park, 134
Cliston, see Clyston
Clopton, John, squire, 84
Clyston (Cliston), Sir Gervoys, bequest to, 83, 84
Coates, Sir Edward F., Bart, 125
Cobham, pottery from, 20
Chatley Farm in, bath-house at, 50, 55
Cobham, Ann, 83
Elizabeth, 83
Reynold, 83, 84
Sir Thomas, of Sterborough, will of, 83
Codington, Richard, and his wife Elizabeth, 131
Elizabeth, 83

Coins : of Ptolemy IV found near Lingfield, 153 ; Roman : of Constantine. found at Ewell, 153, of Gratian, found at Tilford, 42, 54, three *minimissimae*, from Roman villa at Walton-on-the-Hill, 72, 78, of Tetricus II, from Roman villa at Walton-on-the-Hill, 70, 78

Coke, John, 95

Colborne, Hon. Mrs., 133

Colchester (Camulodunum) (Essex), pottery from, 16, 18

Colcoke, Alain, 91

Colepeper (Culpeper), Eleanor, 83 *n*.
  Sir John, 86, 89
  Joyce (Howard), 86, 89, 90
  Margaret (Cotton), 86, 89
  Richard, of Aylesford, 86, 89
  Thomas, 86, 89
  Sir William, 86

Colly, John, 91

Combes (Gombez) : Henry, 93
  Robert, 88
  Thomas, 93
  William, will of, 93 ; his wife Anne, his son William, his sister Julian, 93

Compton Church, bequest to, 94 ; the Oratory, 154-155 ;

Cookson, M. B., 140

Coope, William, 93

Corder, Philip, xv

Cornynestrm, —, 84

Cotton, Sir Thomas, 91
  William, of Oxenhoathe, 86, 89 ; his wife Margaret, *see* Colepeper

Coulsdon, Farthing Down, excavations at, x

Cowden (Kent), 83

Cowper, Henry, his widow Alice, 94

Craces, *see* Guildford

Cranleigh (Cranley) : 88
  land in, 96
  Baynards Park at, visited, ix
  New Park Farm at, visited, ix
  St. Nicholas Church, visited, ix

Creasy, F. J. Randell, his *Peep at Chipstead's* Past reviewed, 158

Crewdson, B., xv

Creyser (Croyser) : Ann (Norbury), 92
  Edith, afterwards Bruyn, 92 ; will of, 92
  William, armiger, of Stoke D'Abernon, will of, 92

Crooksbury Hill, *see* Farnham

Cross, H., F.L.A., 141

Crowhurst, St. George's Church, holy water stoup found in, 156

Croyser, *see* Creyser

Cuddington, Cherry Orchard Farm in, 133
  Diana's Ditch in, 133
  manor of, 131
  Nonsuch, palace of, 131, 133 ; site of, visited, ix
  Nonsuch Park estate, 132

Cuddington, old houses in : Dower House, formerly Harefield, 132 ; Nonsuch Park House, 132

Culpeper, *see* Colepeper

Cutler, Mr., a maltster of Ewell, 130
  Mrs., of Ewell, 129

Cutton, Edmund, 91

Dance, Miss, 143

Darcy, Elizabeth, 86
  Sir Roger, 86

Davey, Mrs., xv

Davies, Edwin, death of, xvi

Dawson, Warren, xv

Dean(e), Sir Richard, priest, 88, 90

Denham, Sir John, Lord Denham, and his wife Dame Elizabeth, 84

Diorite axe from Kingston, 141

Diston, J., 124

Dixon, Sir Nicholas, clerk, 93

Donmowe, *see* Dunmow

Donne, John, the elder, 83

Dorking, Wheatsheaf Inn at, 156 ; the Wheatsheaf Hog, a bequest, 156

Dorling, Rev. E. E., F.S.A., 123 *n*.

Dorset, *see* Hilton

Dunham, Dr. K. C., 141

Dunmow (Essex), Friar of, bequest to, 83

Dunning, G. C., F.S.A., lectures on pottery from Pachesham, Leatherhead, x

Dyckby, John, 91

Eady, Justice Swinfen, 135

Eastwick, *see* Bookham, Great

Edmunds, F. E., 141

Edgeler, William, of Great Bookham, 108

Edwards, H. L., F.A.I., 133

Edwards, James, 126

Effingham, manor of, 87, 88

Eggar, Mrs., 115

Egham, "Great Fosters" house, ix

Elizabeth, Queen, arms of, in Guildhall, Guildford, 97

Ellingworth, Ralph, 91

Elliott (Ellyott, Elyott) :
  Henry, 94
  James, of Great Bookham, 108
  John, 96
  Lawrence, 91

Elmes, Anthony, squire, 94, 95
Elizabeth, 95, 96
Humphrey, 95, 96
Elyott, *see* Elliott
Ennisdale, Lord, ix
Epsom (Ebesham, Ebbisham) :
Downs, racing on, 111
inns : the King's Head, 110, 116 ;
New Inn, afterwards Waterloo
House drapery shop, 111, 116 ;
the Spread Eagle, 110
manor of, 110
medicinal wells in, 110
old houses in : Ashley House, 117 ;
The Cedars, 114 ; Durdans, 110,
111 ; Ebbisham House, 112 ;
in High Street, 116 ; The Hylands, 119 ; Hylands House,
120 ; Mead House, 119 ; Park-
hurst, 113 ; Pitt Place, 111 ;
Richmond House, 115 ; The
Shrubbery, 118 ; in South Street,
118-119 ; The Vicarage, 115 ;
Whitmore's, 121 ; Woodcote
End, 122 ; Woodcote Grove,
formerly Mount Diston, 124 ;
Woodcote Hotel, formerly Wood-
cote Place, 123 ; Woodcote
House, 111
parsonage of, 88
roads in, Ashley Road, 117 ; Chalk
Lane, 123, 124 ; Church Street,
112-115 ; Dorking road, 119-
121 ; High Street, 116 ; South
Street, 118, 119 ; Woodcote
Road, 122
Rosebery Park in, 119
Esdaile, Miss, 114
Esher, Claremont in, grotto at, 134
Essex, *see* Colchester ; Dunmow ;
Pentlow ; Rickling ; St. Osyth ;
Waltham
Estbury, manor of, 96
Estfold, William, mercer and alder-
man of London, 92
Evans, Sir Edward, 1
Evelyn, C. J. A., xv
John, 134
Richard, Lord of manor of Epsom,
110
Mrs., Lady of manor of Epsom, 110
Everard, H. V. H., viii, ix
Ewell : Brickyard, 130
church, visited, ix
flour mills, 125
manor of, granted to Prior and
Convent of Merton, 125
market, licence to hold weekly, 125
old houses in : Bourne Hall (for-
merly Garbrand Hall), 126 ;
Chessington House, 129 ; in

Ewell (contd.)
Church Street, 130 ; Ewell Castle,
131 ; Ewell Grove, 126 ; Ewell
House, 126 ; Fitznells, 127 ; Glyn
House, 126 ; old houses in
High Street, 127-128 ; Malt End
Cottage, 130 ; The Manor House,
125 ; Rectory Farm House, 126 ;
Spring House, 128 ; Tabards,
130 ; Tayles Hill, 125, 126,
excavations at, xiii ; Watch
House, 130 ; Well House, 130
pottery from, 25, 48
Queen Anne inn, 128
roads in : Portway, 125 ; Staneway,
125 ; Stane Street, 147, route of
through, 125
Roman coin found at, 153

Farington, Joseph, 135
Farleigh church, visited, ix
Farmer, Samuel, 131, 132
Farnham : bronze ornament found
at, 144
Crooksbury Hill in, 30, 54
pottery from, 14, 18, 20, 23
Snailslynch kiln site, 44, 54, 81
Tilford, tithing of : Overwey in,
pottery kilns at, 29-56
Farrer, Lord, death of, xvi
Farthing Down, *see* Coulsdon
Featherby, W., 152, 153
Fechinam, *see* Fetcham
Felton, Thomas, of Clerkenwell, 91
Fetcham (Fechinam) church, visited,
ix ; rector of, *see* Hyde
manor of, 92
Ffurde, *see* Ford
Finny, W. St. L., 141
Fitzgarrett, Edward, 86, 90, 91 ; his
wife, Dame Agnes Paston, *q.v.*
Fitzherbert, Mr., 111
Fitzwater, Water, Lord Fitzwater, 84
Flint axe from Titsey, 141
mine at East Horsley, 142
Ford(e) (Ffurde) : Edmund, 91
Erasmus, 87, 88
Richard, 83
Forge, J. W. Lindus, A.R.I.B.A., on
the Grotto, Oatlands Park,
134-140
Fox, John, 85
J., on Stane Street, 147-151
Foxwell, Agnes, 108
France, B. A., 142
Frederick, Duke of York, ownership
of Oatlands Park by, 135, 137,
138
Freeman, E. A., ix, xiv
Frend, W. H. C., xv

Frere, J. A., xv
  Sheppard, F.S.A., 29, 54 ; excavates Roman villa at Walton-on-the-Hill, 65
Freshfield, E., 59
Frimley, pottery from, 20
Frost, Edwin, death of, xvi
Frowch, Thomas, 83

Gardner, Dr. Eric, xv
Gate, Sir Thomas, priest, 94
Gawdye, John, serjeant-at-law, 96
Gayneford, John, 83
Gaynsford, Sir John, of Crowhurst, 88
Genealogists, Society of, 102
Genialis, Antonine, potter, 81
Gerwoys of Clyston, see Clyston
Gibson, Mrs., xv
Gibson, J. H., on the Oratory in Compton Church, 154-155
Gilford, see Guildford
Glass, stained, in the Guildhall, Guildford, 97-101
Glyn, Sir Arthur, Bart., 130
  Miss Margaret H., 130
Godalming, Charterhouse in, Romano-British cemetery at, 26-28, pottery from, 9-25; School Museum, 10
Goldsmyth, Randall, bequest to, 88
Gordon, Rev. C., ix
Gould, R. V., 29
Grant, H. J., 29
Greene, Lord, Master of the Rolls, elected Vice-President, xvi
  Thomas, 94
Greenwich (Kent), Friars of, 85
Grenside, Mrs., 140
Greville, Charles, 138
Grimes, W. F., 44
Guildford (Gilford): Abbot's Hospital, arms of James I and Anne of Denmark in, 100 ; bequest to poor in, 95
  Black Friars of, bequests to, 92-96 *passim*
  Church, Trinity, bequests to, 93, 94
  — St. Mary's, bequests to, 93, 94
  — St. Nicholas, bequests to, 93, 94
  Craces in, 94
  Guildhall in, the stained glass in, 97-101 ; panel containing arms of Queen Elizabeth, 98, of Anne of Denmark, 98-99, of Guildford town, 99-100
  inns: Lion (Lyon), 91 ; Red Lion, 155
  visits of Pepys to, 155
  Mayor of (1589), see Austen

Guildford, Henry de, 155
Gwyn, Nell, at Epsom, 110

Halfarre, Thomas, 96
Hambledon, trial excavations at, xi
Hamilton, Charles, 134, 135
Hampshire, see Alice Holt ; New Forest ; Silchester ; Winchester; Yateley
Hampshire, Henry, 92
Harryson, Laurence, 94
Harvey, John H., F.S.A., lectures on history of excavation sites at Pachesham, Leatherhead, x, on Gothic Builders in Surrey, x ; on An Experiment in Local History, 102-109
Hascombe (Hastcombe), 88
Haslemere, Beech Road in, 2
  Educational Museum, 2
  Romano-British cemetery at, 2-9, 26-28 ; pottery from, 2-25
Hawarde, see Howard
Hawkes, Prof. C. F. C., 26
Hawley, C. D., F.R.I.B.A., xv, 133 ; lectures on beauty in old buildings, x
Henley-on-Thames (Oxon), 94
Henningwer, John, his wife Elizabeth, 96
Henrietta Maria, Queen, 131
Henry VIII, King, and manor of Cuddington, 131
Hertford, see St. Albans
Hiley, F. C. W., viii ; death of, xvi
Hill, Nicholas, 88
  William, 88
Hilton, manor of (Co. Dorset), 91
Hitchin, Mrs., ix
Hofheim, pottery from, 18
Hogsmill river, 125
Holden, John, 87
Holmes, John M., on Romano-British cemeteries at Haslemere and Charterhouse, 1-28
Hooper, Hilda J., on Some Surrey Wills in the Prerogative Court of Canterbury, 82-96
  Dr. Wilfrid, LL.D., F.S.A., gifts to Library, xiv, xv
Hope-Taylor, Brian, excavates at Farthing Down, x, at Hambledon, xi ; on a Saxon pot from Thursley, 152
Hordes, family of, 127
Horne, see Stoke-next-Guildford
Horsley, East, neolithic flint mine at, 142
Houses, old, in Epsom, Ewell and Cuddington, 110-133

Howard (Hawarde) : Charles, 87, 89
Sir Edmund, 86, 87, 89 ; his wife
Joyce, *see* Colepeper
George, 87, 89
Sir George, 90
Henry, 87, 89
Katherine (afterwards Queen), 86,
89
Margaret, 89
Mary, 89
Lord William, 90
Hudson, Walter, 105
Hughes, Edward Hughes Ball, 135
Hull, Dame Alionore, bequest to, 93
Hunt, William Holman, 126
Husewyff, Roger, priest, bequest to,
93
Hyde, Rev. E. C., xiv
Sir Henry, rector of Fetcham
Church, 92
Hylton, Hon. Perdita, xiv

Illingworth, Johane, 87
Ireland, William, armiger, his daugh-
ter Margaret (Leigh), 86
Iron Age pottery from St. George's
Hill Camp, Weybridge, 144-147
key, Roman, from villa at Walton-
on-the-Hill, 78
Iwarbys, family of, 127
Ixworth, manor of (Suffolk), 131

James I, King, at Guildford, 101
Jeffery, John, 91
Johnson, Harman, 91
Dr. Samuel, 138
Johnston, A. B., ix
Rev. H. R. L., ix
P. M., 154
Johnstone, Miss H., Litt.D., ix
Jones, Miss Farewell, xiv
Thomas, of Witley, 94
Jordan, Mrs., 125

Katherine Hill, *see* Artington,
St. Catherine Hill in
Kelycke, Joan, 90
Kent, *see* Chiddingstone ; Cowden ;
Greenwich ; Richborough ;
Speldhurst ; Tong
Kenyon, Sir Frederic, President, pre-
sides at General Meeting, vii
Keton, Robert, 92
King, J. E., 54
Kingefold Woods, 95
Kingston, diorite axe from, 141
Knight, Henry, 86
Kylway, Robert, 96

Lacaille, A. D., lectures on Flint
working, x
Lacelle, Christopher, 91
Laird, Arthur R., xv
Lake, E. J., death of, xvi
Lambert, Sir Henry, his History of
Banstead, 102
Uvedale, his History of Bleching-
ley, vii, 102
Lambeth (Northlambhithe, South-
lamehithe) : 85
Bodley (Boddeles) in, manor of, 91
Church, St. Mary, bequest to, 84 ;
brotherhood of St. Christopher
the elder in, bequests to, 88, 89 ;
Chapel of St. Nicholas in, 85, 89
Harreys field in, 89
Levehurst in, manor of, 86, 87
Stockwell in, 84, 85 ; bequest to
housewives of, 89 ; Chapel, 87
Upgrove manor in, 91
Lampson, Mrs., xiv
Lane, Mrs., viii
Josiah, 135
Langley, Francis, 87, 88
Henry, of Rickling, Co. Essex, 86
Willimo, of Bokenham, 92
Larner, Rev. H. M., xiv
Layham (Leigham) Park, *see* Streat-
ham
Leatherhead, Pachesham in, "The
Mounts" at, excavations at, xii
parish register, transcript of, viii
Lee, *see* Leigh
Lee-Hunt, John, xv
Leger, William, 88
Leigh, *or* Lee (Lygh, Lighe, Legh) :
Agnes, 89, *see* also Paston
Anne (afterwards wife of Sir
Thomas Paston and Edward
Fitzgarrett), 86
Edward, 89, 90
Eleanor, wife of Roger, 85
Elizabeth (Darcy), wife of John,
86, 89
Elizabeth, wife of Sir John, 91
Elizabeth (Langley), wife of Ralph,
86
Frances, 90
George, 87
Dame Isabel (Wurseley), wife of
Richard Culpeper and Sir John
Leigh, 86, 87 ; will of, 89-90
Sir John, of Stockwell, Knight of
the Bath, 85, 86, 90 ; will of,
87-88
Sir John, Knight, son of Ralph
Leigh, 85-89 *passim* ; his will,
90-91
John, of Ridge, 85
John, "of the Rigge," 85, 86

Leigh, *or* Lee (contd.)
  Ralph (Rauf), of Stockwell, brother of Sir John Lee, Knight of the Bath (*q.v.*), will of, 85-87 ; his sons John and Ralph (*q.v.*), his daughters Isabel, 85, 87, Joyce (Stanney), 85, 87, 89, 90, Margaret (Rice), 85, 87, 89, 90 ; his father Ralph, 85, 86
  Ralph, son of Ralph, of Stockwell, 85-91 *passim* ; his son John, 91 ; his daughter Frances, 90
  Richard, 89
  Robert, 85
  Roger, 85, 87, 88
  Thomas, 87
  Thomas a Lee, of Streatham, 90
  William, 87
Leigh manor, *see* Walton-on-Thames
Leigham (Layham) Park, *see* Streatham
Lemprieres, family of, 125
Lethaby, Major T., death of, xvi
Levehurst, *see* Lambeth
Leveson-Gower, Charles, death of, xvi
Levick, Robert, 92
Linch pin, 1st century, found on Stane Street, 150
Lincoln, Earl of, *see* Clinton
Lingfield (Lyngfeld), charities in, 83
  Church of St. Peter, bequest to, 83
  coin of Ptolemy IV found near, 153
  Sterborough (Starborough) Castle in, 83
Littlejohn, Miss J. B., death of, xvi
Livingstone, Dr. David, 115
Lloyd, Henry, Lord of Manor of Ewell, 125
  Mrs., xiv
Local History, experiment in, 102-109
Lolesworth, *see* London, Spitalfields
London : Corporation of, gift from for excavations, xvi
  places in : All Hallows, Barking, 95
  Clifford's Inn, 88
  Gray Friars, bequest to, 87
  Lothbury, Church of S. Margaret in, 91
  Spitalfields (Lolesworth), 95
  The Temple, 88
  The Tower, Royal Church of St. Thomas the Apostle in, 83 ; Ypres Inn in, 84
  Romano-British pottery from, 16, 18
London and Southampton railway, 136
Longe, John, 106
Lord, Rev. P. W., 156
Lowther, A. W. G., F.S.A., Hon. Secretary, 29, 54, 142, 150

Lowther (contd.)
  his "Study of the Patterns on Roman Flue-Tiles," vii
  lectures on excavations at Leatherhead, x
  on Roman villa at Sandilands Road, Walton-on-the-Hill, 65-81
  excavations on Stane Street, 125
  on three stone axes from Ashtead, 141, 142
  on a Bronze Ornament found at St. Catherine's Hill, 143
  on Iron Age pottery from St. George's Hill Camp, Weybridge, 144-147
  describes Saxon spearhead, 152
  on a coin of Constantine found at Ewell, 153
Lovelace, Elizabeth, 90
  John Henry Arthur, 90
  Thomas, 91
Lygh, see Leigh
Lyon Inn, *see* Guildford
Lyngfeld, *see* Lingfield
Lyttleton, Thomas, Lord, 111

Macey, or Macy, *see* Masseye
Madan, Rev. Martin, B.A., 123
Malden, Old, excavations at, xi
Manwoode, Roger, 91
Maps, various, recently added to Library, viii, xiv
Margary, I. D., F.S.A., xiv, 147
  elected Vice-President, xvi
  on a coin of Ptolemy IV found near Lingfield, 153
  on a holy water stoup in Crowhurst Church, 156
  his *Roman Ways in the Weald* reviewed, 157
Mark Oak, *see* Bookham
Marten, Frances, 90
  Marie, 90
Martyn, Dorothy, 87
Marwood, Roger, 91
Masseye, or Macy, John, 108
  William, 108
Master, Capt. C. E. H., viii
Mathewe, Hugh, 84
Mawry, Sir John, clerk, 92
May, Mrs. Doris, J.P., xv
Maynard, John, 95
Merew, see Merrow
Merriman, Commander R. D., xv
Merrow (Merew, Merowe), 88
  Church, bequest to, 94
Merton Abbey, bequest to, 83 ; and grant of manor of Ewell, 125
Messenger, Morgan & May, Messrs., xv
Metcalfe, Margaret, 89
Michell, John, 88

Middlesex, see Syon

Millar, Cecil, 121
W. T., 147

Moffat, Mary, 115
Dr. Robert, 114

Montague, Lord, 91

More, William, armiger, 91
William, of Loseley, 95, 96 ; his daughter Elizabeth (Polsted), 96

Morris, Col. C. E., xv

Morrish, R., F.S.A., ix ; death of, xvi

Mountney, P. J., 28

Mowrtysley, 96

Müller, Miss, ix

Murray, Miss E. M., death of, xvi

Myddleborowe, Richard, 91

Mylenfield Windmill, on Banstead Common, q.v.

Mysters, arms of, 114

Neolithic Flint Mine at East Horsley, 142

New Forest (Hants) pottery industries, 50, 55

New Park Farm, see Cranleigh

Newcastle-under-Lyne, Duke of, see Clinton

Nicholls, A. W., 129

Noks, —, niece of Dame Isabel Leigh, 89

Nonsuch, see Cuddington

Norbury, Sir Henry, 92

North, James, 137
Mr., 151

Northeys, family, at Epsom, 111

Northlambhithe, see Lambeth

Northowe, 88

Oakden, Sir Ralph, xiii

Oakeshott, John, 108

Oatlands, The Chronicles of, 137

Oatlands Park (in parishes of Walton-on-Thames and Weybridge), development of, 134, 135 ; the grotto in, 134-140 ; the Hermitage in, 139

Ockley (Okleigh), 88
manor of Westland in, 88

Onslow, Lord, loans from, to Muniment Room, xiv

Orwin, Dr. and Mrs. C. S., 102

Overwey, in Tilford, see Farnham

Oxfordshire, see Chalgrove ; Henley-on-Thames

Oxted (Oxsted), 88
manorial and estate documents relating to, viii

Pachesham, see Leatherhead

Paddington (Padyngton, Padyngden), manor of, see Abinger

Page, Mr., of Great Bookham, 106

Paget, Clarence G., viii

Pagham (Sussex), 95

Pains Hill, see Walton-on-Thames

Paintings, recently added to Library, xv

Pakker, —, 95

Palmer, Sir Henry, of Lambourne, 82
Mrs. Malyn, 82

Parker, Eric, xi

Parkhurst, John, Lord of the manor of Epsom, 110

Parkyns, John, 95

Parre, William, bequest to, 88

Parrish, E. J., on Investigations on Walton Heath and Banstead Common, 57-64

Paston, Lady (Dame) Agnes, daughter of Sir John Leigh, wife of Edward Fitzgarratt, 90, 91
Edward, 90
Katherine, 90
Sir Thomas, 86, 90

Pater, J. E., 141

Patrick, Major H., xv

Pearce, B. W., F.S.A., 153

Pearson, R. H., lectures on Monumental Brasses, x

Pebble Lane portion of Stane Street, 147

Pembroke, Lady, 91

Pentlow (Essex), manor of (Pentlowhalle), 84

Pepys, Samuel, visits Epsom, 110, Ewell, 125, Guildford, 155

Percival, Dr., 153

Perker, Henry, 95

Perkyn, John, 94

Philps, Miss Clara, of Dorking, 156
John, of Dorking, 156
Sarah, of Dorking, 156
Thomas, proprietor of Wheatsheaf Inn, Dorking, 156

Phoenice Farm, see Bookham, Great

Pickering, W. J., on Council, xv ; gifts to Library, xv

Pigott, R. Mountford, F.R.I.B.A., 140

Pocock, W. W., 59, 60

Polsted, Francis, 95, 96
Henry, brother of Thomas, of Stoke-next-Guildford, 94, 95
Henry, of Albury, son of Thomas of Stoke-next-Guildford, 94 ; will of, 95 ; his wife Alice, 95 ; his son Richard, 95, 96 ; his daughter Joan (Sambourne), 95
John, 94
Thomas, of Stoke-next-Guildford, will of, 94 ; his daughter Margaret and his wife Agnes, 94

Polsted (*contd.*)
Thomas, son of Thomas of Stoke-next-Guildford, 94, 95
Pottery, miscellaneous, from St. George's Hill Camp, Weybridge, 144-147
kilns, 4th century Romano-British, at Overwey, Tilford, 29-56; sites, 30-42, destruction of, 42, 55; operation and distribution of kilns, 42; pottery from, 44-54; organic remains from, 54
Roman, from site round villa on Walton Heath, 64; from villa at Walton-on-the-Hill, 74, 78-81
from Romano-British cemetery at Haslemere, 2-9, at Charterhouse, 9-25
Saxon pot from Thursley, 152
Powell, Miss D. L., 108
Prailand farm, 95
Prest, J. M., on Investigations on Walton Heath and Banstead Common, 57-64
Preston, tithing of, *see* Bookham, Great
Primrose, Archibald Philip, 5th Earl of Rosebery, 111, 124
Prynne, Mrs., death of, xvi
Purtey, Phillipo, 96

Quelch, William, of Great Bookham, 108
Quennell, Col. W. A., death of, xvi

Rackham, Bernard, C.B., F.S.A., on Museum Committee, xiii; on the Stained Glass of Guildford Guildhall, 97-101
Rahbula, E. A. R., F.S.A., 133
Randall, Richard, 96
Rankine, W. F., F.S.A.(Scot.), his "Mesolithic Survey of the West Surrey Greensand," vii; lectures on Flints, x; on a Macehead of Igneous Rock from Ranmore, 141; a Diorite Axe from Kingston, 141; a Polished Flint Axe from Titsey, 141
Ranmore, a macehead found at, 141
Common, 105
Reading (Redinge), St. Giles in, 95
Redinge, *see* Reading
Reid, Sir John Rae, 125
Rice, Eleanor, 90
Henry, 91
Margaret, *see* Leigh
Richard, 90, 91
Thomas, 90, 91
Richinge, *see* Rickling
Rickling (Richinge) (Essex), 86

Ridge (Cheshire), 85
Ridgewood (? Ridgwyke) (Sussex), 95
Ridgwyke (? Ridgewood) (Sussex), 95
Ridyard, G. W., 147
Riley, John, 118
Rither, Domino Henrico, 96
Roads: Pebble Lane, 147; Stane Street, 147-151; see also Epsom *and* Ewell
Rock, igneous, macehead from Ranmore, 141
Roemer, Major C. W. De, 29
Roger, John, of Preston, 108
Richard, 106
Rolts, *see* Bookham, Great
Roman villa at Sandilands Road, Walton-on-the-Hill, 65-81; site, 65; summary of results, 68-72; bath, 70, 74; details of excavations, 72-76; building materials, 76; finds, 78
Roman, *see* also Coins *and* Pottery
Romano-British cemeteries at Haslemere and Charterhouse, 1-28; pottery finds at Haslemere, 2-9, at Charterhouse, 9-25
pottery kilns at Overwey, Tilford, 29-56
Rooper, John, King's attorney, 88
Rosebery, Lord, *see* Primrose
Rosier, Miss A. M., death of, xvi
Rowan, Mrs. A. E., 82
Rowden, Philip, 126
Rowlis, John, of Great Bookham, 108
Rudkin, Major H. R. E., death of, xvi
Russell, Sir Arthur, 137
Ryall of London, *see* London, Tower Royal
Ryde, K. A., A.L.A., ix
Rypon, John, will of, 93; his daughter Margaret and his wife Agnes, 93

Sackville, Jordan de, his wife Ela, 86
St. Albans (Verulamium) (Herts), pottery from, 16
St. Anne's Hill, *see* Weybridge
St. Catherine's Hill, *see* Artington
St. George's Hill, *see* Weybridge
St. Martha's, pottery from, 20
St. Michael, Lawrence, 131
William de, 131
St. Osyth (Osites) (Essex), parsonage of, 95
Sambourne, Thomas, his wife Joan (Polsted), 95
Sanders, William, his daughter Margery (Leigh), 86
Sanderstead, 95
Sandes, Robert, 94

Sandilands Road, *see* Walton-on-the-Hill
Sanger, G. F., xv
Savage, John, 88
Sawyer, William, 88
Saxon burial, probable, at Cheam, 151
    pottery, from Thursley, 152
    spearhead from Cheam, 151
Sayers, W. C. Berwick, xv
Scold's bridle at Walton-on-Thames, 156
Seawell, Thomas Samuel, 108
    Thomas Augustus, 108
Sellick, E. L., on a Dorking bequest, 156
Sewill, Mrs., viii
Sexton, C. E., xv, 101
Seymon, John, 88
Shalford, 88
    Church, bequest to, 94
    lands in, 95
Shalford, John, 88
    Thomas, 88
Sheep Bell House, *see* Bookham, Great
Shere (Sheer, Shyre), lands in, 88, 95
    Tillinghokes wood in, 96
Sherriff, R. C., F.S.A., xvi
Shyre, *see* Shere
Silchester (Hants), pottery from, 12, 15, 16, 18, 22
Simmonds, Richard, 98
Skinner, Mrs. Montague, ix
    Sarah (Wood), 108
    Thomas, 108
    William Wilson, 108
Sleywright, William, 91
Slyfield, *see* Stoke D'Abernon
Slyfield Mill, *see* Bookham, Great
Slyfield, Edmund, 106
Smyth, William, rector of Stoke D'Abernon Church, 92
Snailslynch, *see* Farnham
Somerset, see Williton
Sondford, John, 85
Soppewell, Church of, 92
Southlamehithe, *see* Lambeth
Southland, woods, 95
Speldhurst (Kent), manor of, 95
Spiller, Sir Robert, 101
Spilman (Spylman) : Elizabeth, 87
    John, Serjeant at Law, 88
Spitalfields (Lolesworth), *see* London
Sproule, Lionel, death of, xvi
Spylman, *see* Spilman
Stafford, Humphrey, Earl of Stafford and Duke of Buckingham, 83 n.
Stane Street, portion from Pebble Lane towards Ewell, examined, 147-151 ; finds in, 150

Stanney (Staney) : George, 91
    Joyce, *see* Leigh
Starbourgh, *see* Lingfield, Sterborough Castle in
Statham, John, 96
Stephenson, Mill, F.S.A., 65
Stockwell, *see* Lambeth
Stoke D'Abernon (Stokdabernoun)
    Church, visited, ix ; bequest to, 92 ; rector of (1416), *see* Smyth
    manor of, 92
    Slyfield Manor House, visited, ix
Stoke-next-Guildford, Church (St. John the Evangelist), 93, 94
    Horne meads in, 96
    Stoughton manor in, 96
    Swanmede wood in, 94
    Watforde Close in, 96
Stokes, Sir John, 129
Stompe, Sir James, 91
Stonbrig (?) (Stonebrigg, Stowbrigge), (Kent), church, bequest to, 83, 84
Stone axes, from Ranmore, Kingston and Ashtead, 141, 142
Stoneham farm, 95
Stoughton, *see* Stoke-next-Guildford
Stoughton, Anthony, 96
    George, 96
    Gilbert, will of, 96 ; his wife Marion, 96
    John, 96
    Laurence, 96
Stowbrigge, *see* Stonbrig
Stowe, Sir Francis, 91
Streatham, 90
    manor of Leigham (Layham Park) in, 86, 88, 89
Strodeland, 88
Sturmyn, John, 93
Stuart, P. R., 29
Suffolk, *see* Ixworth
Sumner, Miss, xiii
    Heywood, 55
Surrey, Commissary and Consistory Courts of, records of, viii
    wills, in prerogative Court of Canterbury, 82-96
Surrey Archæological Society :
    Annual General Meeting (1949), vii
    excavations, at Farthing Down, Coulsdon, x ; at Hambledon, xi ; at Pachesham, xii ; at Old Malden, xi ; at Tayles Hill, Ewell, xiii
    excursions, Baynards Park and Cranleigh, ix ; Chertsey, Thorpe and "Great Fosters," Egham, ix ; Chichester, ix ; Ewell, Nonsuch and Cheam, ix ; Stoke D'Abernon and Fetcham, ix ; Warlingham, Farleigh and Addington, ix

Surrey Archæological Society (contd.)
finance, xvi
lectures during 1949, x
Library, gifts to, xiv-xv
Local History Committee's work
during 1949, vii
membership, xvi
Museum and Muniment Room,
xiii-xiv
publications, Vols. XLIX and L,
vii ; special research papers,
vii
Sussex, see Billinghurst ; Pagham ;
Ridgewood ; Yapton
Swanmede, see Stoke-next-Guildford
Swanton, E. W., Curator of Hasle-
mere Museum, 2, 28
Swayne, T. Gatton, xv
Swyft, Peter, 85
Thomas, of Stockwell, will of, 84
Syon (Middlesex), 85

Talworth, John, 92
Tarrant, Mr., 144
Tayles Hill, see Ewell
Thompson, Joseph, 132
Thorpe Church, visited, ix
Thursley, Pitlands Farm, pottery
from, 15
Saxon pot from, 152
Tilford, see Farnham
Tillinghokes, see Shere
Titsey, flint axe from, 141
Todd, K. R. U., on a Neolithic Flint
Mine at East Horsley, 142-143
Tong (Kent), pottery from, 23
Tovey, Duncan, death of, xvi
Trench, G. Mackenzie, xv
Turner, Miss E. M., xiv
S. R., F.R.I.B.A., ix
Tyrrell, Amy, 93
Richard, will of, 92

Ulvan, John, 88
Upgrove manor, see Lambeth

Veall, H., xiv
Vere, Anne, wife of Sir Thomas
Cobham, 83
Aubrey de, 83 n.
Verulamium, see St. Albans
Victoria, Queen, her visit to Oatlands
Park, 137
Vincent, Sir Francis, 106
Vines, see Bookham, Great

Wade, Major A. G., excavates at
Overwey, Tilford, 29, 40, 44
Sir Guy, 96

Wagstaffe, Col. H. W., C.S.I., M.C.,
xvi
Walls, T. K., xi
Walpole, Horace, 135, 137
Waltham (Essex) Abbey, 85
Walton-on-the-Hill, Sandilands Road,
Roman villa at, 65-81
Windmill Bank in, 60, 65
Walton Heath in, investigations of
area adjoining site of Roman
villa, 57-63 ; pottery and other
finds from, 59-63, 64
Walton-on-Thames, church, a scold's
bridle in, 156
Pains Hill in, grotto at, 134, 135
Leigh manor house, 156
Warburton, J. R., on a scold's bridle
in Walton-on-Thames church,
156
Ward-Perkins, Prof. J. B., 144
Warlingham church, visited, ix
Warr, Lord de la, 87
Watforde Close, see Stoke-next-
Guildford
Weeding, Miss D., xvi
Welbeck, Joyce, 89
Margaret, 89
William, 89 n.
Welden, —, niece of Dame Isabel
Leigh, 89
Welton, Sir Thomas, 92
Wentworth, Sir Henry, 86
Werying, John, 85
West, Thomas, 87
West Landon, ? Clandon, q.v.
Westbroke, William, 96
Westland, see Ockley
Westminster, Abbot and Convent of,
89
Weston, Henry, 95
Sir Richard, of Sutton Place, 101
Westwood, Brian, A.R.I.B.A., 140
Norman, A.R.I.B.A., 140
Wey, river, navigation of, 101
Weybridge, St. Anne's Hill, grotto in,
134
St. George's Hill in, 136 ; Camp,
pottery from, 144-147
Wheatley, William, M.A., xiv
Whelar, John, will of, 94 ; his wife
Isabel, 94
Whetill (Whetelle), Mr., 90, 91
Whiffen, Marcus, 134
Whytley, see Witley
Wildwood, manor of, see Alfold
Wilkinson, Mrs., xiii
Williamson, Dr. G. C., 97
Willis, Cloudesley S., F.S.A., xiv
on Old Houses in Epsom, Ewell
and Cuddington, 110-133
John O., 128

Willis (contd.)
William, of Great Bookham, 108
Williton, manor of (Somerset), 91
Wills, Surrey, in Prerogative Court of Canterbury, 82-96
Wilson, Lieut.-Col. J. S., O.B.E., death of, xvi
Dr., F.S.A., ix
Winbolt, S. E., 64, 147
Winchester (Hants) : Cathedral, bequests to, 87, 92, 93, 94
Church of the Abbey of St. Maria in, 86
Windmill Bank, see Walton-on-the-Hill
Witley (Wytley), 94
Wonersh, 95
Wood, Miss M. E., F.S.A., lectures on Norman Domestic Architecture, x
Sarah, afterwards Skinner, 108
Thomas, of Great Bookham, 108
William, of Great Bookham, 108
Woodcote Park, in Ewell, Stane Street at, 147
Woodmansterne, pottery from, 18
Woodward, William, 88

Worplesden church, bequest to, 94
Wotton, 88
pottery from, 20
Wonersh, 88
Wolsey, William, 92
Wratlinge (?), lands in, 95
Wurseley, Otwell, 86
Wyattville, Sir Jeffrey, 132
Wyndham, Sir Thomas, 86, 87

Yapton (Yaxton ?) (Sussex), 95
Yateley (Hants), pottery from, 15, 18
Yates, Edward, F.S.A., 65, 74 ; lectures on Wealden Iron-Working, x
Yaxton (? Yapton) (Sussex), 95
Yngge, David, 95
Yong, William, of Wytham (Berks), 96
York, Duke of, see Frederick
Duchess of, and Oatlands Park grotto, 137, 138
Ypres Inn, see under London, the Tower in

Zeuner, Professor, 153

WS - #0012 - 101022 - C0 - 229/152/13 [15] - CB - 9780332973807 - Gloss Lamination